SUCCESSFUL GARDENING

A - Z of
PERENNIALS

Staff for Successful Gardening (U.S.A.)

Editor: Fiona Gilsenan
Senior Associate Editor: Carolyn T. Chubet
Art Editor: Evelyn Bauer

Contributors
Editor: Thomas Christopher
Editorial Assistant: Tracy O'Shea
Consulting Editor: Lizzie Boyd (U.K.)
Consultant: Dora Galitzki
Copy Editor: Sue Heinemann
Art Associate: Diane Lemonides

READER'S DIGEST GENERAL BOOKS
Editor in Chief: John A. Pope, Jr.
Managing Editor: Jane Polley
Executive Editor: Susan J. Wernert
Art Director: David Trooper
Group Editors: Will Bradbury, Sally French,
Norman B. Mack, Kaari Ward
Group Art Editors: Evelyn Bauer, Robert M. Grant, Joel Musler
Chief of Research: Laurel A. Gilbride
Copy Chief: Edward W. Atkinson
Picture Editor: Richard Pasqual
Rights and Permissions: Pat Colomban
Head Librarian: Jo Manning

The credits that appear on page 176 are hereby made a part
of this copyright page.

Originally published in partwork form.
Copyright © 1990 Eaglemoss Publications Ltd.

Based on the edition copyright © 1990
The Reader's Digest Association Limited.

Library of Congress Cataloging in Publication Data

Reader's Digest Association.
A–Z of perennials / Reader's Digest Association, Inc.
     p.   cm. — (Successful gardening)
   ISBN 0-89577-554-9
   1. Perennials—Encyclopedias I. Title. II. Series.
SB434.R43 1993
635.9'32—dc20   93-26149

Printed in the United States of America

Opposite: Delphiniums, ox-eye daisies, spiky foxgloves, and blue-flowered
centaureas jostle in exuberant companionship.
Overleaf: Yellow coreopsis, blue and white campanulas, purple-leaved *Lobelia
fulgens,* and the woolly spikes of silvery *Stachys lanata* are perennial favorites.
Pages 6-7: Red penstemons, cerise geraniums, and orange-red spheres of
Lychnis chalcedonia join pale blue delphiniums and pink goat's rue.

THE READER'S DIGEST ASSOCIATION, INC.
Pleasantville, New York / Montreal

CONTENTS

Special Features

Perennial Borders   8-14
Graceful grasses   81-84
Sculptural plants   155-158

A–Z of Perennials

Acanthus – Athyrium   16-34
Baptista – Brunnera   35-36
Calamintha – Cynoglossum   37-52
Dactylorhiza – Dryopteris   52-63
Echinacea – Euphorbia   63-72
Festuca – Filipendula   73
Gaillardia – Gypsophila   74-85
Helenium – Hosta   86-95
Incarvillea – Inula   96
Kniphofia   97-98
Lamium – Lythrum   98-107
Macleaya – Monarda   108-115
Nepeta   115
Oenothera – Osmunda   116-118
Paeonia – Pyrethrum   118-144
Ranunculus – Rudbeckia   144-149
Salvia – Symphytum   149-163
Tellima – Trollius   163-167
Valeriana – Viola   168-175
Woodsia   175

PERENNIAL BORDERS

**Herbaceous perennials revel in company —
surrounded by other perennials or mixing happily with
transient annuals and long-lived shrubs.**

The traditional and still highly popular way to cultivate perennial flowers is in a "border" — a long, narrow bed that marks the edges of a path, the foot of a fence or hedge, or perhaps the foundation of a house. Such plantings serve to define and frame the basic landscape design.

The backdrop of a wall, fence, or hedge has an aesthetic value — it sets off the color and texture of the flowers and heightens their visual impact. It also creates a protected space, or a "microclimate," sheltered from cold and drying winds, in which the plants can flourish.

The dimensions of a border — its long sweep and shallow depth — are not only dramatic but also practical. This ribbon of flowers allows the gardener to weed or deadhead without stepping on any plants at the edge.

Years ago the fashion was to segregate perennials in an exclusively herbaceous border. Today gardeners are less dogmatic. They appreciate the ever-changing picture a perennial border presents, as various flowers move in and out of their season of bloom. Yet they also value the continuity that the longer-blooming annuals provide and admire the promptness with which bulbs come into flower in the spring. In addition, modern gardeners often work flowering shrubs, dwarf evergreens, and ornamental grasses into the border to give it backbone and color that lasts through the winter.

Planning a border

Study the proposed site carefully. A sunny or lightly shaded spot, reasonably protected from prevailing winds, with a fertile, well-drained but moisture-retentive soil is best. Few perennials are fussy about soil type or situation, but as you plan, check the entries on the following pages to make sure that perennials you want to mix are in fact compatible.

Draw up a plan to scale. Mark any relatively permanent plants such as trees and shrubs first. Perennials in bold groups of three to seven plants should be plotted next. While arranging them, keep in mind ease of viewing. Try to put the taller plants toward the rear and to cluster ground-hugging flowers along the front.

The choice of plants is always personal, but other important considerations for each plant are the growth habit, density, height, color, and time and duration of the flowering season.

▼ **Wild informality** Verbascums and heleniums jostle in sheets of golden yellow around a clump of pale, dark-eyed delphiniums, creating an exuberant semiwild display.

▲ **Color coordination** The ordered formality of a purple-blue border plan gains dramatic strength from the variations in flower and leaf forms. The tall and graceful flower spikes of speedwell *(Veronica longifolia)* above narrow fresh green foliage relieve the severity of the dark green spiny leaves that clothe the stiff stems of globe thistle *(Echinops).*

◀ **Foliage effects** In mixed borders of shrubs and herbaceous perennials, striking foliage plants add long-lasting impact. *Hosta* 'Frances Williams' holds center stage in this group. Its huge yellow-edged leaves contrast in shape and color with the long and narrow pleated foliage of slender-stemmed false hellebore *(Veratrum nigrum),* which towers above a low clump of golden grass.

▲ **Mixed borders** Set against a background of deciduous trees and flowering shrubs, hardy perennials in full summer color mingle happily with shrub roses and stately lilies. Low-growing edging plants nestle close to a lime-green froth of lady's mantle (*Alchemilla mollis*). The tall, slender spires of verbascums add visual punctuation marks.

▶ **Woodland setting** The light shade of open woodland, with its leafy soil, is the preferred habitat of such moisture lovers as green and variegated hostas and native ferns, arching over moss-covered outcrops. Such perennial joys as purple-leaved heucheras, majestic foxgloves, and pink-flowered physostegias also thrive here.

▲ **Foxglove columns** Rising from an immaculately edged lawn, against a hazy background of pale blue irises, perennial foxgloves (*Digitalis* species) hold their dense flower spires aloft unaided by sticks or canes. Their life span is comparatively short, but they are easily perpetuated from seed to delight the eye again with their colors of pure white, clear pink, and rosy carmine. Deadheading prevents them from exhausting themselves and often results in a second, late-summer burst of bloom.

▶ **Planned continuity** Old-time favorites like Russell lupines and *Iris pallida* have their one glorious, if brief, show of color in early summer. Thereafter, clever planning shifts the interest to a foreground planting of the silver-marbled *Pulmonaria saccharata* and a backcloth of the plume poppy (*Macleaya microcarpa*), whose handsome foliage is topped in late summer with clouds of yellowish-white flowers.

▲ Rose companions The bare stems of standard 'Ballerina' roses are concealed in this mixed border. The dense underplanting includes deep purple lavenders, pink alstroemerias, and the silver-leaved, scarlet-headed flowers of perennial campion (*Lychnis flos-jovis*).

▼ Dependable perennials Long-lived and reliable, many perennials perform to perfection year after year. Among these are the popular red-hot pokers (*Kniphofia*) in stunning yellow and orange, the white-flowered *Chrysanthemum maximum* (syn. *Leucanthemum maximum*), and the violet *Salvia* × *superba*.

▲ **Late-summer color** Yellow and pink predominate in this herbaceous border. The clear yellow tasseled plumes of solidago vie for attention with tall, flat-headed achilleas and clear pink phlox seen against a tripod-trained vivid purple clematis.

◄ **Herbaceous splendor** The middle of summer is celebrated in this border scene of pale blue delphinium spires, dark pink penstemons, pastel-colored campanulas, and exotic-looking, but tough, golden orange daylilies *(Hemerocallis)*. In the center, a clump of goat's rue *(Galega officinalis)* adds brushstrokes of pale pink.

Wall plant The accommodating euphorbias are superb foliage plants that can thrive in very poor soils.

A–Z of Perennials

The descriptions of hardy perennials on the following
pages are arranged in alphabetical order by
the plants' botanical names, which are internationally
used and recognized. Where they exist, common
English names are also given, with cross-references
to the botanical names of the plants. It is well worth
getting to know plants by their botanical names,
for only in that way is it possible to be certain of
specifying a particular type. A species may contain
one or more hybrids, varieties, or cultivars that vary
from the original type. For example, they may bear
flowers that are double, larger, a different color, or
especially fragrant.

Most perennials are herbaceous plants that die back
in the fall and send up new growth in the spring; a
few have evergreen foliage. The range of sizes, shapes,
and colors is vast, with plants to suit every type of
garden. Most adapt easily to any type of soil, but nearly
all perennials benefit from thoroughly dug, humus-rich,
well-drained soil.

The flowering period of a particular plant may be brief
or extend over several months. By using the plant
descriptions as a guide, you can plan a display where
some plants are in full bloom while others are still
forming buds and still others are putting on height and
spread before preparing for the flowering season.

In general, most perennials need little maintenance,
apart from mulching in spring with organic matter,
keeping the bed free of weeds, and ensuring an adequate
water supply. Most perennials should be lifted and
divided every 4 or 5 years to prevent overcrowding.

Acanthus

bear's breeches

Acanthus spinosissimus

❏ Height 3-4 ft (90-120 cm)
❏ Planting distance 3 ft (90 cm)
❏ Flowers summer
❏ Any deep, well-drained soil
❏ Sunny or lightly shaded site
❏ Herbaceous
❏ Zones 7-10

Grown as much for its immense glossy dark green leaves as for its summer display of white and purple flowers, bear's breeches is a magnificent border plant. The flowers look striking on their upright 1½ ft (45 cm) long spikes, and they are suitable for fresh or dried flower arrangements.

Popular species

Acanthus mollis reaches a height of 4 ft (1.2 m) and has mid- to dark green leaves, broader and smoother than those of *Acanthus spinosissimus*. The white flowers have pinkish-purple bracts.
Acanthus spinosissimus reaches a height of up to 4 ft (1.2 m). The spiny leaves are deeply cut and hairy, and the white and purple flowers have green bracts.

Cultivation

Plant in fall or early spring in deep, well-drained soil in a sunny or lightly shaded site.
Propagation Sow seeds in early spring in flats of seed-starting medium in a cold frame. When the seedlings show two or three true leaves, prick them out, 6 in (15 cm) apart, into a nursery bed. Grow for 2 years before planting in their permanent positions.

Alternatively, take 3 in (7.5 cm) long cuttings of the thicker roots between mid- and late winter.
Pests/diseases Trouble free.

Achillea

yarrow

Achillea millefolium 'Cerise Queen'

❏ Height 4-60 in (10-150 cm)
❏ Planting distance 10-48 in
  (25-120 cm)
❏ Flowers early to late summer
❏ Well-drained garden soil
❏ Sunny site
❏ Herbaceous or evergreen
❏ Zones 3-9

Flat, wide heads or loose, rounded clusters of little daisy flowers set against a delicate undercoat of ferny, aromatic leaves make yarrow one of the most popular and reliable of perennials. Tolerant of drought and demanding little attention, the larger species are good border plants and long-lasting as cut flowers; the shorter types are suitable for edging or as ground cover.

Popular species

Achillea clypeolata, with near-silvery filigree and aromatic leaves, is evergreen. It grows to a height of 18 in (45 cm), with a spread of 16 in (40 cm). During summer, it bears tightly packed heads, up to 5 in (12.5 cm) wide, of tiny deep yellow flowers. For best performance it should be divided and replanted annually in spring. The outstanding hybrid, 'Moonshine,' probably a hybrid between *Achillea clypeolata* and *A. taygetea,* is taller, at 2 ft (60 cm), with silver-gray foliage and flower heads that retain their clear yellow color for some time.
Achillea filipendulina has a height and spread of 3-4 ft (90-120 cm), with compact clusters of 6 in (15 cm) wide lemon-yellow flowers. The leaves are gray-green. Some common cultivars include 'Coronation Gold' (flat, deep yellow flower heads)

Achillea × lewisii 'King Edward'

and 'Gold Plate' (deep yellow flowers on 5 ft/1.5 m stems). All are good for drying.
Achillea × lewisii 'King Edward' is a dwarf hybrid, 4-6 in (10-15 cm) high and 8 in (20 cm) wide, that forms a neat mound. The foliage is gray-green, and the buff-yellow flower heads, up to 2½ in (6 cm) wide, are produced from late spring to early fall.
Achillea millefolium has deep green leaves and flat, 4 in (10 cm) wide heads of tiny white to cerise flowers. It grows to 2-2½ ft (60-75 cm). Some improved cultivars include 'Cerise Queen' (intense cherry-red flowers) and 'Flower of Sulfur' (bright yellow flowers and more delicate foliage).
Achillea ptarmica, or sneezewort, spreads rapidly. It carries 2-4 in (5-10 cm) wide clusters of loose daisylike white flowers and has narrow tapering, toothed mid-green leaves. It grows to 2 ft (60 cm) high and has a spread of 15 in (38 cm). Some popular cultivars include 'The Pearl,' with loose white button-shaped double flowers that appear in late summer, and 'Perry's White,' up to 2½ ft (75 cm) tall with double white flowers.
Achillea taygetea has pale yellow flat flower heads set against silver-gray and evergreen foliage. They are long-lasting as cut flowers. It stands 1½ ft (45 cm) high

Achillea ptarmica 'The Pearl'

Achillea 'Galaxy hybrid'

and has a spread of 6 in (15 cm). *Achillea tomentosa,* useful for ground cover, reaches up to 9 in (23 cm) high with a 1 ft (30 cm) spread. The downy gray-green leaves are long and narrow; the dense, bright yellow flower heads are 3 in (7.5 cm) wide.

Cultivation

Plant in fall or early spring in any well-drained garden soil in a sunny site. Cut faded flower stems back to ground level in late fall.

Propagation In early spring divide into portions with four or five young shoots and replant. Alternatively, sow seeds in a cold frame in early spring. Prick out the seedlings when large enough to handle and transfer them to an outdoor nursery bed when well developed. Move the young plants to their flowering positions in midfall or the following spring.

Pests/diseases Trouble free.

Achillea filipendulina 'Gold Plate'

Aconitum
monkshood

Aconitum carmichaelii 'Kelmscott Variety'

- ❏ Height 3-4 ft (90-120 cm)
- ❏ Planting distance 16-18 in (40-45 cm)
- ❏ Flowers midsummer to early fall
- ❏ Moist, deep soil
- ❏ Sunny or lightly shaded site
- ❏ Herbaceous
- ❏ Zones 3-7

Monkshood is a border plant with large and glossy, deeply cut leaves and tall spikes of blue, violet, lavender, white, or pale pink hooded flowers. The plant is poisonous.

Popular species
Aconitum carmichaelii (syn. *A. fischeri*) grows 3 ft (90 cm) tall and bears violet-blue flower spikes in late summer. Cultivars include 'Arendsii' (4 ft/120 cm; amethyst-blue) and 'Kelmscott Variety' (lavender-violet).
Aconitum 'Ivorine' is of hybrid origin, 3 ft (90 cm) tall, with large leaves and yellow-white flowers.
Aconitum napellus, 3½ ft (1 m) tall, has deep blue flowers and leaves with pointed segments. Cultivars include 'Albus' (off-

Aconitum 'Ivorine'

white blooms) and 'Carneum' (pale shell-pink).

Cultivation
Plant in fall or early spring in moist, deep soil in partial shade.
Propagation Divide in fall or early spring.
Pests/diseases Trouble free.

Actaea
baneberry

Actaea spicata

- ❏ Height 1½-4 ft (45-120 cm)
- ❏ Planting distance 1½-3 ft (45-90 cm)
- ❏ Flowers late spring to early summer
- ❏ Rich, moist soil
- ❏ Shaded site
- ❏ Herbaceous
- ❏ Zones 3-7

Baneberries have attractive leaves, flowers, and berries and thrive in mixed borders and by the waterside. They quickly form wide clumps of handsome foliage, deeply divided and fernlike, sometimes with rounded lobes. All species of *Actaea* bear small, fluffy spikes of bluish-white flowers in late spring and early summer, but it is for their showy clusters of berries in the fall that these perennials are chiefly grown. The common name "baneberry" is truly descriptive — while all parts of the plants are poisonous if eaten, the berries are particularly so.

Popular species
Actaea pachypoda (syn. *A. alba*) grows to a height of 2-3 ft (60-90 cm) and has an average spread of 1½ ft (45 cm). The leaves are fernlike, the flowers white, and by late summer the plant bears prominent clusters of pea-sized white berries on thick scarlet stalks.
Actaea rubra resembles *A. pachypoda* but grows more upright, spreading to 2 ft (60 cm). The late-summer berries are glossy

Adiantum
maidenhair fern

Actaea rubra

red, on slender stalks. The plant is sometimes wrongly listed as *Actaea spicata rubra* or *nigra*.

Actaea spicata has a height and spread of 1½ ft (45 cm). The dark green toothed leaves are attractive, and the white flower clusters more conspicuous than on any of the other species. So, too, are the large, glistening black berries — which are the most poisonous.

Cultivation
Baneberries love rich, moisture-retentive soil and shade, although they will tolerate some sun if the ground is kept moist. Plant them during frost-free weather in October or March.

Propagation Divide and replant congested clumps in fall or early spring.

Pests/diseases Slugs and snails may attack emerging shoots in spring.

Adiantum pedatum

❑ Height 6-18 in (15-45 cm)
❑ Planting distance 9-24 in (23-60 cm)
❑ Foliage plant
❑ Moist, rich soil
❑ Semishaded site
❑ Herbaceous or semievergreen
❑ Zones 3-9

Maidenhair fern unfurls in spring to form a mass of delicate foliage. It is a good foil for flowering plants and looks attractive beneath trees.

Popular species
Adiantum pedatum has purple stalks bearing drooping leaflets, which form a cloud of light green foliage, darkening slightly as they mature. It is 1½ ft (45 cm) tall and 2 ft (60 cm) wide. It dies after the first frost.

Adiantum venustum has coppery pink fronds in spring, which turn light green and then blue-green as it matures. Fully grown it is 10 in (25 cm) tall and 9 in (23 cm) wide.

Cultivation
Plant in midspring in semishade in moist soil enriched with com-

post and leaf mold. Plant the rhizomes of *Adiantum pedatum* no more than 1 in (2.5 cm) deep, and those of *Adiantum venustum* ½ in (12 mm) deep. Top-dress with compost or shredded bark.

Propagation Divide in early spring or early fall. Pot out in a shady place and keep moist.

Pests/diseases Trouble free except for occasional slugs.

AFRICAN LILY — see
Agapanthus

Adiantum venustum

Agapanthus
African lily

Agapanthus campanulatus

❏ Height 2-3 ft (60-90 cm)
❏ Planting distance 2 ft (60 cm)
❏ Flowers late summer to early fall
❏ Any fertile, well-drained soil
❏ Sunny, sheltered site
❏ Hardy or marginally hardy; deciduous or evergreen
❏ Zones 8-10

The large rounded and loose flower clusters of the African lily lend an exotic air to the late-summer garden. Borne on tall and sturdy stems above clumps of narrow, strap-shaped midgreen leaves, the flowers are excellent for cutting, and the seed heads are good for dried arrangements. The hybrid varieties are generally hardier than supposed and can be grown in the open garden in the milder South and West; in other areas they succeed best in a sunny and sheltered position, with winter protection over the fleshy roots. African lilies are also ideal for growing in tubs and other deep containers.

Popular species
Agapanthus campanulatus is 2-2½ ft (60-75 cm) tall, with deciduous leaves. It is moderately hardy and bears relatively flat clusters, 4 in (10 cm) or more wide, of pale blue trumpet flowers. The slightly taller cultivar 'Isis' is a richer blue.
Agapanthus 'Headbourne Hybrids' are more readily available than the species and hardier. The flower stems, growing to 2½ ft (75 cm) high above mounds of deciduous foliage, are topped with perfect wide spheres of pale blue to deep violet-blue flowers.

Agapanthus 'Headbourne Hybrids'

Other named hybrids have intensely blue or pure white flowers, such as 'Bressingham White.' *Agapanthus praecox* (syn. *A. umbellatus)* is an evergreen species and not reliably hardy. Under suitable conditions it grows about 3 ft (90 cm) tall and produces large heads of pale or bright blue flowers; white cultivars also occur.

Cultivation
Plant in April, setting the fleshy crowns at least 2 in (5 cm) deep, in fertile, well-drained soil or in compost. All species and varieties require full sun and preferably shelter from strong winds. Once established, the roots resent disturbance and should be left alone until overcrowding makes division necessary. No staking is needed, but cut the stems down to the leaf mounds after flowering unless you want them for dried arrangements. In cold gardens, protect the plants with a deep winter mulch.
Propagation Divide and replant the roots in April or May or raise new plants from bought or saved seed sown in midspring at a tem-

perature of 55-59° F (13-15° C). Prick out the seedlings into flats when large enough to handle. Transfer the young plants singly to pots of potting medium. They will take a couple of years to reach flowering size and should be overwintered in a frost-free greenhouse.
Pests/diseases Generally trouble free.

Alchemilla

lady's mantle

Alchemilla mollis

❏ Height 6-18 in (15-45 cm)
❏ Planting distance 9-15 in (23-38 cm)
❏ Flowers late spring to early summer
❏ Moist, well-drained soil
❏ Sunny or partially shaded site
❏ Herbaceous
❏ Zones 3-7

A frothy mass of tiny, delicate star-shaped flowers and pale silvery green long-lasting foliage make *Alchemilla* a favorite with gardeners and flower arrangers alike. The flowers range in color from pale yellow to lime-green, and the leaves are rounded or divided into narrow leaflets. *Alchemilla* is a versatile perennial — it harmonizes gently with many other plants and spreads rapidly by self-sown seed, making it useful both for ground cover in partial shade and at the front of a border, perhaps spilling over onto a path.

Popular species

Alchemilla alpina has pale green, silvery leaves divided into narrow leaflets and green flowers gathered in clusters. It reaches a height of 9 in (23 cm) and has a spread of 9-12 in (23-30 cm).
Alchemilla erythropoda has a height of 6 in (15 cm) and a spread of 10 in (25 cm). The leaves have a bluish tinge, and the flowers are pale yellow, sometimes tinged red in late summer.
Alchemilla mollis, the most well-known species, has loose, cloudy sprays of yellow-green flowers in intricately branched heads. The leaves have rounded lobes with serrated edges and are covered with a fine down, which traps dew, making them glisten in early-morning sunlight. *A. mollis* grows up to 1½ ft (45 cm) tall and 15 in (38 cm) wide.

Cultivation

Plant in midfall or early spring in a sunny or partially shaded position in any moist but well-drained garden soil. Cut back flowering stems to 1 in (2.5 cm) above the ground after flowering.

The plant self-seeds readily, so cut off flower heads before they go to seed to prevent it from becoming invasive.

Propagation Sow in early spring in seed-starting medium in a cold frame. Prick out the seedlings and harden off in a nursery bed. Plant out in permanent positions in midfall or early spring.

Alternatively, divide and replant immediately in midfall or early spring.

Pests/diseases Generally trouble free.

ALKANET — see *Anchusa*
ALPINE ASTER — see *Aster*

Alchemilla erythropoda

Anaphalis

pearly everlasting

Anaphalis triplinervis 'Summer Snow'

❏ Height 1-3 ft (30-90 cm)
❏ Planting distance 1-1½ ft (30-45 cm)
❏ Flowers midsummer to early fall
❏ Well-drained soil
❏ Sunny or partially shaded site
❏ Herbaceous
❏ Zones 3-8

Anaphalis, a showy border plant, has flat white flower heads with yellow eyes and tapering silver or gray leaves. It is popular in fresh or dried arrangements.

Popular species
Anaphalis margaritacea has loose, pearly white flowers in late summer and gray-green leaves. It grows up to 3 ft (90 cm) high.
Anaphalis triplinervis grows 1½ ft (45 cm) high. The undersides of the silvery leaves are woolly. Small, bunched heads of flowers appear in late summer. A popular cultivar is 'Summer Snow,' grown for its crisp flower heads.
Anaphalis yedoensis has closely bunched flowers from midsummer to early fall, when the gray-green leaves turn a straw color. It grows up to 2½ ft (75 cm) tall.

Cultivation
Plant in early fall or midspring in a sunny site in well-drained soil or in dry shade.
Propagation Divide in early fall or midspring, or take 2-3 in (5-7.5 cm) cuttings of basal shoots in mid- to late spring and root in a cold frame.
 Sow seeds in early spring to midspring in a cold frame. Harden off seedlings in a nursery bed and plant out in midfall or early spring.
Pests/diseases Trouble free.

Anchusa

alkanet, bugloss

Anchusa azurea

❏ Height 3-5 ft (90-150 cm)
❏ Planting distance 1-1½ ft (30-45 cm)
❏ Flowers early summer
❏ Any fertile garden soil
❏ Sunny site
❏ Herbaceous
❏ Zones 3-8

Anchusa azurea (syn. *A. italica*) provides a vivid long-lasting display of summer color. It is seen at its best when planted in groups. Scores of tiny saucer-shaped flowers, each with a white or yellow eye, are borne on narrowly branching upright spikes and rise in clouds of vivid blue above coarse midgreen foliage. The flowers appear on the top third of the plant, drawing attention away from the leaves. These grow on bristly stems, looking coarse and rather unattractive after the flowers die away. Alkanet is short-lived, but self-seeds easily.

Popular cultivars
A few popular cultivars have been developed from *Anchusa azurea.* 'Dropmore' grows up to 4 ft (1.2 m) tall and has deep blue flowers; 'Little John' has brilliant blue flowers and reaches a height of 1½ ft (45 cm); 'Loddon Royalist' grows to a height of 3 ft (90 cm) and has deep blue flowers similar in color to gentians; 'Opal' has sky-blue flowers on stems up to 4 ft (1.2 m) tall.

Cultivation
Plant in midfall or early spring in any fertile and deep garden soil in a sunny site. Support the stems with twiggy sticks and remove the upper half of the stems after flowering to encourage a further display. Cut down old stems in midfall.
Propagation Increase by root cuttings taken in mid- or late winter. Root them in flats of seed-starting medium in a cold frame and set out in a nursery bed in late spring when new shoots have appeared. Plant out in permanent positions in midfall.
Pests/diseases Generally trouble free.

Anemone

Japanese anemone

Anemone tomentosa

- ❑ Height 2-4 ft (60-120 cm)
- ❑ Planting distance 2 ft (60 cm)
- ❑ Flowers early spring to fall
- ❑ Fertile, well-drained, moisture-retentive soil
- ❑ Partially shaded site
- ❑ Herbaceous
- ❑ Zones 5-8

Japanese anemone *(Anemone × hybrida,* syn *A. japonica* or *A. elegans)* provides fine color late in the flowering season when many other plants are past their best. These anemones look good under trees, where the petals of the palest cultivars seem almost translucent in the light shade. Nodding blooms, in white or shades of rose-pink with yellow stamens, open out flat when mature; they are held in loose, open clusters above dark green lobed leaves. The foliage, dense at the bottom of the plant, becomes lighter and smaller-leaved further up, leaving the upper 1-2 ft (30-60 cm) almost bare of leaves. The plants are free flowering after their first year.

Popular species

Anemone hupehensis, a pink-flowered Chinese species, is similar to the hybrids in bloom and habit but flowers a week earlier.

Anemone × hybrida comes in many colors. 'Alba' has large white flowers and grows up to 3 ft (90 cm) high; 'Alice' is a delicate light pink; 'Bressingham Glow' is

Anemone hupehensis

Anemone × hybrida 'Louise Uhink'

Anthemis

anthemis

Anthemis tinctoria

Anthemis cupaniana

a small cultivar, 3 ft (90 cm) tall, with rose-red semidouble flowers; 'Honorine Jobert' has white flowers and grows up to 3 ft (90 cm) tall; 'Kriemhilde' has blush-pink semidouble blooms; 'Lady Gilmour' has pendent, almost double, pink flowers on branching stems; 'Louise Uhink' has white single blooms; 'Queen Charlotte' has pale pink semidouble flowers. *Anemone tomentosa* is similar to *A. × hybrida,* but with vinelike leaves and single pale pink flowers. It grows to 2½ ft (75 cm) and is invasive.

Cultivation

Plant in early fall or early spring in fertile well-drained, but moisture-retentive soil, in light shade.
Propagation Divide and replant during suitable weather in early fall or early spring.

Take root cuttings during winter and root in a cold frame. When three leaves have developed, line out the young plants in nursery rows and plant out in early fall of the next year.
Pests/diseases Flea beetles may eat small holes in the leaves of seedlings. Caterpillars eat the leaves, flower buds, and stems of older plants. Aphids may infest stems and leaves, making them sticky and sooty. Several virus diseases may cause symptoms such as stunted growth, yellowing or distorted leaves, and flowers of poor size and color.

❏ Height ½-2½ ft (15-75 cm)
❏ Planting distance 1-1½ ft (30-45 cm)
❏ Flowers early to late summer
❏ Any well-drained soil
❏ Sunny site
❏ Herbaceous
❏ Zones 4-7

The fernlike leaves of anthemis make a light and aromatic setting for its daisylike white, yellow, or orange flowers, which appear from early to late summer.

Popular species

Anthemis cupaniana has finely dissected gray leaves and white flowers. It forms a spreading cushion up to 1 ft (30 cm) high and 15 in (38 cm) wide.
Anthemis nobilis (common chamomile), grows to 9 in (23 cm) high and spreads to a 15 in (38 cm) wide mat of finely dissected, mossy and aromatic midgreen foliage with small white flowers.
Anthemis sancti-johannis has bright orange flowers and lobed, gray-green hairy leaves. It grows up to 1½ ft (45 cm) high and 15 in (38 cm) wide.
Anthemis tinctoria (golden marguerite) has golden yellow flowers and deep green toothed leaves. It grows up to 2½ ft (75 cm) tall and 1½ ft (45 cm) wide.

Cultivation

Plant decorative species in early fall or early spring in a sunny spot in any ordinary well-drained soil. Cut down old flower stems in early fall.
Propagation Increase *A. nobilis* from cuttings of lateral shoots that are 3 in (7.5 cm) long between late spring and late summer, and root in a cold frame. Plant out in early fall or early spring.

Take 2-3 in (5-7.5 cm) long cuttings of basal shoots of decorative anthemis in early spring to midspring. Root in a cold frame and plant out in early fall to midfall. Alternatively, divide and replant.
Pests/diseases Trouble free.

Anemone x hybrida 'Queen Charlotte'

Aquilegia

columbine

Aquilegia vulgaris 'McKana Hybrids'

Aquilegia flabellata 'Nana'

Aquilegia vulgaris 'Nora Barlow'

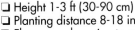

- ❏ Height 1-3 ft (30-90 cm)
- ❏ Planting distance 8-18 in (20-45 cm)
- ❏ Flowers early spring to early summer
- ❏ Well-drained, moist garden soil
- ❏ Partially shaded site
- ❏ Herbaceous
- ❏ Zones 3-9

Columbine is an old-fashioned plant with dainty spurred white, pink, yellow, blue, or red flowers and delicate light gray to gray-green foliage. It is a long-lived plant, but tends to cross-pollinate and produce variable color forms.

Popular species

Aquilegia canadensis grows to 2 ft (60 cm) high and spreads to 1 ft (30 cm). It has distinctive lemon-yellow flowers with bright red spurs in early summer.

Aquilegia flabellata grows up to 1½ ft (45 cm) tall and produces white to violet-blue flowers from early spring to late spring. 'Nana' has lilac and cream flowers, and 'Nana Alba' is pure white.

Aquilegia vulgaris is less popular than the numerous cultivars developed from it. They include 'Crimson Star,' up to 1½ ft (45 cm) tall with crimson and white flowers, and 'McKana Hybrids' and 'Mrs. Scott Elliott,' both up to 3 ft (90 cm) tall, with cream, red, blue, yellow, or pink flowers. 'Nora Barlow' has double flowers, without spurs, colored plum-red, shading to pink and green.

Cultivation

Plant in early fall or early spring in moist, but well-drained, humus-rich soil in a sunny or partially shaded site.

Propagation Sow seeds in mid- to late summer, or in early spring in a cold frame. Alternatively, divide and replant immediately in early fall.

Pests/diseases Leaf miners may burrow into leaves, and aphids cause distorted leaves.

Artemisia

artemisia

Artemisia schmidtiana 'Nana'

- ❏ Height 2-60 in (5-150 cm)
- ❏ Planting distance 9-36 in (23-90 cm)
- ❏ Flowers midsummer to midfall
- ❏ Any well-drained soil
- ❏ Sunny site
- ❏ Herbaceous perennials and deciduous or evergreen subshrubs
- ❏ Zones 4-8

Once used as a herbal remedy for ailments, artemisia is grown for its cloud of silver foliage, which has a pleasant sharp aroma when crushed. Artemisia is a lovely specimen plant and can also act as a foil for darker-foliaged plants. Shorter types are useful as edging. The plumelike flowers, insignificant in most species, appear from early fall to midfall.

Popular species

Artemisia abrotanum (southernwood) is a shrubby deciduous plant up to 4 ft (1.2 m) tall, with downy gray leaves and clusters of yellow flowers in fall.

Artemisia absinthium (wormwood) is a deciduous shrub, 3 ft (90 cm) high and wide, grown for its silver-gray filigree foliage.

Artemisia lactiflora is an herbaceous species with midgreen parsleylike foliage forming a clump 5 ft (1.5 m) high and 1½ ft (45 cm) wide. Fragrant, white flower plumes appear in early fall to midfall and are good for cutting.

Artemisia lanata (syn. *A. pedemontana*) is a shrubby evergreen forming gray-green cushions 2 in (5 cm) high and 9 in (23 cm) wide. It bears yellow flowers from midsummer to early fall.

Artemisia ludoviciana, an herba-

Artemisia ludoviciana

ceous species up to 4 ft (1.2 m) high, has woolly whitish-green leaves and plumes of silver-white brown-topped flowers in early fall to midfall.

Artemisia schmidtiana 'Nana,' a shrubby evergreen, forms a 3-5 in (7.5-13 cm) dome of silver-gray leaves, with dull yellow flowers in woolly silver bracts in early fall.

Artemisia splendens, a deciduous subshrub, has dainty silvery foliage; it grows to 1 ft (30 cm) high and 1½ ft (45 cm) wide.

Artemisia stellerana, a shrubby, grayish-white-leaved evergreen, bears tiny yellow flowers in late summer. 'Silver Brocade' is up to 1 ft (30 cm) tall with deeply lobed, felted white leaves.

Cultivation

Plant herbaceous species during midfall or early spring in light, well-drained soil in full sun. *A. lactiflora* requires a moisture-retentive soil.

Plant shrubby species in any well-drained garden soil in early spring to midspring.

Propagation Divide and replant herbaceous species in midfall or early spring. With shrubby species, take 3-4 in (7.5-10 cm) semihardwood cuttings with a heel in late summer and root them in a coid frame. Plunge pots outdoors in a sheltered bed and plant out the following spring.

Pests/diseases Rust shows as pale brown spots that later turn into almost black pustules.

Artemisia stellerana 'Silver Brocade'

Arum
arum

Arum italicum 'Pictum'

- ❏ Height 1½ ft (45 cm)
- ❏ Planting distance 1 ft (30 cm)
- ❏ Flowers spring
- ❏ Fertile, moisture-retentive soil
- ❏ Partial shade
- ❏ Herbaceous
- ❏ Zones 6-9

A close relative of the distinctive wildflower known popularly as Lords-and-Ladies (*Arum maculatum*), the garden form *Arum italicum* 'Pictum' is becoming increasingly popular. Its lovely gray and green marbled foliage provides winter interest, and its scarlet spikes of berries, though poisonous, bring welcome spots of brilliant color. The cultivar 'Marmoratum' has less heavily marbled leaves.

The stemless spear-shaped leaves appear in a clump in early fall as the berries ripen. They survive the winter, dying off in the spring, soon after the yellowish-green spathes of flowers appear.

Cultivation
Plant the tubers 4 in (10 cm) deep in fertile, moisture-retentive soil in fall. Light shade is preferable, though sun is tolerated, provided the soil is moist.

Propagation Lift the tubers in early fall and divide the offsets. Replant immediately.

Pests/diseases Trouble free.

Aruncus
goatsbeard

Aruncus dioicus

- ❏ Height 3-6 ft (90-180 cm)
- ❏ Planting distance 2 ft (60 cm)
- ❏ Flowers early summer
- ❏ Deep, moist loamy soil
- ❏ Partial shade
- ❏ Herbaceous
- ❏ Zones 3-7

Aruncus is grown for its silky plumes of creamy white flowers, which rise over and contrast gracefully with the bold light to midgreen compound leaves. Rough to the touch, the foliage is effective throughout the growing season. The poisonous, but ornamental seed heads appear only on female plants.

A large shrublike plant, *Aruncus* is suitable either as a specimen or in association with other plants, perhaps in partial shade at the rear of a border. It looks particularly effective close to water.

Popular species
Aruncus dioicus (syn. *Aruncus sylvester)* carries tall plumes of creamy white flowers over a 5 ft (1.5 m) clump of handsome midgreen foliage. The cultivar 'Glasnevin' reaches a height of 4 ft (1.2 m) and bears plumes of white flowers against light green foliage. 'Kneiffii' is smaller, only up to 3 ft (90 cm) tall, and has finely divided, ferny, dark green leaves.

Cultivation
Plant in midfall or early spring in partial shade in deep, moist loamy soil. Cut the stems down in midfall.

Propagation Divide and replant in spring, though roots and stems are tough and rather difficult to separate.

Pests/diseases Sawfly larvae may eat holes in the leaves, often reducing them to skeletons of veins.

Asarum

wild ginger

Asarum europaeum

❑ Height 5-8 in (12-20 cm)
❑ Planting distance 1 ft (30 cm)
❑ Flowers spring
❑ Rich, moist, slightly acid soil
❑ Shady site
❑ Herbaceous or evergreen
❑ Zones 4-7

Wild ginger is a ground cover for moist, shady places, perhaps under trees in woodland. The heart-shaped leaves grow on long stalks. In spring, bell-like brownish to greenish-purple flowers appear under the foliage, which may be evergreen or herbaceous.

Popular species

Asarum canadense is an herbaceous species. It has downy leaves up to 7 in (18 cm) wide, which may irritate the skin.

Asarum caudatum is a semi-evergreen species with leaves up to 6 in (15 cm) wide.

Asarum europaeum is an evergreen clump-forming and widespreading plant with leathery, rounded 3 in (7.5 cm) wide leaves.

Cultivation

Plant in fall in rich, moist soil in a shady position.

Propagation Divide and replant in fall or early spring.

Pests/diseases Trouble free.

Asphodeline

Jacob's rod, king's spear, yellow asphodel

Asphodeline lutea

❑ Height 3-4 ft (90-120 cm)
❑ Planting distance 1 ft (30 cm)
❑ Flowers late spring
❑ Any well-drained soil
❑ Sunny to lightly shaded site
❑ Herbaceous
❑ Zones 6-8

Asphodeline lutea, still sold by some nurseries under its old name, *Asphodelus lutea,* is a stately border plant with a pleasant fragrance. In late spring stiff spikes, up to 4 ft (1.2 m) tall, are covered with clusters of bright yellow starry blooms with red stamens. The flowers, which last for several weeks, are later replaced by seed heads that look decorative in the garden or as part of an indoor cut-flower arrangement.

The furrowed leaves, grasslike and waxy, are up to 1 ft (30 cm) long, growing in tufts at the base of the flower spikes.

Cultivation

Plant in midfall or early spring in ordinary well-drained soil in a sunny position. Take care not to damage the rhizomatous roots.

Propagation Divide in early fall and replant immediately.

Alternatively, sow seed in a cold frame in spring. Pot on and plant out in permanent positions the following spring.

Pests/diseases Generally trouble free.

Asplenium

spleenwort

Asplenium trichomanes

❏ Height 9-24 in (23-60 cm)
❏ Planting distance 10-24 in (25-60 cm)
❏ Foliage plant
❏ Shady site
❏ Rich, moist soil
❏ Evergreen
❏ Zones 3-6

Asplenium is an attractive fern providing year-round interest for shady places in borders or woodland, walls, and rock gardens. The long, graceful fronds resemble broad glossy straps, tough frilled ribbons, or double-curving rows of tiny disks.

Popular species

Asplenium adiantum-nigrum (black spleenwort), 9 in (23 cm) high and wide, is named for the purple-black stalks clothed with finely cut, glossy green fronds.
Asplenium scolopendrium, syn. *Phyllitis scolopendrium* (hart's-tongue fern) has tonguelike fronds and thrives in woodland or shady borders. It reaches a height of 2 ft (60 cm), with a spread of 1 ft (30 cm). Some popular cultivars include 'Crispum' (curled fronds and wavy edges), 'Cristatum' (fronds with tassels at the tips), 'Kaye's Lacerate' (deep-cut edges), and 'Undulatum' (wavy edges).
Asplenium trichomanes (maidenhair spleenwort) has a height and spread of 10 in (25 cm). It can be planted in rock gardens or the crevices of walls and has black stalks with round green lobes.

Cultivation

Plant smaller species in vertical or sloping crevices among rocks or stones during damp weather in midspring or early fall. *A. trichomanes* needs lime. Plant other species in moist, well-drained garden soil in a shady site in midspring.
Propagation Sow the dustlike spores in early spring or mid- to late summer. Or lift, divide, and replant in spring.
Pests/diseases Slugs can attack the fronds.

Aster

aster

Aster amellus 'Mauve Beauty'

❏ Height 15-72 in (38-180 cm)
❏ Planting distance 6-18 in (15-45 cm)
❏ Flowers summer to late fall
❏ Any fertile, well-drained garden soil
❏ Sunny, open site
❏ Herbaceous
❏ Zones 4-8

Asters earn their place in the border with a burst of varied late-summer to fall color — white, blue, purple, pink, red, or lilac — when earlier-flowering perennials are past their best. Each daisylike bloom is a mass of starry petals around a yellow center. Borne in clusters, each flower can measure as much as 2 in (5 cm) wide or as little as ⅓ in (8 mm). The foliage, which provides a strong foil to the colorful flowers, is gray-green, midgreen, or dark green, with rather hairy, narrow leaves.

Border species look outstanding in any fall border. They have an upright habit and are heavily branched toward the top, with many leaves and flowers. They include the popular New York asters in a variety of clear, bright colors. Because they deteriorate quickly, for the best effect New York asters should be divided and replanted at least every 2 years. All asters are excellent for cut-flower arrangements.

Popular species

Aster amellus (Italian aster) is up to 2 ft (60 cm) high and 15 in (38 cm) wide with rough gray-green leaves. The flowers, up to 2½ in

Aster novi-belgii 'Patricia Ballard'

(6 cm) wide, appear on woody stems in late summer and early fall. The species has been superseded by such popular cultivars as 'King George' (violet-blue), 'Mauve Beauty' (mauve), 'Nocturne' (lavender), 'Pink Zenith' (clear pink), and 'Sonia' (rose-pink).

Aster cordifolius is up to 4 ft (1.2 m) tall with sprays of silvery blue flowers, each ¾ in (2 cm) wide.

Aster ericoides (heath aster) is up to 3 ft (90 cm) tall with midgreen leaves. It bears numerous tiny white or pink-edged flowers on slender multibranched stems in early fall to midfall. Cultivars include 'Blue Star' (palest blue), 'Silver Spray' (white), and 'Ringdove' (rosy-purple).

Aster × frikartii is a hybrid that is 2½ ft (75 cm) high with orange-centered blue flowers from late summer to midfall and rough, dark green leaves. Cultivars include 'Jungfrau' (lilac-blue), 'Mönch (lilac-blue and free flowering), and 'Wonder of Staefa' (pale lavender).

Aster linosyris grows up to 2 ft (60 cm) tall with dull green leaves and small, buttonlike bright yellow flowers in dense clusters from late summer to early fall. 'Gold Flake' is a bright cultivar.

Aster novae-angliae (New England aster) is a 4 ft (1.2 m) tall species with pink to purple flowers in loose clusters on woody stems in early fall. Some cultivars include 'Alma Potschke' (salmon-pink), 'Harrington's Pink' (clear pink), 'Mt. Everest' (white), 'September Ruby' (ruby-red), and 'Treasure' (lilac).

Aster novi-belgii (New York aster) is up to 4 ft (1.2 m) tall, with deep green leaves and clusters of flowers on branched stems in early fall to midfall. Tall cultivars include 'Ada Ballard' (lavender-blue), 'Alert' (deep crimson), 'Autumn Glory' (semidouble, red), 'Coombe Violet' (violet), 'Eventide' (semidouble, violet-blue), 'Marie Ballard' (double, light blue), 'Patricia Ballard' (semidouble, pink), and 'White Lady' (white). Dwarf cultivars, up to 1 ft (30 cm) tall, include 'Jenny' (double, violet-purple), 'Kristina' (pure white), 'Lady in Blue' (semidouble, blue), 'Little Pink Beauty' (semidouble, pink), 'Snowsprite' (white), and 'Victor' (lavender).

Aster thomsonii 'Nanus' is up to 15 in (38 cm) tall with lavender-blue flowers in late summer to midfall and gray-green leaves.

Aster tongolensis (syn. *A. subcaeruleus*) is up to 1½ ft (45 cm) tall with hairy, dark green leaves

Aster novi-belgii 'Alert Dwarf'

Aster amellus 'King George'

and bright blue-purple flowers in midsummer. The cultivar 'Napsbury' has deep blue flowers.

Cultivation

Plant in any fertile, well-drained garden soil in a sunny area in midfall or early spring. The soil must not dry out in late summer and fall when the plants are in flower. Support the taller asters with twiggy sticks.

Propagation Divide and replant in midfall or early spring for vigorous outside growth. To raise large numbers of plants, pull the clumps apart into single shoots in early spring to midspring and plant 6 in (15 cm) apart. Divide *A. novi-belgii* like this annually.

Pests/diseases Powdery mildew appears as a white powder on the leaves. Aster wilt affects many species and cultivars, particularly *A. novi-belgii*. The stems may turn brown and wither, and the shoots wilt and die. *A. novae-angliae* and its cultivars seem to be immune.

Aster × *frikartii* 'Wonder of Staefa'

Astilbe
astilbe

Astilbe × arendsii 'Fanal'

❏ Height 8-48 in (20-120 cm)
❏ Planting distance 1-2 ft (30-60 cm)
❏ Flowers early to late summer
❏ Rich, moist soil
❏ Sunny or partially shaded site
❏ Herbaceous
❏ Zones 4-8

The fluffy, long-lasting flower spires of *Astilbe,* in white, cream, pink, lilac, and red, rise above lush, deeply cut foliage. Ideal for damp borders, it looks particularly effective near water.

Popular species
Astilbe × arendsii grows 2-4 ft (60-120 cm) high and has dark green fernlike foliage and a wide range of flower colors. Cultivars include 'Deutschland' (white), 'Fanal' (deep red), 'Federsee' (rosy red), 'Hyacinth' (rose-pink), 'Irrlicht' (pure white), and 'Red Sentinel' (brick-red).
Astilbe chinensis, up to 3 ft (90 cm) tall, has rose-pink to purplish blooms and coarse-toothed leaves. The dwarf cultivar 'Pumila,' 1½ ft (45 cm) high, has midgreen ferny

Astilbe × arendsii 'Deutschland'

foliage and purplish-pink flowers.
Astilbe × crispa, 8 in (20 cm) tall, has midgreen, crinkly leaves and white, pink, or pale red flowers.
Astilbe simplicifolia, up to 1 ft (30 cm) high, has arching white or pink flower plumes, which rise above deeply cut leaves. 'Sprite' has shell-pink flower sprays that last for weeks.

Cultivation
Plant in midfall or early spring in rich, permanently moist soil in sun or partial shade. Give twiggy support to tall cultivars in windy sites.
Propagation Divide and replant every 3 years in early spring to midspring.
Pests /diseases Trouble free.

Astilbe chinensis 'Pumila'

Astrantia

masterwort

Astrantia major

❏ Height 1-3 ft (30-90 cm)
❏ Planting distance 9-15 in (23-38 cm)
❏ Flowers early to late summer
❏ Moist, fertile soil
❏ Partially shaded or sunny site
❏ Herbaceous
❏ Zones 4-7

Astrantia has been a favorite in gardens since the 16th century. Its starry flowers of white, pink, or greenish-pink are surrounded by white, green-and-white or plum-colored bracts and are held in small clusters above clumps of coarsely dissected leaves. It grows up to 3 ft (90 cm) tall and is suitable for fresh or dried cut-flower arrangements. The flowers are up to 2½ in (6 cm) wide.

Popular species

Astrantia carniolica, up to 2 ft (60 cm) high, has midgreen finely divided leaves and white flowers in mid- to late summer, tinged with pink and surrounded by white bracts. The cultivar 'Rubra' is 1 ft (30 cm) high with purple-red flowers and bracts in midsummer.
Astrantia major grows up to 3 ft (90 cm) tall and has greenish-pink, rose, or white blooms and pink-purple bracts in early summer to midsummer. 'Variegata' has cream-edged leaves.
Astrantia maxima, up to 2 ft (60 cm) tall, has bright green leaves and shell-pink flowers with pink bracts in early summer to midsummer.

Cultivation

Plant in midfall or early spring in moist, fertile garden soil. A partially shaded site is best, but a sunny site will do if the soil stays reasonably moist in summer. Use twiggy sticks to support plants.
Propagation Divide and replant from midfall to early spring. Or sow seeds in early fall in a cold frame. Prick out in spring and plant out in a nursery bed in early summer to midsummer. Plant out into permanent positions the following spring.
Pests/diseases Trouble free.

Astrantia major 'Variegata'

Athyrium

lady fern

Athyrium felix-femina

❏ Height 1-3 ft (30-90 cm)
❏ Planting distance 1½-3 ft (45-90 cm)
❏ Foliage plant
❏ Moist, humus-rich soil
❏ Lightly shaded site
❏ Herbaceous
❏ Zones 3-6

In the light shade of a border the delicate fronds of *Athyrium* resemble green lace. This fern is at its best in spring, when the fresh young fronds unfurl in a cloud of dainty foliage on darker stalks. The lady fern, *Athyrium felix-femina,* is up to 2 ft (60 cm) high and wide, with fresh green fronds. Many cultivars have been developed from it, including 'Veroniae Cristatum,' with curled and roughly triangular fronds, and 'Victoria,' with finely cut, crested fronds forming a lattice-work effect.

Cultivation

Plant in midspring or early fall in light shade in a humus-rich soil. Keep moist at all times. Lift and replant when the rootstock pushes above ground.
Propagation Sow the dustlike spores at any time, or divide and replant in midspring.
Pests/diseases Generally trouble free.

AVENS — see *Geum*
BABY'S BREATH — see *Gypsophila*
BALLOON FLOWER — see *Platycodon*
BANEBERRY — see *Actaea*

Baptisia
false indigo

Baptisia australis

❑ Height 2-4 ft (60-120 cm)
❑ Planting distance 1½ ft (45 cm)
❑ Flowers early summer
❑ Deep, moist soil
❑ Sunny site
❑ Herbaceous
❑ Zones 3-9

False indigo thrives in rough places. *Baptisia australis,* an erect, leafy perennial grows about 4 ft (1.2 m) high, with blue-green trifoliate leaves. In early summer it produces slender indigo-blue spikes of sweet-pea-like flowers, which are good for cutting.

Cultivation
Plant in midfall or early spring, in deep, moist soil and full sun. Once established, the roots resent disturbance.
Propagation Sow seeds in mid-spring, outdoors or in a cold frame. Transfer seedlings to a nursery bed and grow on for two years.
Pests/diseases Trouble free.

BARRENWORT — see
Epimedium
BEAR'S BREECHES — see
Acanthus
BEDSTRAW — see *Galium*
BELLFLOWER — see
Campanula

Bergenia
bergenia

Bergenia cordifolia

❑ Height 12-18 in (30-45 cm)
❑ Planting distance 1-2 ft (30-60 cm)
❑ Flowers late winter to early summer
❑ Any garden soil
❑ Sunny or partially shaded site
❑ Evergreen
❑ Zones 3-8

The leathery, slightly glossy leaves of *Bergenia* provide bold mid- to dark green year-round ground cover, tinted red or purple in winter. From late winter to early summer, clusters of white or pale pink to deep purple-red bell-shaped flowers rise over the foliage on tall, straight stems.

Popular species
Bergenia cordifolia, up to 1½ ft (45 cm) tall, has drooping heads of lilac-rose flowers on reddish stems from early spring until early summer. The glossy green crinkly-edged leaves are up to 10 in (25 cm) long. The creeping rootstock forms close ground cover and edgings. The cultivar 'Purpurea' has purplish leaves in winter and pink-purple flowers.
Bergenia crassifolia, up to 1 ft (30 cm) high, has tinted red leaves in winter; lavender-pink flowers appear in January.
Bergenia purpurascens (syn. *B. delavayi),* up to 15 in (38 cm) high, has loose heads of purple-pink to pink flowers. The leaves are reddish in winter.
Garden hybrids and cultivars include 'Abendglut,' or 'Evening

Bergenia purpurascens

Glow' (magenta-crimson flowers and heart-shaped leaves that turn maroon in winter); 'Ballawley' (deep carmine-pink); and 'Silverlight' (white above broad leaves that turn bronze-red in winter). 'Baby Doll,' only 1 ft (30 cm) tall, bears dense clusters of pale pink flowers.

Cultivation
Plant well-rooted plants in mid-fall or early spring in almost any soil in sun or partial shade, setting the plants 1 ft (30 cm) apart. Bergenias thrive in quite damp soils next to water and also do well in dry soil, although growth

Bergenia 'Silverlight'

Blechnum
hard fern

Blechnum spicant

❑ Height ½-2 ft (15-60 cm)
❑ Planting distance 1-1½ ft (30-45 cm)
❑ Foliage plant
❑ Moist, well-drained, lime-free soil
❑ Shady, sheltered position
❑ Evergreen
❑ Zones 7-10

Hard ferns have tough, leathery, dark green fronds resembling rosettes of curving double combs. They are very hardy evergreen foliage plants but hate alkaline soils. These plants do best in the Northwest.

Popular species
Blechnum penna marina (dwarf hard fern), up to 6 in (15 cm) tall, spreads from creeping rhizomes, making it suitable for rock gardens. It has narrow fronds.
Blechnum spicant (common deer fern) is up to 2 ft (60 cm) tall with densely set narrow fronds.

Cultivation
Plant in spring, in moist, well-drained acid soil, sheltered from drying winds. Mulch annually in spring with shredded bark.
Propagation Divide and replant in spring or early fall.
Pests/diseases Trouble free.

Brunnera
Siberian bugloss

Brunnera macrophylla

❑ Height 1-1½ ft (30-45 cm)
❑ Planting distance 1½ ft (45 cm)
❑ Flowers late spring to early summer
❑ Lightly shaded site
❑ Moist, fertile soil
❑ Herbaceous
❑ Zones 3-7

Brunnera macrophylla (syn. *Anchusa myosotidiflora*) is a handsome border plant, with heart-shaped, mat green leaves, setting off a cloud of blue forget-me-not-like flowers. Useful for ground cover, popular cultivars include 'Langtrees' (leaves spotted with silver) and 'Variegata' (white-splashed leaves).

Cultivation
Plant in midfall or early spring in moist fertile soil. *Brunnera* tolerates sun, if the soil does not dry out, but prefers light shade. On variegated forms, remove any stems that revert to green.
Propagation Divide and replant in mid- to late fall. Or take root cuttings in mid- to late fall and root in a cold frame. Plant out in a nursery bed in late spring to early summer. Plant out in the flowering site in fall.
Pests/diseases Trouble free.

Bergenia purpurascens

is slow in dry conditions. Lift and divide only when overcrowded. Remove stems after flowering.
Propagation Divide and replant in fall or early spring.
Pests/diseases Leaf spot fungus may blotch leaves. Slugs may be a problem.

BETONY — see *Stachys*
BISHOP'S HAT — see *Epimedium*
BLACK SNAKEROOT — see *Cimicifuga*
BLANKET FLOWER — see *Gaillardia*
BLAZING STAR — see *Liatris*

BLEEDING HEART — see *Dicentra*
BLUE-EYED GRASS — see *Sisyrinchium*
BONESET — see *Eupatorium*
BOWLES' GOLDEN GRASS — see *Carex*

BUGBANE — see *Cimicifuga*
BUGLOSS — see *Anchusa*
BURNET — see *Sanguisorba*
BURNING BUSH — see *Dictamnus*
BUTTERCUP — see *Ranunculus*
CALAMINT — see *Calamintha*

Calamintha

calamint

Calamintha nepeta

❑ Height 1 ft (30 cm)
❑ Planting distance 1 ft (30 cm)
❑ Flowers late summer to midfall
❑ Gritty, well-drained soil
❑ Sunny site
❑ Herbaceous
❑ Zones 5-9

Calamintha nepeta (syn. *C. nepetoides)* is a long-flowering member of the mint family, with a pleasant minty aroma to the leaves that is irresistible to bees. It forms a bushy mound up to 1 ft (30 cm) high and wide, with deep green leaves about 1 in (2.5 cm) long. From late summer profuse small pale lilac, tubular-shaped flowers appear in whorls along erect, leafy stems.

Cultivation
Plant in midspring in gritty, well-drained soil in a sunny site.

Propagation Divide and replant in spring, or sow seeds in a cold frame. Prick out seedlings into a nursery row and move the plants to permanent sites the following spring.

Pests/diseases Generally trouble free.

Campanula

bellflower

Campanula trachelium

❑ Height ½-5 ft (15-150 cm)
❑ Planting distance 9-24 in (23-60 cm)
❑ Flowers late spring to late fall
❑ Well-drained, fertile soil
❑ Sunny or partially shaded site
❑ Herbaceous
❑ Zones 3-8

The nodding blooms of bellflower *(Campanula)* were a familiar sight in Shakespeare's day and before. Many species have truly bell-shaped flowers; in others they are formed like cups or stars. The delicate flowers bloom singly on branching stems or are held in loose or tight clusters, or in spikes. The flowers come in shades of blue, violet, lavender, pink, and white, and the foliage is gray-green to mid- or dark green. Hundreds of bellflower species exist, including perennial, biennial, and annual types. Those described here are perennials suitable for growing in bold groups in herbaceous and mixed borders; some are invasive and should be sited with care.

Popular species
Campanula alliariifolia grows up to 2 ft (60 cm) high and has spikes of creamy white flowers in early summer to midsummer.
Campanula barbata (bearded bellflower) is a short-lived species up to 1½ ft (45 cm) high. It forms rosettes of lance-shaped, hairy midgreen leaves and single stems bearing one-sided panicles of nod-

Campanula persicifolia

ding bell-shaped flowers in early summer. They range in color from bluish purple to white and are distinguished by the long wooly hairs that protrude from the bells.
Campanula carpatica is an alpine species, 9-12 in (23-30 cm) tall, and too invasive for any but the largest of rock gardens. It is, however, admirably suited for front edging of borders and beds, where the leaf clumps quickly form neat mounds of midgreen, gently toothed ovate leaves. In mid- and late summer, the plants are densely covered with showy cup-shaped flowers, 1-2 in (2.5-5 cm) wide, in shades of blue and purple. Numerous cultivars are available, including 'Blue Carpet' (blue dwarf), 'Blue Clips' (medium blue), 'Wedgewood White' (white), and 'White Star' (white).
Campanula glomerata (clustered bellflower) is up to 1½ ft (45 cm) high with dense clusters of erect purple bell-shaped flowers on rigid leafy stems from late spring to midfall. Good cultivars include 'Joan Elliott' (purple) and 'Superba' (violet).
Campanula lactiflora (milky bellflower) is up to 5 ft (1.5 m) tall with sprays of bell-shaped light lavender-blue or milk-white flowers in early summer to midsummer. Cultivars include 'Alba' (white), 'Loddon Anna' (soft pink), 'Pouffe' (up to 10 in /25 cm

Campanula portenschlagiana

high with profuse lavender-blue flowers), and 'Prichard's Variety' (deep lavender-blue).

Campanula latifolia (giant bell-flower) has tubular purple-blue flowers on erect stems in mid-summer and grows to 5 ft (1.5 m). Cultivars include 'Gloaming' (smoky blue) and 'Macrantha' (dark purple).

Campanula persicifolia, syn. *C. grandis* or *C. latiloba* (peach-leaved bellflower), has evergreen basal leaves and slender stems up to 3 ft (90 cm) high with clustered saucer-shaped white, blue, or purple-blue flowers from early to late summer. Cultivars include 'Alba' (white), 'Coerulea Coronata' (semidouble, purple-blue), 'Percy Piper' (deep blue), and 'Telham Beauty' (large, light blue).

Campanula portenschlagiana, syn. *C. muralis*, is an invasive plant, growing up to 6 in (15 cm) high. It is best grown in crevices in walls or paths. Deep purple, bell-shaped flowers are borne from midsummer to late fall.

Campanula poscharskyana is a rampant species that grows up to 6 in (15 cm) tall and 1½ ft (45 cm) wide. Sprays of lavender-blue starry flowers appear in succession from midsummer to late fall.

Campanula pyramidalis (chimney bellflower) is a very hardy, but short-lived perennial species best grown as a biennial because flowering deteriorates in the second year. The 4 ft (1.2 m) tall stems are clothed with rich green heart-shaped leaves under the broad spikes of blue or white bells in midsummer.

Campanula trachelium, syn. *C. urticifolia* (nettle-leaved bell-flower), has nettlelike leaves and purple-blue flowers in late summer. It is up to 2 ft (60 cm) high.

Cultivation

Plant in early fall or midspring in well-drained, fertile garden soil in a sunny or partially shaded site sheltered from winds. Tall cultivars need staking.

Propagation Sow seeds in midfall or early spring to midspring in a cold frame. Line taller species out in nursery rows and plant out in midfall. Grow smaller species on in pots until they are ready for planting out.

Divide and replant cultivars in midfall or early spring to mid-spring. Or take cuttings of non-flowering basal shoots that are 1-2 in (2.5-5 cm) long in mid- to late spring and root in a cold frame. Pot and treat as seedlings.

Pests/diseases Slugs and snails may damage leaves and shoots. Rust fungus may affect leaves.

CAMPION — see *Lychnis*

Campanula lactiflora

Campanula latifolia

Campanula persicifolia 'Alba'

Carex

sedge

Carex stricta 'Bowles' Golden'

- ❏ Height 1-4 ft (30-120 cm)
- ❏ Planting distance 1-3 ft (30-90 cm)
- ❏ Foliage plant
- ❏ Moist soil
- ❏ Sun or light shade
- ❏ Herbaceous or semievergreen
- ❏ Zones 6-9

Sedges are grasses with green to yellow, sometimes variegated, arching foliage. Smaller species can edge beds and borders, while larger species are good specimen clumps around ponds. Tiny flowers appear on spikes with leafy bracts.

Popular species
Carex morrowii (Japanese sedge) is up to 1 ft (30 cm) tall. Cultivars include 'Aureo Variegata' (leaves striped golden yellow) and 'Variegata' (leaves striped white). *Carex pendula* (great drooping sedge), up to 4 ft (1.2 m) tall, has broad yellow-green leaves and produces attractive pendent seed heads in fall.
Carex stricta 'Bowles' Golden' is up to 2 ft (60 cm) tall. Its golden yellow leaves become green in late summer.

Cultivation
Plant in fall or spring in any well-drained, but moisture-retentive soil. *C. pendula* prefers constantly moist soil.
Propagation Divide and replant in spring. Or sow in early spring in a cold frame. Harden off in a nursery bed; plant out in fall.
Pests/diseases Trouble free.

CARNATION — *Dianthus*

Catananche

cupid's dart

Catananche caerulea

- ❏ Height 1½-2½ ft (45-75 cm)
- ❏ Planting distance 15-18 in (38-45 cm)
- ❏ Flowers mid- to late summer
- ❏ Light, well-drained soil
- ❏ Sunny site
- ❏ Herbaceous
- ❏ Zones 3-9

The soft blue flowers of *Catananche caerulea* (cupid's dart) are carried high over its sparse narrow-leaved foliage. Shaped like double daisies on wiry stems, with deep blue centers and papery calyxes, the flowers are suitable for both fresh and dried flower arrangements. The plant is up to 2½ ft (75 cm) high and looks decorative in borders. Cultivars include 'Major' (larger flowers in a richer shade of blue) and 'Perry's White.'

Cultivation
Plant in early fall or midspring in a sunny position in light, well-drained soil. Support the stems in exposed positions.
Propagation Sow seeds during mid- to late spring in a cold frame. Prick out into flats, then into a nursery bed; move to permanent positions in fall.
Increase cultivars by taking root cuttings in early spring and rooting in a cold frame.
Pests/diseases Generally trouble free.

CATMINT — see *Nepeta*
CELANDINE POPPY — see *Stylophorum*

Centaurea

knapweed

Centaurea macrocephala

Centaurea dealbata 'Steenbergii'

❏ Height 1½-4 ft (45-120 cm)
❏ Planting distance 1-2 ft (30-60 cm)
❏ Flowers late spring to early fall
❏ Any fertile, well-drained soil
❏ Sunny site
❏ Herbaceous
❏ Zones 3-7

Handsome thistlelike flower heads in shades of blue, lilac, rosy to deep pink, or bright yellow make the *Centaurea* a striking border plant. Deeply cut leaves form a low-growing clump; they may be deep green, silvery, or gray-green backed with silver.

Popular species

Centaurea dealbata (perennial cornflower), up to 2 ft (60 cm) high, has gray-green, silver-backed leaves. Its rose-pink flowers bloom in summer. Cultivars include 'John Coutts' (pale yellow center) and 'Steenbergii' (white center).

Centaurea hypoleuca growing 1½ ft (45 cm) high, has grayish-green deeply cut leaves. Pink cornflowerlike blooms open from late spring to late summer.

Centaurea macrocephala grows up to 4 ft (1.2 m) tall and has very large yellow thistlelike flowers in early summer to midsummer. *Centaurea montana,* is up to 2 ft (60 cm) tall, with deep green hairy leaves and thinly petaled blue flowers from late spring to early summer.

Centaurea pulchra 'Major,' 3 ft (90 cm) tall, bears pink flowers.

Cultivation

Plant in midfall or early spring in any fertile, well-drained soil in a sunny position.

Propagation Divide and replant every third or fourth year in midfall or early spring. Or sow seeds in midspring in a cold frame. Prick out into flats and grow on in a nursery bed. Pot seedlings of *C. dealbata* and *C. hypoleuca* singly and plunge pots outdoors. Move plants to flowering sites in midfall; overwinter pot-grown species in a cold frame; plant out in final positions next midspring.

Pests/diseases Powdery mildew appears as a white coating on leaves, stems, and flowers.

Centaurea montana

Centranthus

red valerian

Centranthus ruber and *C. r.* 'Albus'

❏ Height 1½-3 ft (45-90 cm)
❏ Planting distance 1 ft (30 cm)
❏ Flowers late spring to late summer
❏ Well-drained soil
❏ Sunny position
❏ Herbaceous
❏ Zones 5-8

Distinctive reddish-pink flower heads top *Centranthus ruber.* This strong, upright plant thrives in alkaline soil, producing a long-lasting display of small star-shaped flowers held in upright clusters. The broad fleshy leaves are gray-green and up to 4 in (10 cm) long; they can smell unpleasant when bruised. If allowed to grow on walls, the plant's powerful woody roots may split open brickwork.

Centranthus ruber reaches a height of 3 ft (90 cm) and spreads across an area 1 ft (30 cm) wide. 'Albus' (white flowers) and 'Coccineus' (red) are cultivars.

Cultivation

Plant in early spring to midspring in a sunny site in any well-drained, even poor, soil. Alkaline soils are particularly suitable. Cut down dead growth in fall.

Propagation Sow seeds between midspring and early summer, either where the plants are to flower or in a seed bed. If the seeds are sown in the flowering site, thin to the required distance; if in a seed bed, transplant while the plants are quite small.

Pests/diseases Generally trouble free.

CHAMOMILE — see *Anthemis*

Chelone

turtlehead

Chelone obliqua

❏ Height 2-3 ft (60-90 cm)
❏ Planting distance 1-2 ft (30-60 cm)
❏ Flowers midsummer to early fall
❏ Deep, well-drained moist soil
❏ Sunny or partially shaded site
❏ Herbaceous
❏ Zones 3-8

The pink or deep rose flowers of *Chelone* are gathered in spikes, shaped like colorful turtles' heads. These upright perennials are good additions to fall borders.

Popular species

Chelone lyonii, up to 3 ft (90 cm) tall, has clusters of pink flowers. *Chelone obliqua,* up to 2 ft (60 cm) high, has deep rose flower spikes above dark green foliage.

Cultivation

Plant in early fall or early spring in a sunny or partially shaded position in any deep, well-drained moist soil.

Propagation Sow seeds in early spring (at 59°F/15° C) under glass or in a cold frame in midspring. Prick out into a nursery bed and plant out in permanent positions 1½-2 years after sowing.

Pests/diseases Generally trouble free.

CHECKER MALLOW — see *Sidalcea*
CHINESE LANTERN — see *Physalis*
CHRISTMAS ROSE — see *Helleborus*

Chrysogonum

chrysogonum

Chrysogonum virginianum

❏ Height ½-1 ft (15-30 cm)
❏ Planting distance 8 in (20 cm)
❏ Flowers late spring to midfall
❏ Moist, well-drained soil
❏ Partially shaded or sunny site
❏ Evergreen in the South
❏ Zones 5-9

The starry golden flowers of *Chrysogonum virginianum* stand out vividly against its dense, bright green toothed foliage throughout the long flowering season from late spring to mid-fall. Suitable for brightening up the front of a border, it roots where it touches the soil and spreads to an attractive carpet.

Cultivation

Plant in ordinary well-drained soil in a partially shaded position or in sun.

Propagation Divide and replant in early spring.

Alternatively, sow seeds in late spring or early summer, but expect variation in leaf size and flower color.

Pests/diseases Generally trouble free.

Chrysanthemum

chrysanthemum

Semipompon chrysanthemum

Spoon-petaled chrysanthemum

Pompon chrysanthemum

❏ Height ½-6 ft (15-180 cm)
❏ Planting distance 1-2 ft (30-60 cm)
❏ Flowers early summer to late fall
❏ Well-drained soil
❏ Sunny site
❏ Hardy and half-hardy; herbaceous
❏ Zones 4-9

Chrysanthemums owe their popularity to their enormous diversity. The flowers come in shades of red, yellow, white, purple, pink, mauve, or bronze. They range from the plain, daisylike form to the more elaborate types developed by horticulturists — rayed petals with pincushionlike centers, petals curving up, petals curving down, or petals massed tightly together to create a ball of color. In some types the flowers are small and gathered in loose clusters on branching stems; in others each stem bears one huge single bloom.

The simplest type of chrysanthemum produces daisylike flowers, which are usually white with yellow centers, but also come in shades of pink or purple. They include annual, bedding, and rock garden types as well as the border chrysanthemums described here.

The huge selection known as florists' chrysanthemums offers a much wider variety of color and flower form, lasting well into fall. In mild areas, particularly in sheltered gardens in the South, late-flowering varieties may still be in bloom at the beginning of winter. In cold gardens and in the North, late-flowering florists' chrysanthemums are best grown in pots that can be stood outside during the summer; by the end of September they should be moved into a greenhouse.

Anemone-flowered chrysanthemum

Single chrysanthemum

Florists' chrysanthemums are hybrids of complex parentage and are suitable for growing in beds, borders, or pots. Left alone, they produce sprays of flowers up to 2½ in (6 cm) wide. Disbudded, however, they produce magnificent long-stemmed single blooms, each measuring 5 in (12 cm) wide or more. They are not reliably hardy. In mild areas, they may survive the average winter, but second-year plants produce less impressive floral displays. They are best raised annually from basal cuttings taken from roots, lifted from the garden in late fall, and overwintered in a frost-free greenhouse or cold frame. Perennial border chrysanthemums are fully hardy and can be left in their permanent flowering positions.

Popular species

Chrysanthemum haradjanii, now called *Tanacetum haradjanii* (syn. *T. densum* 'Amanum'), which reaches up to 6 in (15 cm) high, is grown for its silvery fern-like foliage. It has small yellow, button flowers, but these are best removed. The plant is suitable for bedding designs and as an accent at the front of a border.

Chrysanthemum leucanthemum, syn. *Leucanthemum vulgare* (ox-eye daisy or moon daisy), is an ultra-hardy border perennial. It reaches a height of 2 ft (60 cm) and has a profusion of white daisy-like flowers in early summer.

Chrysanthemum parthenium, now called *Tanacetum parthenium* (feverfew), is a hardy but short-lived perennial species usually grown as an annual. From 8-18 in (20-45 cm) high, it has light green aromatic leaves and a profuse show of yellow or white anemone-type flowers. Popular cultivars include 'Golden Ball' (golden yellow; 10 in/25 cm high) and 'Ultra Double White' (white; 1½ ft/45 cm high).

Chrysanthemum × *rubellum* has fragrant pink, yellow-eyed daisy flowers in late summer to early fall. It grows up to 2½ ft (75 cm). Cultivars include 'Clara Curtis' (clear pink), 'Dutchess of Edinburgh' (muted red), and 'Mary Stoker' (soft yellow).

Chrysanthemum serotinum, now called *Leucanthemella serotinum* (Hungarian or giant daisy), is up to 6 ft (1.8 m) high, bearing white flowers with a greenish-yellow center in late fall. It is suitable for growing at the back of borders.

Chrysanthemum × *superbum*, syn. *Leucanthemum maximum* (the Shasta daisy) grows up to 3 ft (90 cm) tall with white daisy flowers in mid- to late summer. The leaves are dark green and toothed. Some cultivars include 'Aglaya' (semidouble, white), 'Cobham Gold' (double, creamy with light yellow center), 'Esther Read' (double, white), 'Polaris' (clean white), 'Snowcap' (20 in/50cm high, white), and 'Wirral Supreme' (double, white).

Florists' types

Florists' chrysanthemums have pungent deep green leaves divided into rounded lobes and can be grown in borders, beds, pots, or greenhouses. Florists' chrysanthemums belong to one of two main types — the large/medium or the spray type.

LARGE/MEDIUM TYPES are disbudded, which encourages the development of one very large bloom per stem, sometimes reaching a width of 7 in (18 cm). The plants themselves are 4-5 ft (1.2-1.5 m) high. They are classified according to type of bloom.

Incurve: Close, firm petals, curving in on each other to form a perfect globe. Hybrids include 'Gillette' (solid creamy white), 'Honey Ball' (golden orange), 'Indian Chief' (deep red with gold reverse), 'Love Affair' (pink petals, deep lavender on inside), 'Mustang' (orange-

Korean chrysanthemum

Chrysanthemum rubellum 'Clara Curtis'

Spray-type anemone-flowered chrysanthemum

Chrysanthemum (Tanacetum) haradjanii

Chrysanthemum × superbum

bronze), 'Royal Pageant' (rosy purple), and 'Trail Blazer' (white).

Reflexed: Petals fall outward and downward, overlapping like feathers on a bird. Hybrids include 'Black Magic' (deep purple), 'Kansas' (scarlet-bronze), 'Paint Box' (brilliant orange), 'Peace' (pastel yellow), 'Sheer Pink' (deep pink), 'Solitaire' (ivory-white), and 'Typhoon' (crimson with gold).

Intermediate: Petals curve loosely or are incurved toward the top and reflexed below. Hybrids include 'Eroica' (deep purple), 'Good News Bronze' (bronze), 'Matador' (dark red), 'Promenade' (pink), and 'Silken Flame' (brilliant orange).

Anemone: A pincushionlike center ringed with petals. Hybrids include 'Cloverlea Sunshine' (yellow with orange disk), 'Daybreak' (apricot-orange), and 'Dorothy Mechin' (large, lavender-pink).

SPRAY TYPES, up to 4 ft (1.2 m) high, produce sprays of smaller flowers, each up to 2½ in (6 cm) wide, and has one of the following types of flower heads.

Double: The center of the flower is hidden by petals. Popular hybrids include 'Anthem' (dwarf, yellow) and 'Gordon Taylor' (brilliant red).

Single: Five or less rows of petals around a central disk. Popular hybrids include 'Baroque' (white with purple band), 'Lucido' (crimson with green center), and 'Marguerita' (white).

Anemone hybrids include 'Daymark' (white), Regatta' (bright yellow with green center), and 'Wall Street' (lavender with deep purple center).

Others: Petals shaped like spoons or quills, giving a spidery appearance. Hybrids include 'Bullseye' (yellow florets with a circle of red around green center) and 'Fantasy' (purple tips with cream tubes).

Pompon: Clusters of small tightly packed heads on plants up to 1 ft (30 cm) high. Hybrids include 'Carillon' (lavender pink), 'Frolic' (purple), 'Kelvin Mandarin' (deep orange), 'Kelvin Victory' (red center shading to light pink), and 'Ping Pong' (white).

Korean: Single or double flowers up to 2 in (5 cm) across. Hardier than other florists' chrysanthemums, they can be left in permanent beds in most areas.

Cultivation

For florists' chrysanthemums, take out shallow planting holes in moist, well-drained humus-rich soil in late spring. Stake the tall varieties and tie in the plants as they grow. When a plant is 6-8 in (15-20 cm) tall, pinch out the growing tip to stop further upward growth and hasten the development of lateral-flowering shoots. Except on spray types, allow only six flowering stems to develop on each plant.

To obtain large blooms, remove all buds and side shoots except the center (crown) bud on each stem. This type of disbudding should start from midsummer onward, or when the side shoots are about ¾ in (18 mm) long. Cut all stems down after flowering; lift the crowns before the first hard frost and overwinter in a greenhouse or cold frame.

Plant border chrysanthemums from early fall to midspring in a sunny position in well-drained, fertile soil. *C. rubellum* may produce such large flower clusters that the plants need support. Cut back all perennials to ground level after flowering.

Propagation To propagate florists' chrysanthemums, start the overwintered crowns (stools) into growth in late winter. Take

Incurved chrysanthemum

Reflexed chrysanthemum

2-2½ in (5-6 cm) basal cuttings in early spring and root in a propagator or glass-covered box. Transfer rooted cuttings singly to 3 in (7.5 cm) pots of potting medium and keep them cool. Pot on as necessary when roots fill the pots, and plant out in the flowering positions when all danger of frost is past.

Propagate border chrysanthemums by basal cuttings that are 2-3 in (5-75 cm) long in midspring and root in a cold frame. Plant out when well rooted. Or lift and divide established clumps in spring.

Pests/diseases Chrysanthemum leaf miner tunnels into leaf tissues, producing irregular mines, which disfigure and weaken the plants.

Leaf spot appears on the leaves as circular black or brown spots up to 1 in (2.5 cm) in diameter.

Powdery mildew forms a spotty white covering on leaves, stems, and flower buds.

Rust shows as pinhead-size red-brown powdery pustules on the undersides of leaves. The disease spreads rapidly.

Slugs and snails may feed on the leaves, stems, and flowers.

Intermediate chrysanthemum

Cimicifuga
bugbane

Cimicifuga racemosa 'Atropurpurea'

Clematis
clematis

Clematis integrifolia 'Hendersonii'

❑ Height 2-6 ft (60-180 cm)
❑ Planting distance 1-1½ ft (30-45 cm)
❑ Flowers late spring to early fall
❑ Moist, fertile, preferably alkaline soil
❑ Sunny site
❑ Herbaceous
❑ Zones 3-7

❑ Height 2-6 ft (60-180 cm)
❑ Planting distance 1½-3 ft (45-90 cm)
❑ Flowers midsummer to early fall
❑ Moist, rich soil
❑ Lightly shaded site
❑ Herbaceous
❑ Zones 3-8

Bugbane *(Cimicifuga)* has sometimes drooping, sometimes gently upright, feathery spikes of rather fluffy white or cream flowers, set against midgreen ferny leaves divided into many leaflets. The flowers are suitable for cutting.

Popular species
Cimicifuga americana has fluffy white wandlike flower spikes up to 2 ft (60 cm) tall above 4 ft (1.2 m) high leaf clumps.
Cimicifuga japonica has drooping stems of feathery snow-white flowers and shiny lobed leaves. It grows up to 4 ft (1.2 m) tall.
Cimicifuga racemosa (black snakeroot) has graceful spikes of feathery white flowers on 4-6 ft (1.2-1.8 m) tall plants in mid- to late summer. The cultivar

'Atropurpurea' has purplish leaves and purple stems with white flower spikes.
Cimicifuga simplex, up to 4 ft (1.2 m) high, has spikes of white flowers in early fall. Cultivars include 'Elstead Variety' (lilac buds, white flowers) and 'White Pearl' (pearly white flowers).

Cultivation
Plant during suitable weather in midfall or early spring. While *Cimicifuga* grows in dry soil, it thrives in a lightly shaded spot in rich, moist soil. Stems need support only in exposed positions. Once planted it should not be disturbed except to divide the roots for propagation.
Propagation Divide and replant in midfall or early spring. Or sow seeds in a cold frame in fall. Germination can be slow.
Pests/diseases Trouble free.

CINQUEFOIL — see *Potentilla*
CLARY SAGE — see *Salvia*

The ever-popular clematis group, usually thought of as climbers, includes several perennials that can fill the border with an outstanding display of flowers, which are later replaced by fluffy seed heads. The flowers are in shades of blue, purple, white, or sometimes pink and are often fairly small. They may be starry, narrowly bell-shaped, or flat with distinctive stamens. Often they bear no resemblance to the typical flower of climbing clematis.

Popular species
Clematis × durandii is a very hardy sprawling plant that will climb up to 6 ft (1.8 m) tall if given support. In late summer it produces nodding dark violet flowers up to 4 in (10 cm) wide, with cream stamens.
Clematis heracleifolia has loose spikes of strongly scented, fairly small, narrowly bell-shaped purple-blue flowers in late summer. The leaves are dark green and the plant is subshrubby, sprawling across an area of up to 4 ft (1.2 m), with a height of 3½ ft (1 m) if supported. Cultivars include 'Crépuscule' (azure with a light

Clematis heracleifolia davidiana 'Wyevale'

Coreopsis

coreopsis

Coreopsis grandiflora 'Sunburst'

❑ Height ½-3 ft (15-90 cm)
❑ Planting distance 1-1½ ft (30-45 cm)
❑ Flowers late spring to early fall
❑ Fertile, well-drained soil
❑ Open, sunny site
❑ Herbaceous
❑ Zones 4-9

scent), *davidiana* (large, violet-blue with a light scent), and 'Wyevale' (flax-blue and fragrant flowers).

Clematis integrifolia has veined midgreen leaves and small, nodding indigo-blue flowers from early summer to early fall. Only 3 ft (90 cm) tall, it will sprawl across an area 5 ft (1.5 m) wide unless supported. Some cultivars include 'Hendersonii' (larger, deep blue) and 'Rosea' (pink).

Clematis recta produces a mass of small, scented, starry white flowers in late spring to early summer. They are followed by silky seed heads. This species, which is poisonous, has dark green leaves. It grows up to 4 ft (1.2 m) high. A cultivar is 'Purpurea' (copper-purple leaves when young).

Cultivation

Plant in a sunny border in midfall or late spring. Herbaceous clematises do well in any moist, fertile soil but thrive in alkaline soils. *C. recta* and its cultivars need support. The plant looks attractive climbing up low-growing shrubs. *Clematis integrifolia* usually needs twiggy sticks for support.

Mulch annually in spring, using compost, shredded bark, or well-decayed manure. Cut back the stems of *C. heracleifolia* and *C. recta* to about 6 in (15 cm) above ground level in midfall or early spring.

Propagation Take basal cuttings that are 3 in (7.5 cm) long in mid- to late spring and root in a cold frame. Pot singly and plunge pots into an outdoor nursery bed. Plant out into permanent positions from midfall onward.

Pests/diseases Slugs may eat young shoots. Aphids may infest growing points. Earwigs may eat ragged holes in petals and leaves.

COLUMBINE — see *Aquilegia*
COMFREY — see *Symphytum*
CONEFLOWER — see *Echinacea* and *Rudbeckia*
CORALBELLS — see *Heuchera*

Perennial *Coreopsis* has daisy-like flowers that shine out cheerfully against the mid- to bright green deeply cut foliage and look just as attractive arranged in a vase. The plants withstand pollution and are generally long-lived, trouble-free border subjects.

Popular species

Coreopsis auriculata has flowers that are 2 in (5 cm) wide, blotched maroon in the cultivar 'Superba.' It grows about 1½ ft (45 cm) tall, but the cultivar 'Nana' reaches a height of only 6 in (15 cm) and is suited to the front of a border.

Coreopsis grandiflora (tickseed) is a robust but sometimes short-lived species that grows up to 1½ ft (45 cm) high. It has narrow, deeply toothed midgreen leaves. The bright yellow flowers, up to 2½ in (6 cm) wide, are borne on long stems from early summer to late summer. The flowers are good for cutting. Some cultivars are 'Goldfink' (6-8 in/15-20 cm in height; bright yellow; longer-lived), 'Mayfield Giant' (3 ft/90 cm; orange-yellow), and 'Sunburst' (2½ ft/75 cm; rich yellow, double).

Coreopsis verticillata is a long-lived species up to 2 ft (60 cm) high. It is upright and bushy with

Cortaderia

pampas grass

Cortaderia selloana 'Pumila'

❏ Height 5-10 ft (1.5-3 m)
❏ Planting distance 5-6 ft (1.5-1.8 m)
❏ Flowers late summer to fall
❏ Any well-drained, fertile soil
❏ Reasonably sheltered sunny site
❏ Evergreen
❏ Zones 8-10

The ornamental grass *Cortaderia selloana* provides an impressive focal point, as well as year-round interest. In late summer it produces upright 2-2½ ft (60-75 cm) creamy plumes on stout stalks over a clump of slender, arching, and rough-edged leaves.

Popular cultivars

'Gold Band' is up to 5 ft (1.5 m) tall with leaves narrowly striped in gold and green.

'Pumila', more compact than the species with a maximum height of 5 ft (1.5 m), is suitable for small gardens.

'Rendatleri' has purplish-silver plumes and grows as high as 8 ft (2.4 m).

'Sunningdale Silver' grows up to 10 ft (3 m) high and has large, loose white plumes.

Cultivation

Plant in midspring in any well-drained, fertile soil in a reasonably sheltered sunny site, either on a lawn or among shrubs. Wear gloves when removing dead leaves in spring as the edges are sharp.

Propagation Divide and replant in midspring.

Pests/diseases Generally trouble free.

Coreopsis verticillata

finely divided, bright green ferny leaves. The profuse show of clear yellow, 1 in (2.5 cm) wide flowers lasts from early summer to early fall. Cultivars include 'Golden Showers' (syn. 'Grandiflora'; rich yellow flowers), 'Moonbeam' (soft, muted yellow flowers), and 'Zagreb' (bright golden flowers).

Cultivation

Plant from midfall to early spring in any fertile and very well-drained garden soil in an open, sunny site. *C. grandiflora* should be staked with twiggy sticks at an early stage. The cultivar 'Sunburst' is very short-lived unless cut back after flowering.

Propagation Divide in midfall or early spring, making sure that each portion has a number of shoots. Replant immediately in permanent position.

Alternatively, sow seeds in open ground in midspring; prick out into a nursery bed and grow on. Transfer to the flowering site from midfall onward.

Pests/diseases Spittlebugs exude a frothy mass in leaf axils and suck sap from the stems. Slugs may eat leaves and flowers.

CORNFLOWER—see *Centaurea*

Corydalis

corydalis

Corydalis lutea

Cotyledon

lamb's tail

Cotyledon oppositifolium

❏ Height 6 in (15 cm)
❏ Planting distance 2 ft (60 cm)
❏ Flowers late spring to early summer
❏ Free-draining soil
❏ Shady site
❏ Evergreen
❏ Zones 5-7

Lamb's tail *(Cotyledon simplicifolia,* syn. *Chiastophyllum oppositifolium)* is grown partly for the texture and color of its interesting leaves and partly for its elegant flower racemes. This rosette-forming succulent provides a creeping, self-rooting mat. The light to midgreen fleshy leaves are oval and lightly toothed. In late spring to early summer, stems of yellow flowers arch over the foliage, adding to the color and textural interest.

Lamb's tail can be grown in clusters in walls and crevices.

Cultivation
Plant in any free-draining soil with added grit, in a cool, shady site, surrounded by fine gravel.
Propagation Take 2-3 in (5-7.5 cm) softwood cuttings during early summer. Let the cut surfaces heal for 1-2 days before placing in a rooting medium.
Pests/diseases Mealy bugs may cause conspicuous cottony tufts of white wax on young growth.

COWSLIP — see *Primula*

❏ Height 10-15 in (25-38 cm)
❏ Planting distance 1 ft (30 cm)
❏ Flowers from late spring to late fall
❏ Well-drained, fertile garden soil
❏ Shady or partially shaded site
❏ Herbaceous
❏ Zones 5-7

Corydalis is a soft, entrancing little plant with pale, delicate foliage decorated with a profuse and long-lasting show of quaint tubular, spurred flowers. Some species seed themselves freely and are often seen growing in old walls and brickwork.

Popular species
Corydalis cheilanthifolia grows about 10 in (25 cm) high and is of neat tufted habit. It is the least invasive of the species and suitable for ground cover, edging, and container growing. The attractive ferny foliage is tinted bronze-purple and handsomely shows off the dense spikes of bright yellow flowers that appear from late spring to fall.

Corydalis lutea (common yellow corydalis) grows up to 1 ft (30 cm) tall. It has fernlike light green leaves and displays yellow flowers on arching stems from midspring until late fall. It is often seen on old walls and can be invasive.

Cultivation
Plant in early spring in any good, well-drained garden soil, in sun or light shade. *C. lutea* will grow in deep shade, and a rich soil encourages even more self-sown seedlings. For best results, grow the species in ordinary, even poor soil and pull up unwanted seedlings as soon as they appear.
Propagation Sow seeds in a cold frame in late winter to early spring or in early fall to midfall. Prick out when the first true leaf appears, as the root is very brittle on older seedlings. Pot individually and overwinter in a cold frame. Plant out in early spring to midspring. *C. lutea* can also be sown directly in the permanent site.
Pests/diseases Generally trouble free.

Crambe

flowering sea kale, giant sea kale

Crambe cordifolia

- ❏ Height 4-6 ft (1.2-1.8 m)
- ❏ Planting distance 2-3 ft (60-90 cm)
- ❏ Flowers late spring to summer
- ❏ Fertile, well-drained soil
- ❏ Sunny site
- ❏ Herbaceous
- ❏ Zones 6-8

Crambe cordifolia is a magnificent plant for larger gardens. It has enormous dark green heart-shaped leaves, irregularly lobed and toothed, measuring up to 2 ft (60 cm) long. In summer the great mound of foliage supports a charming cloud of tiny white cross-shaped flowers held in widely branching sprays about 3 ft (90 cm) across.

In large borders *Crambe cordifolia* is useful for concealing a spring-flowering shrub that looks dull in summer. It also makes an imposing specimen plant.

Cultivation

Plant in fall or spring in fertile, well-drained soil in a sunny site protected from strong winds. Mulch the root area annually in late spring. Cut back to ground level in fall.

Propagation Sow seeds in a cold frame in spring. Prick out the seedlings singly into pots and plant out in a nursery bed when well rooted. Grow on for a year before transferring the young plants to their permanent sites; they should flower in their third year. Alternatively, take root cuttings in spring.

Pests/diseases Slugs and snails eat young leaves.

CRANESBILL — see *Geranium*
CREEPING CHARLIE — see *Lysimachia*

Crepis

hawk's beard

Crepis aurea

- ❏ Height 4-9 in (10-23 cm)
- ❏ Planting distance 9-12 in (23-30 cm)
- ❏ Flowers early summer to early fall
- ❏ Any well-drained soil
- ❏ Sunny site
- ❏ Herbaceous
- ❏ Zones 7-9

The pink or coppery orange dandelionlike flowers of hawkweed *(Crepis)* look pretty in a rock garden, but they are just as welcome as edging to the front of an herbaceous border. The plant is very hardy and will grow in very poor soil, provided it is in a sunny position.

Crepis incana

Popular species

Crepis aurea, up to 6 in (15 cm) high, has light green dandelion-like leaves and produces coppery-orange flowers from midsummer to early fall.

Crepis incana, up to 9 in (23 cm) high, has hairy gray-green leaves and soft pink flowers from mid- to late summer. It is clump forming and ideal for edging.

Cultivation

Plant in any well-drained soil in a sunny position from late summer to early fall.

Propagation Sow seeds in midspring in a cold frame. Prick out in flats, or pot singly; transplant to permanent positions in late summer or early fall. Alternatively, divide and replant in midspring.

Pests/diseases Generally trouble free.

CUPID'S DART — see *Catananche*

Cynoglossum

hound's tongue

Cynoglossum nervosum

❏ Height 2 ft (60 cm)
❏ Planting distance 1 ft (30 cm)
❏ Flowers late spring to summer
❏ Rich, well-drained soil
❏ Sunny or lightly shaded site
❏ Herbaceous
❏ Zones 4-8

Cynoglossum nervosum forms a dome up to 2 ft (60 cm) high of softly textured midgreen leaves, which are hairy and narrowly tongue-shaped. In late spring to summer many intensely blue flowers, which look rather like forget-me-nots, rise over the foliage on branching stems. The plant is easy and accommodating.

Cultivation
Plant in midfall or early spring in a sunny or lightly shaded position in moderately rich, well-drained soil. Support *C. nervosum* with twiggy sticks and cut the stems down to ground level in fall.
Propagation Sow seeds in early spring to midspring in a cold frame. Prick out into a nursery bed and grow on; plant out in fall. Or divide and replant in midfall or early spring.
Pests/diseases Generally trouble free.

Dactylorhiza

marsh orchid

Dactylorhiza elata

❏ Height 1½-2 ft (45-60 cm)
❏ Planting distance 1 ft (30 cm)
❏ Flowers early summer to midsummer
❏ Humus-rich, moist soil
❏ Partially shaded site
❏ Marginally hardy; herbaceous
❏ Zones 7-9

With a little care and suitable conditions, *Dactylorhiza,* a member of the Orchid family, will produce its lovely flowers in a border. These beautiful upright plants have lance-shaped leaves, sometimes speckled with brown and forming a sheath around the stem. The lobed flowers are in shades of purple, magenta, or red.

Popular species
Dactylorhiza elata, up to 2 ft (60 cm) tall, has dull green leaves and dense clusters of deep lilac-purple, slightly speckled flowers. *Dactylorhiza foliosa* is up to 1½ ft (45 cm) high with shiny green leaves and red-purple flowers. *Dactylorhiza majalis* (broad-leaved marsh orchid), which grows to 1½ ft (45 cm) high, has heavy chocolate markings on the leaves.

Cultivation
Plant in fall or spring in humus-rich soil in semishade. Keep constantly moist.
Propagation Divide and replant the rhizomes in the fall.
Pests/diseases Trouble free.

DAISY, PAINTED — see *Chrysanthemum*
DAME'S VIOLET — see *Hesperis*
DAYLILY — see *Hemerocallis*
DEAD NETTLE — see *Lamium*

Delphinium

delphinium

Delphinium × *elatum* 'Blue Springs'

Delphinium × *belladonna* 'Lamartine'

❏ Height 15-96 in (38-240 cm)
❏ Planting distance 1-2 ft (30-60 cm)
❏ Flowers early summer to midsummer
❏ Deep, rich, nonacid soil
❏ Sunny, preferably sheltered site
❏ Herbaceous
❏ Zones 4-8

The dense flower spikes of the taller *Delphinium* varieties rise like stately Roman columns. Lower-growing varieties have a graceful branching appearance.

Spurred flowers cluster around upright stems, above the mid- to dark green deeply divided foliage. Famous for their dazzling range of blues, the flowers come in pinks, purples, yellows, reds, or whites, often with a contrasting central eye, or "bee." Delphiniums are short-lived and need care, but worth the effort.

Popular species

Delphinium × *belladonna*, 3½-4½ ft (1-1.4 m) high, bears mainly white to dark blue flowers on slender, branching stems from early summer. Cultivars, usually listed as Belladonna delphiniums, include 'Lamartine' (deep violet) and 'Moerheimii' (white).

Delphinium × *elatum*, growing 3-8 ft (90-240 cm) tall, has sturdy stems topped by dense spikes of flattish flowers, sometimes with black or white central bees. Superior new strains include the Pacific Hybrids and New Century Hybrids, 4-5 ft (1.2-1.5 m) tall, with majestic flower spikes in shades of white, pink, blue, and purple. Popular Pacific Hybrids include 'Black Knight' (dark purple, almost black), 'Blue Bird' (medium blue with a white bee), 'Blue Springs' (3 ft/90 cm tall; blue and lavender), and 'Fantasia' (15 in/38 cm; white, lavender, or blue, with a creamy white bee). The Connecticut Yankee series includes 'Baby Doll' (pale purple flowers with pale yellow centers), 'Blue Fountains' (blue,

white, and purple flowers), and 'Blue Tit' (indigo flowers with black centers). The Mid-Century hybrids include 'Ivory Towers' (white), 'Moody Blues' (light blue), 'Rose Future' (pink), and 'Ultra Violet' (dark blue).

Delphinium grandiflorum, up to 2 ft (60 cm) tall, has violet-blue flowers on branching stems in midsummer.

Delphinium nudicaule, up to 2 ft (60 cm) tall, has orange-red cup-shaped flowers in airy spikes.

Cultivation

Plant in early fall or early spring in rich, deep soil in a sunny, preferably sheltered site. Stake taller plants in midspring.

Propagation For *elatum* and *belladonna* groups, take basal cuttings that are 3-4 in (7.5-10 cm) long in midspring and root in a cold frame. Grow on in nursery rows and plant out in early fall. Or divide and replant in early spring to midspring.

All perennial species can be raised from seeds sown in the permanent bed in summer or early fall. Obtain the seeds, which are short-lived, from a reliable source to ensure true breeding to type.

Pests/diseases Snails and slugs may eat shoots. Stem and root rots cause wilt. Powdery mildew shows as a white coating.

Delphinium × *elatum* 'Fantasia'

Delphinium × *elatum* 'Blue Bird'

Delphinium × *elatum*

Delphinium × *elatum* 'Black Knight'

Dianthus

border carnations, pinks

Dianthus × *arvernensis*

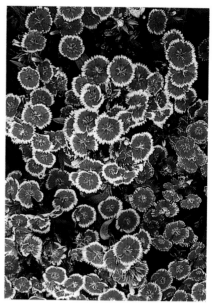

Dianthus 'Telstar Picotee'

❑ Height: carnations, 1-3 ft (30-90 cm);
   pinks, 3-18 in (7.5-45 cm)
❑ Planting distance 6-18 in (15-45 cm)
❑ Flowers late spring to midfall
❑ Well-drained, neutral or alkaline soil
❑ Sunny site
❑ Carnations — moderately hardy;
   evergreen
❑ Pinks — very hardy; evergreen
❑ Zones 3-9

Few garden flowers are more delightful than pinks or more elegant than carnations. Usually scented, they come in numerous shades and color combinations. These plants are true classics, whose beauty has fascinated gardeners and flower arrangers since Roman times, when the blooms were woven into garlands for festivals.

Pinks are generally smaller than carnations and are usually scented. The blooms, carried on erect and dainty stems, are either single, consisting of five slightly overlapping petals, or double. There are four color classifications: self (all one color), bicolor

(the base of each petal has a patch of dark, contrasting color), laced (the contrasting patch is extended in a band near the edge of each petal), and fancy (speckles or stripes of contrasting color). Pinks are very versatile and can be grown in rock gardens, at the edge of a border, as fill-in plants, on walls, or in beds, containers, or window boxes. Some types flower twice, once in summer and again in fall.

Border carnations grow up to 3 ft (90 cm) tall. Their large, heavy flowers, which are not always scented, may measure over 3 in (7.5 cm) wide. They are borne on stout stems, which need to be staked. There are four main color classifications: self (all one color), fancy (a single color background — white, yellow, or apricot — with stripes or flecks in a contrasting color), picotee (white or yellow ground color with a contrasting color around the edge of every petal), and clove (any color or color combination; there is a

very distinctive clove scent).

Popular pinks

MODERN PINKS *(Dianthus × allwoodii)* are the very successful result of crossing a perpetual-flowering carnation with an old-fashioned pink. Fast growing, these border pinks flower profusely in early summer to midsummer and again in early fall to midfall. They grow up to 1½ ft (45 cm) high and have grassy gray-green leaves. Popular hybrids and cultivars include 'Baby Treasure' (shell-pink with a scarlet eye), 'Constance' (white with maroon lacing), 'Danielle' (salmon-red), 'Doris' (very pale salmon-pink), 'Patience' (fringed pink, with a red eye), 'Robin' (bright coral-red), 'Telstar Hybrids' (mixed colors, white to scarlet, many with contrasting eyes), and 'War Bonnet' (double, maroon).

MINIATURE PINKS, of complex parentage, are up to 6 in (15 cm) tall and suitable for rock gardens, raised beds, or containers. They include 'Agatha' (semidouble, pink with a scarlet eye), 'Mars' (double, deep pink), and 'Wink' (white).

Dianthus alpinus, a rock pink, is up to 4 in (10 cm) high. It forms mid- to deep green mats of foliage and from late spring to late summer produces pale pink to purple flowers, each with a paler eye surrounded by a ring of purple spots. *Dianthus arenarius* grows up to

Dianthus nardiformis

Dianthus deltoides 'Flashing Light'

1 ft (30 cm) high, with a dense green or gray-green mat of leaves. The flowers are white with fringed petals and green eyes. They appear from early to late summer.

Dianthus × arvernensi (Auvergne pink) forms a mound of leaves up to 3 in (7.5 cm) high and is good for rock gardens. The flowers, which appear on branched stems in late spring to midsummer, are rosy pink with toothed edges.

Dianthus deltoides (maiden pink) up to 1 ft (30 cm) high, looks pretty in crevices in paving. It has narrow, mid- to deep green leaves, sometimes flushed with purple. The flowers, appearing from early summer until fall, range in color from red to pink to white. Popular cultivars include 'Albus' (white), 'Brilliant' (bright rose-pink), 'Flashing Light' (crimson), 'Samos' (brilliant carmine with dark purple leaves), and 'Wisley Variety' (carmine with dark green foliage).

Dianthus gratianopolitanus, syn. *D. caesius* (Cheddar pink), is ½-1 ft (15-30 cm) high and creeps to form a gray-green mat up to 1 ft (30 cm) wide. It is excellent for a rock garden. The fringed flowers are pink.

Dianthus nardiformis, a 4 in (10 cm) tuft of slender branching stems with bristlelike leaves, bears plum-colored blossoms of notched, bearded petals in summer. Unusually heat tolerant, it is winter hardy to zone 6.

Dianthus pavonius (syn. *D. neglectus),* 4-9 in (10-23 cm) high, forms a dense gray-green tuft of foliage and produces pale pink to crimson flowers, which are buff-colored on the undersides, from midsummer to late summer.

OLD-FASHIONED PINKS are developed in part from *Dianthus plumarius.* They are slow growing, reaching 15 in (38 cm), with gray-green leaves. The flowers appear in midsummer. Popular hybrids and cultivars include 'Dad's Favorite' (white with purple-maroon lacing), 'Excelsior' (carmine with a darker eye), 'Inchmery' (pale pink), and 'Mrs. Sinkins' (double, white).

Dianthus superbus, 9-18 in (23-45 cm) tall, has midgreen leaves and white or pale to deep lilac blooms from midsummer.

Popular carnations

Dianthus caryophyllus has gray-green grasslike foliage and clusters of often clove-scented, dull purple blossoms on stems up to 1½ ft (45 cm) high in midsummer. It is the main parent of the many border carnations with smooth-petaled flowers that measure up to 2 in (5 cm) wide, or more if the plants are disbudded.

Some popular border carnations include 'Aqua' (double, white), 'Beatrix' (pale pink), 'Candy Dish' (double, pink streaked red), 'Danielle Marie' (double, salmon), 'Desmond' (large, dark red), 'Doris' (pink with red eye), 'Essex Witch' (fringed, semidouble, pink), 'Helen' (double, deep salmon-pink), 'Her Majesty' (large, double, white), 'Ian' (double, red), 'Luminette' hybrids (mixed colors, fragrant, strong stems for cut flowers), 'Old Spice' (fringed, salmon pink), 'Snowbank' (shaggy, double, white), 'Spotlight' (double, crimson-vermilion), and 'War Bonnet' (double, maroon).

Cultivation

Plant pinks and border carnations in spring or fall, in ordinary well-drained soil, alkaline to neutral, and in full sun. Stake carnations and tall pinks with bamboo canes. Do not mulch, or water except during excessively dry spells. Do not feed carnations that are short-lived; they are best perpetuated from layering every 2 years. Old pinks benefit from a spring feeding of a complete fertilizer.

In midspring, pinch out the tips of any young pinks if they do not

Dicentra
bleeding heart

Dicentra spectabilis 'Alba'

❏ Height 9-30 in (23-75 cm)
❏ Planting distance 1-1½ ft (30-45 cm)
❏ Flowers spring to midsummer
❏ Well-drained, humus-enriched soil
❏ Partially shaded site, sheltered from wind and frost
❏ Herbaceous
❏ Zones 3-9

The distinctive red, deep pink, or white blooms of *Dicentra* look like dangling hearts, each with a pendent drop formed by protruding inner petals. The flowers hang from stems arching over a mound of deeply cut gray-green, blue-green, or bright green foliage. These graceful plants range in height from 9-30 in (23-75 cm) and flower in spring and early summer — occasionally later.

Dicentra is an extremely picturesque specimen plant, and it looks delightful in a border. *Dicentra spectabilis* is the most commonly grown species. This species tends to die back and disappear below ground after flowering. It looks best when it is combined with other plants chosen to fill in the gaps left by dying plants.

Popular species

Dicentra eximia (fringed bleeding heart) forms a clump that grows up to 1½ ft (45 cm) tall and 1 ft (30 cm) wide. It has gray-green foliage and bright rose-pink flowers on drooping stems from spring to midsummer. Popular cultivars include 'Alba' (white flowers), 'Luxuriant' (bright green foliage and brick-red flowers on 1 ft/30 cm compact plants), 'Stuart Boothman' (gray-green leaves and flesh-pink blooms), and 'Zestful' (up to 20 in/50 cm tall with soft pink flowers).

Dicentra formosa (western bleeding heart), up to 1½ ft (45 cm) high and wide, has bright green leaves on long stalks and pink flowers from late spring to early summer. Some popular hybrids between this and other species include 'Adrian Bloom' (pink-red), 'Bountiful' (deep pink with blue-green leaves), and 'Sweetheart' (white).

Dicentra spectabilis (common bleeding heart), up to 2½ ft (75 cm) high and 1½ ft (45 cm) wide, has gray-green leaves. The rose-

'Scarlet Luminette' (border carnation)

produce several side shoots naturally. Carnations usually do not need pinching in the same way, but pinch out buds on all flowering stems to leave only the top or crown buds.

Propagation Increase pinks from cuttings of side shoots during summer and root in a cold frame. Pot on in individual pots. Layer carnations and pinks in mid- to late summer and sever the layers after 6-8 weeks. Plant immediately in their final sites.

True species can be raised from seed in late spring or early summer; seedlings are often variable.

Pests/diseases Root rot and crown rot may occur in poorly drained soils. Red spider mites may be troublesome in dry soils. Powdery mildew appears as a fine white powder.

'Mrs. Sinkins' (old-fashioned pink)

Dictamnus

burning bush, dittany

Dictamnus albus

Dicentra spectabilis

red flowers, plumper than those of other species, have glistening white protruding inner petals. The flowers appear in late spring and early summer. The cultivar 'Alba' has pure white flowers.

Cultivation

Plant in midfall or early spring in any well-drained garden soil enriched with organic matter in a partially shaded site sheltered from spring frosts and strong winds. Keep well watered, especially in periods of drought. Once well established, leave the plants alone as the brittle roots resent disturbance.

Propagation Divide and re-plant in midfall or early spring if overcrowding makes this necessary. At the same time of year take root cuttings that are 3-4 in (7.5-10 cm) long. Root in a cold frame, grow on in a nursery bed, and plant out in their permanent positions in midfall. These new plants, like divisions, may take a year or two to become established.

Alternatively, germinate seeds indoors in early spring at a temperature of 59° F (15° C). Harden off the seedlings in a cold frame and plant out in their permanent positions early in the following spring.

Pests/diseases Generally trouble free.

❑ Height 2-3 ft (60 -90 cm)
❑ Planting distance 1½-2 ft (45-60 cm)
❑ Flowers early summer to midsummer
❑ Well-drained soil
❑ Sunny site
❑ Herbaceous
❑ Zones 3-8

Dictamnus albus (syn. *D. fraxinell*) is a showy plant forming a bush of lush dark green toothed leaves, which smell of lemons when crushed. Dense spikes of white or pink flowers, laced with a darker pink, are borne from early summer to midsummer and later replaced by seedpods. All parts of this poisonous plant, particularly the seed heads and flowers, give off an inflammable vapor. On a hot, still summer evening, a lighted match held near a flower will cause a slight pop as the volatile oils ignite — hence the name *burning bush*. Some cultivars include 'Purpureus' (pink with red stripes) and 'Rubra' (rose-purple).

Cultivation

Plant in midfall or early spring in a sunny site. The soil should be well drained. Do not disturb the plants, particularly the large ones, once established. Cut back the stems to their base in mid- to late fall.

Propagation In late summer or early fall, sow freshly gathered seeds thinly in a seed bed outdoors. Transplant the seedlings to their flowering positions two years later from midfall onward. Plants may take 3 to 4 years to flower.

Pests/diseases Generally trouble free.

Digitalis

perennial foxglove

Digitalis grandiflora

❏ Height 1-4 ft (30-120 cm)
❏ Planting distance 6 in (15 cm)
❏ Flowers late spring to late summer
❏ Any moist, well-drained garden soil
❏ Partial shade
❏ Herbaceous
❏ Zones 3-8

The upright stems of perennial foxglove carry columns of lovely bell-shaped yellow or pink flowers. Beneath them are mid- to dark green oval leaves, which become larger near ground level.

Perennial foxgloves are attractive plants for lightly shaded borders and are especially suited to woodland and wild-garden cultivation, where they often become naturalized.

Foxgloves should be propagated frequently as many seed-raised plants tend to produce shorter and sparser flower spikes after the second or third year.

Popular species

Digitalis grandiflora (syn. *D. ambigua),* 2-3 ft (60-90 cm) high,

Digitalis × mertonensis

is a long-lived and reliable species with soft, hairy leaves and, in mid- to late summer, slightly arching stems of soft yellow flowers. These blooms are 2 in (5 cm) long and are often frequented by bees.

Digitalis lutea, 2-3 ft (60-90 cm) high, has yellow ¾ in (18 mm) long flowers on tapering spikes from late spring to midsummer. The glossy lance-shaped leaves are finely serrated.

Digitalis × mertonensis is a hybrid between *D. grandiflora* and the common foxglove, the biennial *D. purpurea.* It grows 2-4 ft (60-120 cm) high. From late spring to midsummer it produces densely packed tapering spikes of flowers that are 2 in (5 cm) long and the color of crushed strawberries. Frequent division of this short-lived foxglove hybrid is recommended.

Cultivation

Plant in midfall or midspring in partial shade in any good moist

garden soil. Remove the faded spikes after flowering to encourage the formation of side shoots that will produce shorter spikes later. In midfall cut plants down to ground level.

Perennial foxgloves, particularly *D. × mertonensis,* are short-lived and biennial in habit.

Propagation Scatter seeds outside in late spring or early summer, gently raking them in. A thin covering of fine compost improves seed germination. Transplant the seedlings to a nursery bed. Space them 6 in (15 cm) apart and move to the flowering positions in early fall.

Pests/diseases Plants grown in overwet soil may develop crown rot and root rot in winter. Affected plants show discolored leaves, dying-back of stems, and finally collapse. New plants should be grown in a different site with improved soil conditions.

DITTANY — see *Dictamnus*

Doronicum

leopard's-bane

Doronicum pardalianches

- ❏ Height 8-36 in (20-90 cm)
- ❏ Planting distance 9-18 in (23-45 cm)
- ❏ Flowers midspring to midsummer
- ❏ Deep, moist soil
- ❏ Sun or partial shade
- ❏ Herbaceous
- ❏ Zones 4-7

Doronicum cordatum 'Magnificum'

Doronicum cordatum 'Miss Mason'

In midspring leopard's-bane *(Doronicum)* is a mass of wiry-stemmed brilliant yellow daisy-like flowers over low clusters of midgreen to rich bright green, usually heart-shaped leaves.

Leopard's-bane dies down in hot weather, so it is best grown in combination with plants that will fill the gap it leaves.

Popular species

Doronicum cordatum (syn. *D. columnae* or *D. cordifolium),* up to 1 ft (30 cm) high, has bright green kidney-shaped leaves and single, golden yellow flowers in mid- to late spring. Popular cultivars include 'Magnificum' (golden yellow; 2-3 in/5-7.5 cm wide) and 'Miss Mason' (bright yellow; up to 2½ in/6 cm wide; clump forming).

Doronicum pardalianches (great leopard's-bane) is a robust species up to 3 ft (90 cm) tall with tufts of broad, pale green basal leaves. The bright yellow flowers, up to 3 in (7.5 cm) wide, appear from late spring to midsummer.

Doronicum plantagineum, up to 2 ft (60 cm) tall, produces golden yellow flowers from midspring to early summer. The bright green leaves are heart-shaped and slightly hairy. Cultivars include 'Harpur Crewe' (syn. 'Excelsum') with several golden yellow flowers per stem.

Cultivation

Plant in midfall or early spring in sun or partial shade in deep, moist soil. Plants in exposed sites may need support.

Propagation Divide and replant in midfall or early spring.

Pests/diseases Powdery mildew appears as a white powdery coating on the leaves. Slugs and snails may devour young plants.

Dryopteris

shield fern, wood fern

Dryopteris filix-mas

- ❏ Height 1½-4 ft (45-120 cm)
- ❏ Planting distance 2-4 ft (60-120 cm)
- ❏ Foliage plant
- ❏ Rich, moist soil
- ❏ Shady site
- ❏ Deciduous or evergreen
- ❏ Zones 5-9

Dryopteris is an attractive group of ferns, some of which grow wild in America. The delicate, pale fronds lighten shady corners of the garden, where they thrive in moist soil. Often the fronds are evergreen.

Popular species
Dryopteris affinis (syn. *D. pseudomas)* is known as golden-sealed male fern. Up to 4 ft (1.2 m) tall, it is semi-evergreen. The large, arching fronds are golden green when young, darkening to rich green with scaly golden stems. This fern tolerates dry soil. The cultivar 'Cristata,' commonly called 'The King', has large crests on fronds up to 3 ft (90 cm).
Dryopteris cristata (crested wood fern) grows up to 3 ft (90 cm)

high, with erect and spreading fronds, leathery in texture. It thrives in boggy ground.
Dryopteris dilatata (syn. *D. austriaca)* is known as broad wood fern. Up to 4 ft (1.2 m) tall and 2 ft (60 cm) wide, it is deciduous, with elegant, arching fronds that have a broad triangular shape. It grows particularly well by water. The cultivar 'Recurvata' grows up to 2 ft (60 cm) tall.
Dryopteris erythrosora (autumn fern) is a striking plant up to 2 ft (60 cm) high. The broad triangular fronds are pink and coppery when young, maturing to dark green, and the fruiting dots are red. It is fully evergreen.
Dryopteris filix-mas (male fern), up to 3 ft (90 cm) high, is a robust deciduous species, with light green fronds on brownish stalks. It tolerates dry, poor soils, sunny sites as well as deep shade, and is useful for ground cover, looking particularly attractive in wild gardens. Some cultivars include 'Crispa Cristata' (to 18 in/45 cm

high with crisped fronds), 'Cristata' (up to 16 in/40 cm with crisped and crested fronds), and 'Linearis Polydactyla' (upright with finely cut fronds).
Dryopteris marginalis is up to 2½ ft (75 cm) tall with bluish-green leathery evergreen fronds growing from a fairly woody crown.

Cultivation
Plant in early to midspring in light or deep shade in humus-rich, acid to neutral soil that is moist or even boggy for varieties of the crested wood fern.
Propagation Divide and replant the crowns in midspring.

Alternatively, sow the dustlike spores thinly in potting soil and germinate under glass in a greenhouse. Keep moist. Prick out and pot the sporelings singly when large enough to handle. Plant out in fall or spring.
Pests/diseases Generally trouble free.

Echinacea
coneflower

Dryopteris filix-mas

Echinacea purpurea 'Robert Bloom'

❏ Height 2-4 ft (60-120 cm)
❏ Planting distance 1½ ft (45 cm)
❏ Flowers midsummer to early fall
❏ Any fertile, well-drained soil
❏ Sunny site
❏ Herbaceous
❏ Zones 3-8

The long-lasting flowers of *Echinacea purpurea* (purple coneflower) have drooping daisylike petals in a deep shade of dusky pink, surrounding prominent cone-shaped centers. These splendid flowers are set against rough, lance-shaped midgreen leaves, with slightly toothed edges. They look magnificent in any sunny flower bed and are excellent for cutting.

Popular cultivars
'Bressingham Hybrids,' up to 3 ft (90 cm) tall, provide a mixture of pink-purple shades.
'Crimson Star' is 2 ft (60 cm) tall with crimson flowers.
'The King,' up to 4 ft (1.2 m) tall, has coral-maroon flowers.

'Robert Bloom,' up to 3 ft (90 cm) tall, has intense cerise-purple flowers.
'White Lustre' grows up to 3 ft (90 cm) tall, with white flowers.

Cultivation
Plant in midfall or early spring in any fertile, well-drained soil in a sunny site.

Propagation Divide and replant in midfall or early spring.

Take root cuttings in late winter and root in a cold frame. Plant out in a nursery bed when young leaves appear and then into final positions from midfall onward.

Alternatively, sow seeds in early spring in a sunny, cool room at a temperature of 55° F (13° C). Prick out into flats and harden off before setting outdoors in a nursery bed in early to late summer. Plant them out in midfall; or sow them in a sunny bed in midfall.

Pests/diseases Generally trouble free.

Echinops

globe thistle

Echinops humilis 'Taplow Blue'

- ❑ Height 3-5 ft (90-150 cm)
- ❑ Planting distance 2 ft (60 cm)
- ❑ Flowers midsummer to early fall
- ❑ Any ordinary well-drained soil
- ❑ Sunny position
- ❑ Herbaceous
- ❑ Zones 4-8

Globe thistle is a striking plant with dense, perfectly globular and prickly, deep purple to blue-green flower heads. Set off by jagged, metallic thistlelike leaves, the blooms provide long-lasting architectural interest for borders.

A useful plant, globe thistle tolerates poor soil and drought. The flower heads may be cut and dried for winter decoration.

Popular species

Echinops banaticus, up to 4 ft (1.2 m) high, has slender, spiny, dark green leaves that are downy on the undersides. Globular heads of gray-blue flowers, about 1 in (2.5 cm) wide, are borne on branching stems in midsummer to late summer.

Echinops humilis grows up to 5 ft (1.5 m) high and has dark green, almost spineless, wavy-edged leaves, cobwebby above and hairy beneath. Blue flowers appear from late summer to early fall. The best cultivar is 'Taplow Blue,' up to 4 ft (1.2 m) high, with soft blue flowers and gray-green leaves.

Echinops ritro reaches a maximum height of 4 ft (1.2 m) and is more compact than *E. humilis.* Its deep gray-green leaves do not have spines and are downy on the undersides. The steel-blue to dark mauve-blue flowers appear in mid- to late summer and are up to 2 in (5 cm) wide. 'Veitch's Blue' has richer blue flowers.

Cultivation

Plant in midfall or early spring in any ordinary well-drained garden soil. In windy spots, stake the tall stems to prevent them from toppling over. Cut the stems down to ground level in midfall.

Propagation Divide the roots during suitable weather in midfall or early spring.

Insert root cuttings in a container of sandy soil in late fall to early winter and overwinter them in a cold frame. In spring transplant rooted cuttings to a nursery

Echinops ritro 'Veitch's Blue'

bed and plant them out in the fall.

Alternatively, sow seeds outdoors in midspring in a sunny position. Prick out the seedlings into nursery rows, finally setting them out in their permanent positions in fall.

Pests/diseases Generally trouble free.

Epimedium

barrenwort, bishop's hat

Epimedium × youngianum

❏ Height 8-12 in (20-30 cm)
❏ Planting distance 12-15 in (30-38 cm)
❏ Flowers midspring to midsummer
❏ Moist, humus-rich soil
❏ Cool, partial shade
❏ Semievergreen or evergreen
❏ Zones 5-8

Epimedium perralderianum

Epimedium × rubrum

In moist shady places *Epimedium* provides a lustrous carpet of richly tinted foliage. In spring the new leaves, heart-shaped and sometimes toothed, are fresh green, tinted red or pink. As summer advances a network of veins develops and the leaves deepen in color, reaching the height of their beauty in fall, when they become suffused with yellow, red, orange, and bronze tints. The plants make marvelous year-round ground cover.

The spurred, saucer-shaped flowers are white, pink, carmine, violet, red, or yellow, though in many species they are hidden within the carpet of leaves.

Popular species

Epimedium grandiflorum (syn. *E. macranthum*) a semi-evergreen up to 1 ft (30 cm) tall and wide, has long-spurred white, pink, red, or violet flowers up to 2 in (5 cm) wide in midsummer. *Epimedium perralderianum*, an evergreen up to 1 ft (30 cm) high and 15 in (38 cm) wide, has bright green and bronze-red leaves that turn copper-bronze in winter. It bears sprays of yellow flowers in midsummer.
Epimedium pinnatum, an evergreen 1 ft (30 cm) tall and wide has midgreen hairy leaves, tinted red in fall. The bright yellow flowers, ¾ in (18 mm) wide, appear in late spring to midsummer. The variety *E. p. colchicum* has larger and more profuse flowers.
Epimedium × rubrum, semi-evergreen and 1 ft (30 cm) high and wide, has midgreen, red-tinted young leaves turning orange and yellow in fall. Crimson flowers appear in late spring.
Epimedium × versicolor 'Sulphureum', a semi-evergreen, 1 ft (30 cm) high, has midgreen, toothed leaves and pendent, pale yellow flowers.
Epimedium × warleyense, a semi-evergreen up to 1 ft (30 cm) tall and wide, has midgreen, red-marked toothed leaves and copper-red flowers in midspring to late spring.
Epimedium × youngianum, a semi-evergreen up to 8 in (20 cm) high and 1 ft (30 cm) wide, has toothed midgreen, red-marked young leaves, flushed orange-red in fall. Pink flowers appear in mid- to late spring. Cultivars include 'Niveum' (pure white flowers) and 'Roseum' (lilac-pink).

Cultivation

Plant in early fall or early spring in partial shade in moist, rich soil. Top dress with well-decayed compost or leaf mold in early spring and remove old leaves.
Propagation Divide and replant in early fall or early spring.

Sow seeds during mid- to late summer in flats of sterilized seed-starting mix in a cold frame. Prick out the seedlings into an outdoor bed. Transfer them to their final positions the following spring.
Pests/diseases Trouble free.

Eremurus
foxtail lily

Eremurus 'Shelford Hybrids'

Eremurus robustus

- ❏ Height 2-10 ft (60-300 cm)
- ❏ Planting distance 2-4 ft (60-120 cm)
- ❏ Flowers late spring to midsummer
- ❏ Well-drained, rich soil
- ❏ Sunny site
- ❏ Herbaceous
- ❏ Zones 6-9

Foxtail lilies are imposing plants for the back of borders. The spikes of star-shaped, pastel-colored flowers, which open from the base upward, work well in formal flower arrangements. They rise above long strap-shaped leaves, which die down in summer.

Popular species
Eremurus elwesii grows 6-8 ft (1.8-2.4 m) tall and forms clumps of light green leaves. Above these, rise elegant yellow-green stems — as much as 4 ft (1.2 m) tall — of fragrant, soft pink flowers. The cultivar 'Albus' is pure white.

Eremurus himalaicus, a very hardy species, reaches a height of up to 4 ft (1.2 m). Spikes, 2 ft (60 cm) tall, of pure white flowers with orange anthers are borne in late spring.

Eremurus olgae grows 4 ft (1.2 m) high and has narrow, pale green leaf clumps. White flower spikes, tinted pale pink, appear in early summer and midsummer.

Eremurus robustus is the tallest species, growing 8-10 ft (2.8-3 m) high and bearing narrow, bright green leaves, 4 ft (1.2 m) long, which die down before the flowers open in early summer. The peach-pink blooms, which have brown and green markings, are borne on spikes up to 4 ft (1.2 m) long.

Eremurus 'Shelford Hybrids' produce sturdy stems up to 7 ft (2.1 m) tall, rising above light green leaves. They flower in early summer and midsummer; the spikes of blooms vary in color from a very pale pink to copper-orange. *Eremurus stenophyllus bungei* is much shorter, up to 3 ft (90 cm), with golden yellow and orange flower spikes that appear in early summer and midsummer.

Cultivation
All *Eremurus* species resent wetness around the roots. Plant them deeply in early to midfall, in humus-rich, well-drained soil. Set the crowns on a layer of sand. They require a sunny site, but one not exposed to early-morning sun. Mulch the crowns annually in early fall with leaf mold or composted manure. Stake tall species and cut all stems down after flowering unless the seed heads are wanted for drying.

Propagation The brittle, fleshy roots resent disturbance, and although the plants can be divided in early fall, they may take several years to recover. The best means of propagation is by sowing mature seeds by late winter or early spring in a greenhouse or a cool, sunny room. Grow the seedlings on in pots in a cold frame for 2-3 years before transplanting them to the permanent sites. Plants that are grown from seeds take 4-6 years to flower.

Pests/diseases Generally trouble free.

Erigeron

fleabane

Erigeron × hybridus

Erigeron pulchellus

Erigeron mucronatus

- ❏ Height 10-24 in (25-60 cm)
- ❏ Planting distance 9-15 in (23-38 cm)
- ❏ Flowers late spring to late summer
- ❏ Moist, well-drained soil
- ❏ Sunny site
- ❏ Herbaceous
- ❏ Zones 4-8

The pretty double or semidouble daisylike flowers of *Erigeron*, set against narrow midgreen or gray-green oval leaves, give it a delicate appearance, which is belied by the plant's hardiness, reliability, and long flowering season.

The outer ring of florets surrounding the yellow centers may be white, pink, yellow, blue, or shades of purple. The plants may be tufted or mat forming. They are good subjects for herbaceous and mixed borders, with the shorter species suitable for front edging. The flowers, which measure up to 2½ in (6 cm) wide, are excellent as cut flowers.

Popular species

Erigeron aurantiacus, which is often short-lived, forms a velvety mat with a maximum height and spread of 10 in (25 cm). It is decorated with orange-yellow flowers in early to late summer. The cultivar 'Sulphureus' is pale yellow. Both the species and cultivar are ideal as edging for flower beds.

Erigeron × hybridus plants have been developed from the species *Erigeron speciosus* and its variety, *E. s. macranthus*. They are very hardy and easy to grow, giving a good display for beds and cutting. They have strong, leafy stems, a profusion of flowers up to 2½ in (6 cm) wide, and usually reach a maximum height of 2 ft (60 cm). Cultivars include 'Azure Fairy' (lilac-blue), 'Darkest of All' (deep violet-blue), 'Dimity' (pink), 'Double Beauty' (violet-blue), Foerster's Darling' (bright-pink), 'Pink Jewel' (light pink), 'Prosperity' (purplish blue, semidouble), and 'Rose Jewel' (lilac-rose).

Erigeron macranthus is a tufted plant, with yellow-centered, purple-blue flowers in midsummer to late summer. The species has a maximum height of 2 ft (60 cm).

Erigeron mucronatus (syn. *E. karvinskianus*) grows up to 10 in (25 cm) high and has white to pale pink flowers. It is suitable for edging, but it self-seeds freely and can become invasive.

Cultivation

Plant in midfall or early spring in a sunny site in any type of moist but well-drained soil. In exposed sites support the plants with twiggy sticks. Remove the dead flowers to encourage further flowering later in the season. Cut the stems down to ground level in fall.

Propagation Divide and replant during suitable weather in midfall or early spring. This should be done every 2-3 years to

Erigeron macranthus

Eryngium
sea holly

Erigeron aurantiacus

prevent overcrowding the plants.

Alternatively, sow seeds in mid- to late spring in pots or flats of seed-starting mix in a cold frame. Prick out the seedlings into flats of potting mix, and when well developed, move them to a nursery bed. Transfer the young plants to their final positions in fall and press them firmly.

Pests/diseases Generally trouble free.

Eryngium alpinum

- ❑ Height 2-4 ft (60-120 cm)
- ❑ Planting distance 1-2 ft (30-60 cm)
- ❑ Flowers midsummer to early fall
- ❑ Ordinary well-drained soil
- ❑ Sunny site
- ❑ Herbaceous or evergreen
- ❑ Zones 5-8

Eryngium is prized by flower arrangers for its spiny leaves and teasellike flower heads. The leaves of these stylish plants may be grayish green, bluish green, or dark green; the flower heads are light blue, steel-blue, or violet-blue and suitable for both cutting and drying.

Popular species
Eryngium alpinum grows up to 2 ft (60 cm) high. It has dark green-blue heart-shaped leaves and stout blue stems bearing metallic blue flower heads with impressive finely divided violet-blue bracts from midsummer to early fall.

Eryngium bourgatii, up to 2 ft (60 cm) tall, has crisp gray-green, white-veined leaves, which are divided into threes, and bluish

Eryngium bourgatii

flowers with narrow steel-blue bracts in mid- to late summer.

Eryngium giganteum, up to 4 ft (1.2 m) tall, has bluish heart-shaped leaves and silvery blue to greenish flowers with long bracts. This species flowers only once, then dies, but it self-seeds readily.

Eryngium maritimum (true sea holly) is up to 1½ ft (45 cm) high

Eupatorium
boneset

Eupatorium purpureum

❏ Height 2-6 ft (60-180 cm)
❏ Planting distance 2-3 ft (60-90 cm)
❏ Flowers midsummer to early fall
❏ Any moist soil
❏ Sun or partial shade
❏ Herbaceous
❏ Zones 4-9

Ideal for large borders and wild gardens, *Eupatorium* is a tall, upright plant with slender mid-green leaves and rounded, fluffy heads of blue-purple, red-purple, or white flowers in midsummer to early fall.

Popular species
Eupatorium cannabinum (hemp agrimony), up to 4 ft (1.2 m) tall, has red-purple flowers in midsummer to early fall. The cultivar 'Plenum' has double flowers.
Eupatorium coelestinum (mist flower), up to 2 ft (60 cm) tall, has blue, violet, or white flowers in midsummer to late summer. It is invasive.
Eupatorium purpureum (Joe Pye weed), up to 6 ft (1.8 m) tall, has vanilla-scented leaves and rose-purple flowers in midsummer to late summer. 'Atropurpureum' has purple-green leaves and rose-lilac flowers.

Cultivation
Plant in midfall or early spring in a sunny or partially shaded site in any fairly moist soil.
Propagation Divide and replant from midfall to early spring.
Pests/diseases Generally trouble free.

Eryngium giganteum

with stiff, deeply cut silver-green leaves. From midsummer to early fall, large silvery bracts surround steel-blue flowers on branching stems.
Eryngium × oliverianum, up to 4 ft (1.2 m) high, has deeply cut, blue-green leaves, bluish flowers, and deep purplish-blue, narrow bracts throughout summer.
Eryngium planum, up to 3 ft (90 cm) tall, has dark green heart-shaped leaves, light blue flowers, and narrow blue-green bracts from mid- to late summer.
Eryngium varifolium, an evergreen up to 2½ ft (75 cm) tall, has rounded dark green leaves with white marbling. The flower heads appear from mid- to late summer and are blue with silver bracts.

Cultivation
Plant in midfall or midspring in a sunny site in ordinary well-drained soil. Slender plants need twiggy sticks for support in exposed sites.
Propagation Take root cuttings in late winter and root in flats of potting soil in a cold frame. When young leaves are well developed, set the plants in nursery rows, then plant them out in their flowering positions in midfall or midspring.
Pests/diseases Generally trouble free.

Euphorbia

spurge

Euphorbia griffithii 'Fireglow'

Euphorbia myrsinites

- ❏ Height ½-4 ft (15-120 cm)
- ❏ Planting distance 15-24 in (38-60 cm)
- ❏ Flowers early spring to late summer
- ❏ Ordinary well-drained soil
- ❏ Sunny site
- ❏ Herbaceous or evergreen
- ❏ Zones 5-9

Grown for their colorful bracts and foliage and for their architectural impact, spurges are excellent plants for poor soil. The narrow to lance-shaped leaves grow on strong stems topped by showy yellow, green-yellow, or orange-red bracts surrounding insignificant flowers. The plants are bushy and may form a rounded clump, a group of columns, or a low, trailing mat. The stems contain a milky sap, which can irritate the skin and eyes.

Popular species

Euphorbia characias, up to 4 ft (1.2 m) high, has column-shaped heads of pale yellow bracts, which are held upright over gray-green, sometimes evergreen, foliage beginning in early spring.

Euphorbia characias wulfenii is similar to *E. characias,* but with yellow-green bracts.

Euphorbia cyparissias (cypress spurge) has pale green narrow leaves. Only 1 ft (30 cm) tall, it is useful for ground cover, spreading over an area 2 ft (60 cm) wide. The bracts, which appear from mid- to late spring are green-yellow. This species thrives in alkaline soil.

Euphorbia epithymoides (syn. *E. polychroma),* up to 1½ ft (45 cm) high, forms a compact evergreen dome of bright green leaves, reddish in fall, with profuse bright yellow beads of bracts that are 3 in (7.5 cm) wide in late spring.

Euphorbia griffithii 'Fireglow,' up to 2½ ft (75 cm) tall, has pink-veined bright green leaves and brilliant orange-red bracts in late spring and early summer.

Euphorbia myrsinites is only 6 in (15 cm) tall but trails over an area up to 16 in (40 cm) wide. It has fleshy, blue-gray evergreen leaves, tightly packed and spiraled along the arching stems, which are topped with greenish-yellow bracts in spring.

Euphorbia palustris, up to 3 ft (90 cm) high, has canary-yellow bracts in early summer to midsummer.

Euphorbia robbiae has upright heads of greenish-yellow bracts in early summer to midsummer. It forms a dense, dark green evergreen mound up to 2 ft (60 cm) high and wide. It thrives in shade.

Euphorbia sikkimensis, up to 4 ft (1.2 m) high, has midgreen leaves which are bright red when young. Yellow bracts appear in summer.

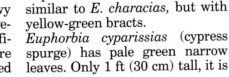

Euphorbia robbiae

Euphorbia epithymoides

Euphorbia characias

Cultivation
Plant in early fall or midspring in a sunny site in any ordinary well-drained soil.

Set out only small plants of *E. characias* as large specimens resent disturbance.

Propagation Sow seeds in early spring in a cold frame. Prick out into nursery rows; in fall, transplant to final positions.

Alternatively, take terminal cuttings that are 3 in (7.5 cm) long in midsummer or propagate any division in early fall or midspring.

Pests/diseases Shoots damaged by cold winds or frosts may be infected by Botrytis, or gray mold.

EVENING PRIMROSE — see *Oenothera*
EVERLASTING PEA — see *Lathyrus*
FALSE HELLEBORE — see *Veratrum*
FALSE INDIGO — see *Baptisia*
FALSE SOLOMON'S SEAL — see *Smilacina*
FALSE SPIKENARD — see *Smilacina*
FEATHER GRASS — see *Stipa*
FESCUE — see *Festuca*

Festuca

fescue

Festuca glauca

❑ Height 6-9 in (15-23 cm)
❑ Planting distance 6 in (15 cm)
❑ Flowers early summer to midsummer
❑ Light, well-drained soil
❑ Sunny site
❑ Evergreen
❑ Zones 5-9

Fescue *(Festuca glauca,* syn. *F. ovina glauca)* forms a dense domed tuft of tough blue-gray blades of grass 6-9 in (15-23 cm) tall. In early summer to midsummer the clumps sprout purplish tufted flower spikes, but you may want to remove these as the plant tends to lose its neat shape when in flower. The spikes later turn a sandy color.

This plant is ideal for the front of a border, providing year-round foliage interest. It is also useful for planting between conifers.

Cultivation
Plant in early fall or midspring in a sunny site, preferably in light, well-drained soil. In late spring the developing flower heads may be cut off if the plants are being used primarily for foliage interest. If the flower heads are left on, remove the dead flowers before they can shed their seeds.
Propagation Sow seeds in midspring in light soil in the open. Prick out the seedlings in small groups of three or four when large enough to handle and set in nursery rows. Plant out in early fall.

Alternatively, divide and replant in early fall or midspring.
Pests/diseases Generally trouble free.

FEVERFEW — see
Chrysanthemum

Filipendula

meadowsweet

Filipendula purpurea

❑ Height 2-8 ft (60-240 cm)
❑ Planting distance 1½-2 ft (45-60 cm)
❑ Flowers early to late summer
❑ Any ordinary well-drained soil
❑ Sunny or partially shaded site
❑ Herbaceous
❑ Zones 3-9

Meadowsweet is a stately perennial with white or pink flower plumes rising over a lush mound of mid- to dark green toothed, palmate leaves. The taller species stand elegantly at the back of borders, and most species thrive by water, mingling well with other waterside plants. The plumes are good for flower arrangements.

Popular species
Filipendula kamtschatica has fragrant fleecy white plumes of flowers in midsummer to late summer and midgreen leaves divided like hands. It grows up to 8 ft (2.4 m) high. The variety 'Rosea' has reddish pink flowers.
Filipendula purpurea (syn. *Spiraea palmata),* up to 4 ft (1.2 m) tall, has hand-shaped dark green leaves with white hairs beneath. The flower plumes are rose-pink fading to pale pink or white. They are borne in airy clusters in midsummer.
Filipendula rubra 'Venusta,' 7 ft (2.1 m) tall, has deep pink flowers on branching stems from mid- to late summer, and lobed, midgreen leaves.
Filipendula ulmaria is a fragrant species 3-6 ft (90-180 cm) high

Filipendula ulmaria 'Aurea'

with narrow dark green leaves that are hairy underneath. Branching, flattened heads of creamy white flowers appear from early to late summer. The cultivar 'Aurea,' 2 ft (60 cm) high, has golden foliage.
Filipendula vulgaris 'Flore Pleno' (dropwort) is the double-flowered form of the wild species. Up to 2 ft (60 cm) high, it has a froth of creamy white flowers.

Cultivation
Plant in midfall or early spring in a sunny or partially shaded spot in any ordinary soil that does not dry out in summer. However, *F. vulgaris* thrives in full sun and prefers a well-drained, particularly alkaline soil. *F. ulmaria* 'Aurea' needs moist soil and partial shade.
Propagation Divide and replant in fall.

Alternatively, sow seeds in pots of seed-starting medium in late winter to early spring at a temperature of 50-55° F (10-13° C). In early summer to midsummer set the seedlings in nursery rows; plant out in fall.
Pests/diseases Powdery mildew may cause a white coating on the leaves.

FLAX — see *Linum*
FLEABANE — see *Erigeron*
FOAMFLOWER —see *Tiarella*
FOUNTAIN GRASS — see *Pennisetum*
FOXGLOVE — see *Digitalis*
FOXTAIL LILY — see *Eremurus*
FRINGECUP — see *Tellima*

Gaillardia

blanket flower

Gaillardia 'Goblin'

- ❏ Height 2-2½ ft (60-75 cm)
- ❏ Planting distance 1½ ft (45 cm)
- ❏ Flowers early summer to midfall
- ❏ Well-drained soil
- ❏ Sunny site
- ❏ Herbaceous
- ❏ Zones 3-9

Blanket flower *(Gaillardia aristata,* or *G. × grandiflora)* forms a clump of many-petaled bright orange, red, or bronze flowers. These are often bicolored, with yellow, brown, or purple central eyes. The narrow leaves are gray-green. The plant is relatively short-lived.

Some cultivars include 'Burgundy' (deep wine-red), 'Dazzler' (yellow with maroon center), and 'Goblin' (yellow and red).

Cultivation
Plant blanket flowers from early to late spring in light, well-drained soil in a sunny site.
Propagation Sow seeds outdoors in late spring to early summer; prick off seedlings and grow on. Plant out in early spring to midspring of the following year.

Alternatively, sow seeds under glass in late winter or early spring at a temperature of 59° F (15° C). Prick out, harden in a cold frame, and plant out.
Pests/diseases Downy mildew can cause browning of the leaves.

Galax

galax

Galax urceolata

- ❏ Height 1-1½ ft (30-45 cm)
- ❏ Planting distance 1 ft (30 cm)
- ❏ Flowers early summer
- ❏ Acid soil
- ❏ Shaded site
- ❏ Evergreen
- ❏ Zones 5-8

The intense red-bronze winter foliage of *Galax urceolata* (syn. *G. aphylla)* forms a glossy, eye-catching carpet for planting in moist shade, perhaps in a woodland setting. The leaves, which grow in rosettes, are broadly heart-shaped and dark green in summer, turning red in fall. Slender spikes of tiny white flowers rise over the low-growing leaf clumps in early summer.

Cultivation
Plant in midfall or early spring in acid, rich soil in shade.
Propagation Divide and replant in midfall or early spring.
Pests/diseases Generally trouble free.

Galega

Goat's rue

Galega officinalis

- ❏ Height 3-5 ft (90-150 cm)
- ❏ Planting distance 2-2½ ft (60-75 cm)
- ❏ Flowers early summer to midsummer
- ❏ Well-drained soil
- ❏ Sunny site
- ❏ Herbaceous
- ❏ Zones 3-7

Goat's rue *(Galega officinalis)* is a vigorous bushy plant for the back of a border. Deeply divided light green foliage forms a bush 3-5 ft (90-150 cm) high and up to 2½ ft (75 cm) wide. In early summer to midsummer, tiny round lilac-blue flowers appear on 6-12 in (15-30 cm) spikes. Cultivars include 'Alba' (white), 'Her Majesty' (soft lilac-blue), and 'Lady Wilson' (purple and cream).

Cultivation
Plant in midfall or early spring in sun in well-drained soil. Goat's rue looks best planted in groups of three or more. In rich soil the plants may sprawl and should be supported with twiggy sticks.
Propagation Sow seeds in midspring in a sunny spot in the open. Prick out into a nursery bed when large enough to handle and plant out in midfall, or propagate by division in midfall or early spring.
Pests/diseases Powdery mildew causes foliage to turn gray.

Galium

sweet woodruff, bedstraw

Galium odoratum

❏ Height 10 in (25 cm)
❏ Planting distance 3 ft (90 cm)
❏ Flowers late spring to early summer
❏ Well-drained but moisture-retentive soil
❏ Lightly shaded site
❏ Herbaceous
❏ Zones 4-8

Sweet woodruff (*Galium odoratum*, formerly called *Asperula odorata*) is a vigorous sweet-smelling ground-cover plant, which spreads over an area up to 3 ft (90 cm) wide. The deep green bristle-tipped leaves grow in whorls in sets of six, seven, or eight. Tiny white flowers, suitable for cutting, appear in small clusters at the end of each leafy stem in late spring and early summer.

Cultivation
Plant from midfall to early spring in well-drained but moisture-retentive soil, ideally in the light shade cast by overhead trees.
Propagation Divide and replant in midfall or early spring.
Pests/diseases Generally trouble free.

GARDENER'S GARTERS — see *Phalaris*

Gaura

gaura

Gaura lindheimeri

❏ Height 3-4 ft (90-120 cm)
❏ Planting distance 1½ ft (45 cm)
❏ Flowers midsummer to midfall
❏ Well-drained soil
❏ Sunny site
❏ Herbaceous
❏ Zones 5-9

A bushy and graceful plant, *Gaura lindheimeri* is useful in borders because of its long flowering season, which lasts from midsummer well into fall. The thin but erect stems have sparse, narrow blue-green leaves and are studded with delicate star-shaped flowers that open white from rose-pink buds. Extremely hardy, the plant is sometimes short-lived, especially in cold and wet soils. It is easily raised from seed, often flowering in the first year.

Cultivation
Plant in groups of three or more in midspring in any light and well-drained soil in full sun, preferably protected from strong winds. *Gaura* thrives in dry, sandy soils. Remove the faded flowering stems to encourage further blooms and cut all stems back to ground level in late fall.
Propagation Sow seeds in midspring where the plants are to flower and thin out the seedlings to 1½ ft (45 cm) spacings.
Pests/diseases Generally trouble free.

GAYFEATHER — see *Liatris*

Gentiana

gentian

Gentiana lutea

❏ Height 2-5 ft (60-150 cm)
❏ Planting distance 1-1½ ft (30-45 cm)
❏ Flowers mid- to late summer
❏ Deep, rich moist soil
❏ Sunny or lightly shaded site
❏ Herbaceous
❏ Zones 6-9

The trumpets of many gentians are favorites in rock gardens, but two species are more suitable for herbaceous and mixed borders.

Popular species
Gentiana asclepiadea (willow gentian), up to 2 ft (60 cm) tall, has glossy leaves and blue trumpet flowers on long stems.
Gentiana lutea, up to 5 ft (1.5 m) tall, has large ovate, veined leaves. Bright yellow starry flowers grow in whorls on tall stems, followed by attractive seed heads.

Cultivation
Plant gentians in early spring to midspring. If soil is moist, they will thrive in full summer sun. *G. asclepiadea* prefers light shade.
Propagation Sow ripe seeds before midfall and place in a cold frame. Chilling before planting often speeds germination. Prick out seedlings when large enough to handle and later pot them singly. Keep the young plants in the frame, or plunge pots outdoors until ready to plant out in permanent positions. Or divide and replant in early spring.
Pests/diseases Generally trouble free.

Geranium

cranesbill, geranium

Geranium × 'Johnson's Blue'

- ❏ Height 4-36 in (10-90 cm)
- ❏ Planting distance 6-24 in (15-60 cm)
- ❏ Flowers late spring to midfall
- ❏ Any ordinary well-drained soil
- ❏ Sunny or partially shaded site
- ❏ Herbaceous or evergreen
- ❏ Zones 4-8

True geraniums — not to be confused with pelargoniums, their more tender cousins, which are usually grown in pots — are among the most charming and well-known garden plants, with simple saucer-shaped flowers held over a rounded, bushy mass of foliage.

These tough plants have palmate, sometimes deeply divided, leaves. Usually midgreen, the leaves may be dark green, gray-green, or silver-green in some species.

The soft, long-lasting flowers, about 1-2 in (2.5-5 cm) wide, are saucer-shaped and always have five petals. They appear in informal clusters or in twos, threes, or fours and may be in many different shades of pink, purple, blue, or white. Many species have pale flowers with deeper veining, while others have flowers of a deeper hue, including an unusual and intense shade of magenta-pink. *Geranium phaeum* has almost black flowers. Combined with care, such species can form an exciting display. The flower is followed by a seed head shaped like a crane's bill, which gives the plant one of its common names.

Depending on height, geraniums can be grown in borders, beds, or rock gardens. Some are excellent for ground cover and as edging, while others thrive in the moist, shady conditions of open woodland.

Popular species

Geranium cinereum, up to 6 in (15 cm) high and 1 ft (30 cm) wide, has tufts of downy gray-green kidney-shaped leaves cut into five or seven wedge-shaped lobes. Profuse deep pink flowers, with darker centers and stripes, appear from late spring until mid-

Geranium × *oxonianum* 'A.T. Johnson'

fall. Cultivars include 'Ballerina' (lilac-pink flowers, dark centers, red veins) and 'Laurence Flatman' (large pink flowers, heavily marked with crimson).

Geranium cinereum sub-caulescens is up to 6 in (15 cm) high and about 1 ft (30 cm) wide, with round lobed gray-green leaves and profuse black-centered

Geranium cinereum 'Laurence Flatman'

Geranium pratense

Geranium clarkei 'Kashmir White'

77

Geranium × magnificum

magenta flowers from late spring to midfall. Some cultivars include 'Guiseppii' (strong crimson-purple) and 'Splendens' (salmon-pink).

Geranium dalmaticum, up to 6 in (15 cm) high and 2 ft (60 cm) wide, forms a dense cushion of lobed, glossy midgreen leaves, tinted red and orange in fall. Dainty clusters of light pink flowers, about 1 in (2.5 cm) wide, appear from early to late summer. 'Album' has white flowers, tinged pink.

Geranium endressii, 1½ ft (45 cm) high, is useful for ground cover. It has midgreen palmate, deeply divided leaves and pale pink flowers, lightly veined red, from late spring to late summer. Cultivars include 'A.T. Johnson' (silvery pink), 'Rose Clair' (rose-salmon veined purple), and 'Wargrave Pink' (clear salmon). Some hybrids are 'Claridge Druce' (vigorous; to 20 in/50 cm, with 2 in/5 cm wide lilac-pink flowers) and 'Russell Prichard' (prostrate; fairly hardy; gray-green leaves and carmine flowers).

Geranium himalayense has round midgreen leaves and forms clumps up to 1 ft (30 cm) high and 2 ft (60 cm) wide. Violet-blue, red-veined flowers, 1-1½ in (25-38 mm) wide, appear in early summer to midsummer. The cultivar 'Plenum' (syn. 'Birch Double') has double flowers. 'Johnson's Blue,' a hybrid, has dark-veined, bright lavender-blue flowers.

Geranium ibericum is usually a hybrid between *G. ibericum* and *G. platypetalum,* and should correctly be called *G. × magnificum.* Up to 2 ft (60 cm) high and wide, it has seven-lobed midgreen upright leaves and glossy violet-blue, 1 in (2.5 cm) wide flowers from midsummer to late summer.

Geranium macrorrhizum, up to 1 ft (30 cm) high and 2 ft (60 cm) wide, has semi-evergreen five-lobed midgreen leaves that have a roselike scent when crushed. This hardy species has dark magenta-pink flowers, 1 in (2.5 cm) wide, from late spring to midsummer. Popular cultivars include 'Album' (nearly white) and 'Ingwersen's Variety' (rose-pink).

Geranium phaeum (mourning widow), up to 2 ft (60 cm) high

G. sanguineum striatum 'Lancastriense'

and 1½ ft (45 cm) wide, has small deep maroon-purple to blackish nodding flowers, with backward-pointing petals. This species thrives in shade.

Geranium pratense (meadow cranesbill) grows 2 ft (60 cm) or more high, with an equal spread. It bears midgreen long-stalked leaves with five to seven deeply divided lobes. Small red-veined blue-purple flowers appear from midsummer to early fall. Some

Geranium cinereum subcaulescens 'Splendens'

cultivars include 'Mrs. Kendall Clarke' (pearly gray tinted pink), 'Plenum Album' (double, white, rare), and 'Plenum Coeruleum' (double, pale blue).

Geranium psilostemon (syn. *G. armenum)* forms a bushy mound up to 3 ft (90 cm) high and 2½ ft (75 cm) wide. It has palmate, five-lobed midgreen leaves and a profusion of black-centered, intense magenta-pink flowers from early to late summer. This species tends to flop over when in flower. It needs deep humus-rich soil.

Geranium renardii has soft gray-green puckered leaves forming a clump up to 9 in (23 cm) high and 2 ft (60 cm) wide. Pale lavender flowers, veined violet, appear from late spring to midsummer. This species does best in poor soil.

Geranium sanguineum (bloody cranesbill) grows up to 10 in (25 cm) high and 1½ ft (45 cm) wide and has dark green foliage and 1 in (2.5 cm) wide magenta-pink flowers from early summer to early fall. This vigorous species is excellent for ground cover. Some cultivars include 'Album' (white) and 'Lancastriense' (rose-pink).

Geranium sylvaticum, up to 2½ ft (75 cm) high and 2 ft (60 cm) wide, has seven-lobed silver-green leaves and white-centered violet flowers. Cultivars include 'Album' (white) and 'Mayflower' (pale violet-blue).

Geranium wallichianum, a semi-prostrate species up to 1 ft (30 cm) high and 2 ft (60 cm) wide, has hairy stems and silky, light green leaves that are wedge-shaped and deeply toothed. Its white-centered light blue flowers appear from midsummer to early fall. The cultivar 'Buxton's Blue' has clearer blue flowers with white centers.

Cultivation

Plant geraniums in early fall or early spring in any ordinary well-drained soil in sun or partial shade. *G. cinereum* is best planted in early spring unless the site is sheltered and sunny. Taller species, such as *G. pratense* and *G. psilostemon,* may need twiggy sticks for support, particularly in exposed or shady sites.

Cut back old flowering stems almost to ground level to encourage

Geranium psilostemon

new compact growth and a second flush of flowers.

Propagation Divide the plants or sow seed in fall or early spring. Overwinter in a cold frame and plant the seedlings out in nursery rows for the summer; move them to permanent quarters in the fall.

Pests/diseases Mildew can stunt and discolor leaves.

Geum

avens

Geum × borisii

Geum quellyon 'Lady Stratheden'

❏ Height 1-2 ft (30-60 cm)
❏ Planting distance 1-1½ ft (30-45 cm)
❏ Flowers late spring to early fall
❏ Rich soil
❏ Sunny or partially shaded site
❏ Herbaceous
❏ Zones 5-7

Avens is a cheerful little clump-forming plant, decorated with bright long-lasting flowers. It is suitable for the front of beds.

The saucer- or bowl-shaped single or double blooms come in brilliant shades of yellow, red, or orange. They are set against hairy midgreen, usually rounded leaves held in rosettes or grouped on stalks with one larger leaf at the tip. The flowers are good for cutting, particularly the blooms of varieties of *Geum quellyon*.

Popular species

Geum × borisii, up to 1 ft (30 cm) high and wide, has bowl-shaped orange-scarlet flowers 1¼ in (3 cm) wide set on branching stems. The rosettes of crinkly leaves are useful for ground cover. The hybrid 'Georgenberg' is similar, with apricot flowers suffused red.

Geum quellyon (Chilean avens), up to 2 ft (60 cm) high, has bowl-shaped scarlet flowers about 1 in (2.5 cm) wide. Cultivars, which have larger flowers, are now more commonly grown, including 'Fire Opal' (flame-red, semidouble), 'Lady Stratheden' (yellow, double), and 'Mrs. Bradshaw' (scarlet, semidouble).

Geum rivale (water or purple avens, Indian chocolate), up to 1½ ft (45 cm) high and wide, thrives in wet soil. It has nodding bell-like 1¼ in (3 cm) flowers with yellow-pink petals, veined red-purple, and purple sepals. Its roots can be used to make a chocolate-flavored drink. Cultivars include 'Leonard's Variety' (coppery-pink, flushed orange) and 'Lionel Cox' (gold).

Cultivation

Plant in early fall or early spring in sun or partial shade. Avens will grow in any ordinary garden soil, but they do best in soil enriched with organic matter. *G. rivale* also thrives in moist soil. In exposed sites, *G. quellyon* may need support. Cut the plant stems back to ground level after they have flowered.

Propagation Sow ripe seeds in a cold frame from early to late summer or in late winter to early spring. Prick out when large enough to handle. Overwinter seedlings of summer-sown plants in a cold frame and transfer to nursery rows in spring. Plant out from early fall. Plants sown in spring will be ready for nursery rows that summer and can be planted out in their permanent positions from early fall of the same year.

Cultivars do not breed true from seed and are best increased by division in early spring to mid-spring.

Pests/diseases Trouble free.

GLOBEFLOWER — see *Trollius*
GLOBE THISTLE — see *Echinops*
GOATSBEARD — see *Aruncus*
GOAT'S RUE — see *Galega*
GOLDEN-EYED GRASS — see *Sisyrinchium*
GOLDEN RAY — see *Ligularia*
GOLDENROD — see *Solidago*

GRACEFUL GRASSES

**Perennial grasses add grace and charm
to herbaceous and mixed borders, introducing air
and light to solid flower colors.**

The airy grace of ornamental grasses provides valuable contrast in perennial and mixed borders. These grasses' slender stems and arching leaves, combined with their delicate flower sprays and plumes, make them ideal foils for brilliant flower colors and dark green foliage plants. The shorter ones look good at the front of beds and as edging, while the taller grasses make impressive specimen plants for a lawn.

Leaf color is an important consideration in planning combinations of grasses in borders. Leaves are rarely grass-green, but often come in striking shades of yellow or gold, as in the bright yellow *Milium effusum aureum* or the golden sedge (*Carex stricta* 'Bowles' Golden'). Both of these grasses create pools of sunlight against purple leaves and strong flower colors. Blue-green fountain grass (*Pennisetum orientale*) and *Festuca ovina glauca* look stunning against gray- and silver-leaved plants such as woolly lamb's ears (*Stachys byzantina*).

For edging borders, the Japanese sedge (*Carex morrowii*) forms arching evergreen mounds of bright green narrow leaves, striped white in 'Variegata' and golden in 'Aureo-variegata.'

Grasses should not necessarily be relegated to the background as foils for other perennials. Some make excellent focal points in themselves, with their impressive height and graceful outlines adding architectural dimensions to planting schemes. Pampas grass (*Cortaderia selloana*), with its huge silken flower plumes in fall, is always popular. In moist soil, the 4 ft (120 cm) tall *Carex pendula* is also a striking specimen plant with broad golden yellow leaves and drooping seed heads in fall. Silver grass (*Miscanthus* species) will reach 10 ft (300 cm) in a single season, forming slender clumps of leaves striped yellow or white. In smaller gardens, feather grass (*Stipa* species) is particularly attractive, with its silver and brown plumes.

▼ **Fall plumes** The creamy white and silky plumes of the evergreen pampas grass make an eye-catching focal point in early fall. Here, they tower above the pale russet spikes of the herbaceous silver grass (*Miscanthus sinensis*).

▲ **Silver foil** Sheltered by silver grass, yellow-flowered rudbeckias stand out dramatically against the narrow-leaved *Miscanthus sinensis* 'Gracillimus.' It is accompanied by the popular yellow-banded zebra grass (*Miscanthus sinensis* 'Zebrinus'). Both contrast well with the bronze leaves of the frost-tender castor-oil plant (*Ricinus communis*).

▶ **Feather tops** The dainty plumes of *Pennisetum villosum* tremble in the slightest breeze. They give an airy look to the flat red flower heads of the late-summer perennial *Sedum* 'Autumn Joy' and are excellent for cutting and drying.

◄ **Feather grass** In late summer the arching foliage and dainty silvery yellow flower plumes of feather grass *(Stipa pennata)* introduce a delicate contrast to clumps of green hostas, golden rudbeckias, and waving red spires of *Polygonum.*

▼ **Zebra grass** A tall clump of yellow-speckled *Miscanthus sinensis* 'Zebrinus' dwarfs the spires of pink phlox and a foreground planting of glossy, round-leaved *Bergenia cordifolia.* Although it is herbaceous, the dead foliage can be left to provide winter color and then cut down to the ground in early spring.

▲ Front edging The neat tufts of silver-blue fescues *(Festuca ovina glauca)* form a low evergreen edging, topped in early summer with pale purple flower spikes.

◄ Border sedge The evergreen *Carex buchananii* grows only 2 ft (60 cm) tall and tolerates drier soil than most sedges. It is suitable for mixed borders. Here, it is seen with orange montbretia *(Crocosmia × crocosmiiflora)*.

▼ Bottle brushes Called rose fountain grass because of its purplish flower spikes in early fall, *Pennisetum alopecuroides* is long-lived if grown in a sheltered site and given some winter protection.

Gunnera

gunnera

Gunnera manicata

❏ Height 6-10 ft (1.8-3 m)
❏ Planting distance 10-13 ft (3-4 m)
❏ Flowers midspring to midsummer
❏ Deep, moist soil
❏ Sunny or partially shaded site,
   sheltered from wind
❏ Herbaceous
❏ Zones 7-10

Gunnera manicata is a magnificent waterside plant with large rhubarblike dark green leaves on thick, prickly stems. The green flowers, which turn brown, are massed in enormous cones and partially hidden by the foliage. Clusters of red fruits follow.

Cultivation
Plant in mid- to late spring in sun or light shade in deep, moist soil, preferably with shelter to protect the leaves from wind damage. Do not disturb after planting. Protect the crowns in winter by covering them with the plant's own leaves, weighted down with soil.
Propagation Sow seeds thinly in early spring to midspring in flats of seed-starting medium at a temperature of 61°F (16°C). Prick out into individual containers and overwinter in a frost-free greenhouse. Plant out in spring.

Alternatively, increase by division, using the small crowns that develop around the base and sides of old plants.
Pests/diseases Generally trouble free.

Gypsophila

baby's breath, chalk plant

Gypsophila paniculata

❏ Height 3 ft (90 cm)
❏ Planting distance 2-3 ft (60-90 cm)
❏ Flowers early to late summer
❏ Any well-drained soil
❏ Sunny site
❏ Herbaceous
❏ Zones 3-9

The tiny flowers of baby's breath, as delicate as their name, form a lovely cloud of white or pale pink over a bushy mound of narrow, grasslike gray-green leaves. The slender, branched flower stems of *Gypsophila paniculata* are used in floral displays and bridal bouquets, creating a light cloudy effect around other flowers.

The species, which is also known as chalk plant, grows up to 3 ft (90 cm) high and has gray-green lance-shaped leaves up to 3 in (7.5 cm) long and a profusion of tiny white single flowers held in loose clusters from early to late summer. The best cultivar is 'Bristol Fairy' with double white flowers; some other cultivars include 'Compacta Plena' (up to 1½ ft/45 cm high; double, white), 'Flamingo' (double, pale pink), 'Perfecta' (double, white), and 'Rosy Veil' (1 ft/30 cm high; double, very pale pink).

Cultivation
Baby's breath likes lime but will grow in any well-drained soil in a sunny location. Acid soil should be top-dressed with 2-4 oz (50-100 g) of lime per sq yd/m. Plant in midfall or early spring and provide twiggy support. The fleshy roots grow deep in the soil and resent disturbance once they are established.
Propagation Sow seeds in pots or flats of seed-starting medium in a cold frame in early spring. Prick out the seedlings into flats and later transfer to nursery rows outdoors. Grow on until ready to plant out in midfall or early spring.

Alternatively, increase plants from basal cuttings that are 3 in (7.5 cm) long and taken in mid- to late spring. Insert in flats or containers of potting medium in a cold frame. Or take lateral shoots that are 2-3 in (5-7.5 cm) long in midsummer and root in the same way. In either case, pot in 3 in (7.5 cm) pots. Cuttings taken in spring can be set in nursery rows in summer and will be ready to plant out that fall or the following spring. Summer cuttings should be overwintered in a cold frame.
Pests/diseases Generally trouble free.

HARD FERN — see *Blechnum*
HART'S TONGUE FERN — see *Asplenium*
HAWKWEED — see *Crepis* and *Hieracium*

Helenium
sneezeweed

Helenium autumnale 'Wyndley'

❏ Height 4-6 ft (1.2-1.8 m)
❏ Planting distance 1-1½ ft (30-45 cm)
❏ Flowers late summer to midfall
❏ Any ordinary soil
❏ Sunny site
❏ Herbaceous
❏ Zones 3-8

A robust and striking border plant, sneezeweed *(Helenium autumnale)* produces a mass of broad-petaled daisylike flowers with prominent central cones. The flowers, in shades of yellow, gold, and red, are borne in tall, branching heads over lance-shaped leaves throughout late summer and fall. Hybrids, some of which start to bloom earlier, have now superseded the species.

The free-flowering plants produce long-lasting blooms for indoor floral arrangements.

Popular cultivars
'Butterpat' has pure yellow flowers from late summer to early fall.
'Copper Spray' produces coppery orange flowers from mid- to late summer.
'Moerheim Beauty' bears rich bronze-red flowers from midsummer to early fall.
'Wyndley' produces yellow and orange flowers with brown centers from early to late summer.

Cultivation
Plant from midfall to early spring in a sunny spot in any ordinary soil. In exposed sites support the plants with stakes. Some early-flowering cultivars will produce a second crop of flowers if cut back as soon as the first flush has finished. Cut all the stems back to ground level in late fall.

Propagation Divide and replant every 3 years to maintain the quality and quantity of the flowers. Division can be done in midfall or midspring; set each division in its permanent position.

Pests/diseases Stems, leaves, and flowers may be eaten by slugs. A virus disease may turn the flowers green.

Helenium autumnale 'Copper Spray'

Helianthus
sunflower

Helianthus × multiflorus

❏ Height 4-8 ft (1.2-2.4 m)
❏ Planting distance 1½-2 ft (45-60 cm)
❏ Flowers midsummer to early fall
❏ Well-drained garden soil
❏ Sunny site
❏ Herbaceous
❏ Zones 4-8

Perennial sunflowers are smaller and bushier relatives of the giant annual *Helianthus annuus.* They are useful at the back of beds and provide welcome color in late summer and fall. The daisylike flowers come in shades of yellow, and many of the cultivars are double forms. They are all long-lasting as cut flowers.

Popular species
Helianthus × multiflorus grows up to 6 ft (1.8 m) tall and bears broadly ovate midgreen leaves that are rough to the touch and sharply toothed. The species produces pale yellow flowers, 3 in (7.5 cm) wide, from midsummer. It is generally represented by such cultivars as 'Capenoch Star' (lemon-yellow), 'Flora-Pleno' (double, clear yellow), 'Loddon Gold' (5 ft/1.5 m; fully double, golden yellow), and 'Soleil d'Or' (semidouble, golden yellow).
Helianthus salicifolius (syn. *H. orgyalis),* up to 8 ft (2.4 m) high, has stout stems closely set with

Helichrysum

strawflower

Heliopsis

heliopsis

Helianthus × multiflorus 'Loddon Gold'

Helichrysum 'Sulphur Light'

❑ Height 1 ft (30 cm)
❑ Planting distance 1 ft (30 cm)
❑ Flowers late summer to early fall
❑ Any ordinary well-drained soil
❑ Sunny site
❑ Herbaceous
❑ Zones 6-9

Heliopsis 'Gold Greenheart'

❑ Height 3-4 ft (90-120 cm)
❑ Planting distance 1½-2 ft (45-60 cm)
❑ Flowers mid- to late summer
❑ Any ordinary soil
❑ Sunny site
❑ Herbaceous
❑ Zones 3-9

long, midgreen willowlike leaves. In early fall it bears sprays of golden yellow flowers about 1½ in (38 mm) wide.

Cultivation
Plant in any well-drained garden soil in a sunny spot in mid- to late fall or midspring. Support the stems with stakes or stout canes, and cut them back to ground level when flowering has finished. Divide double varieties every third or fourth year or they may revert to single forms.
Propagation Sow seeds in early spring to midspring in a sunny spot in a nursery bed. Prick out the seedlings and transfer to their permanent positions in late fall.

Divide and replant in midfall or midspring.
Pests/diseases Botrytis ·(gray mold) may cause the flowers to rot in wet weather.

Strawflower *(Helichrysum orientale)* is grown for its narrow, gray-green woolly leaves, topped in late summer by clusters of tiny round, fluffy yellow flowers that are 1½ in (38 mm) wide. This soft-textured plant is only moderately hardy and needs a protected site, perhaps by a wall.

The best hybrid is 'Sulphur Light,' which has light yellow flowers.

Cultivation
Plant in any ordinary sharply drained soil in a sunny spot from late summer to early fall or from mid- to late spring in a sheltered position or at the foot of a south-facing wall. In severe winters protection may be needed.
Propagation Take lateral shoot cuttings that are 2-3 in (5-7.5 cm) long, preferably with a heel, in mid- to late summer. Insert them in a potting medium in a cold frame. Pot on in the following spring. Plant out in the permanent site in fall.
Pests/diseases Patches of white fungal growth on the undersides of the leaves are caused by downy mildew. Leaves may turn yellow and fall prematurely.

The stiff, upright stems and rough midgreen leaves of *Heliopsis helianthoides* set off a lush display of yellow to orange dandelionlike flowers. These are single in the species, but cultivars offer semidouble and double forms. The blooms are 3 in (7.5 cm) wide and excellent for cutting.

Popular cultivars
'Desert King' has single yellow flowers.
'Golden Plume' has double, rich yellow flowers.
'Gold Greenheart' has double, pale yellow flowers with the center tinged green.
'Incomparabilis' has double orange-yellow flowers.
'Patula' has double, golden yellow flowers.
'Summer Sun,' shorter than the species, has double, golden yellow flowers.

Cultivation
Plant in midfall or early spring in any ordinary garden soil in a sunny spot.
Propagation Divide and replant in fall or spring.
Pests/diseases Trouble free.

HELLEBORE — see *Helleborus*
HELLEBORINE — see *Veratrum*

Helleborus

hellebore

Helleborus orientalis hybrids

❏ Height 1-2 ft (30-60 cm)
❏ Planting distance 1-2 ft (30-60 cm)
❏ Flowers early winter to late spring
❏ Deep, well-drained, moist soil
❏ Partially shaded site
❏ Evergreen, deciduous, or herbaceous
❏ Zones 3-8

Hellebores are one of the few garden plants that are at their best in the winter, when many gardens look dull and lifeless. The different species bloom in succession from early winter to late spring. The most popular of these plants is the Christmas rose *(Helleborus niger),* which is as much a symbol of Christmas as holly.

The flowers of hellebores are held singly or in clusters and can be either bell- or cup-shaped. They come in shades of purple, green-yellow, and white and are decorated with yellow or gold anthers. They usually measure about 2 in (5 cm) wide, though *H. lividus* has slightly larger flowers, and *H. foetidus* produces clusters of 1¼ in (3 cm) wide flow-

ers. All are excellent for cutting.

The leaves in most species are evergreen and can be dark, mid-green, or pale green or grayish.

Hellebores enjoy partial shade and are ideal for planting between shrubs. All parts are poisonous.

Popular species

Helleborus atrorubens, grows up

to 1 ft (30 cm) high and 1½ ft (45 cm) wide and has dark green, deeply lobed oval leaves. This species is deciduous except in mild climates. The cup-shaped, 2 in (5 cm) wide flowers, lasting from midwinter to early spring or midspring, are bluish maroon, turning violet.

Helleborus corsicus, syn. *H.*

Helleborus lividus

Helleborus niger

Helleborus foetidus

argutifolius (Corsican hellebore), is a moderately hardy evergreen up to 2 ft (60 cm) high and wide, with grayish, divided toothed leaves. Drooping cup-shaped, 2 in (5 cm) wide yellowish-green flowers appear from early spring to midspring.

Helleborus foetidus (stinking hellebore), up to 2 ft (60 cm) high and wide, has narrow, deeply cut, shiny dark green evergreen leaves. Clusters of drooping bell-shaped pale green flowers, 1¼ in (3 cm) wide, appear from early to late spring, and are sometimes tipped with purple. The plant smells unpleasant.

Helleborus lividus is a semihardy to moderately hardy evergreen plant up to 1½ ft (45 cm) high and 1 ft (30 cm) wide. Pale green leaves with grayish veins are divided into three lobes; the cup-shaped, 2½ in (6 cm) wide flowers are yellowish green, lasting from early spring to midspring.

Helleborus niger (Christmas rose) is up to 1½ ft (45 cm) high and wide. It has dark green leathery leaves, divided into seven to nine lobes. The saucer-shaped, nodding white or pink-tinged flowers with golden anthers appear from early winter to early spring. A cultivar is 'Potter's Wheel' (white flowers that are 5 in/13 cm wide).

Helleborus orientalis (Lenten rose), up to 2 ft (60 cm) high and 1½ ft (45 cm) wide, has broad, prostrate dark green leaves. The cream- to plum-colored flowers, often flecked crimson, are 2-3 in (5-7.5 cm) wide and appear from late winter to early spring. This species is evergreen in mild areas.

Helleborus purpurascens is an herbaceous species up to 1 ft (30 cm) high and 15 in (38 cm) wide. It has midgreen, deeply-lobed leaves. The nodding maroon flowers, 2 in (5 cm) wide, are greenish inside and appear from early spring to midspring.

Helleborus viridis (green hellebore), an herbaceous species up to 1 ft (30 cm) high and 1½ ft (45 cm) wide, has dull green leaves and cup-shaped yellow-green flowers, 2 in (5 cm) wide, from late winter to early spring.

Cultivation

Plant in midfall in partial shade in deep, well-drained but moist soil. *H. foetidus* in particular thrives in shade. Once they are planted, hellebores should not be disturbed.

Propagation Sow seeds when ripe, usually in early summer to midsummer, in flats or containers of seed-starting medium in a cold frame. Prick out the seedlings into a nursery bed. They will be ready to plant out in their permanent positions in the fall of the following year and should flower when they are 2-3 years old.

Pests/diseases Leaf spot may appear as round or oval black blotches. Diseased leaves may wither and die.

Helleborus atrorubens

Hemerocallis

daylily

Hemerocallis 'Pink Damask'

Hemerocallis 'Stafford'

❑ Height 8-48 in (20-120 cm)
❑ Planting distance 1-3 ft (30-90 cm)
❑ Flowers early summer to fall
❑ Any fertile soil
❑ Sunny or lightly shaded site
❑ Herbaceous
❑ Zones 3-9

The lovely flowers of daylilies last only one day, yet the plants produce so many blooms that as one dies a fresh one takes its place, providing a superb display throughout the summer.

Set against clumps of arching, strap-shaped pale to midgreen leaves, the graceful flowers consist of five long petals, sometimes ruffled, forming a widely flared trumpet with yellow or red anthers at the center. The flowers come in many shades of gold, yellow, pink, or red, sometimes with stripes on the petals or contrasting throats. They usually open from early to late summer, with a few varieties flowering in fall. Numerous hybrids are available.

These plants make a fine display in borders, but they are not suitable for cutting.

Popular species

Hemerocallis citrina, up to 3 ft (90 cm) high, has slightly fragrant lemon-yellow flowers, which open at night in mid- to late summer. The blooms are 5 in (13 cm) wide.

Hemerocallis fulva, up to 3 ft (90 cm) high, has rusty orange-red flowers about 3½ in (9 cm) wide in early to late summer.

Hemerocallis hybrids are 2-3 ft (60-90 cm) high and 1½ ft (45 cm) wide. Dwarf varieties, less common than the tall types, are 8-18 in (20-45 cm) high and 1 ft (30 cm) wide. The hybrids produce flowers in a wide range of shades of yellow, orange, apricot, red, and pink. The flower's dominant color may be suffused with another contrasting color. This group includes a large number of cultivars, some with large bold flowers as much as 6 in (15 cm) wide; others have many small flowers only 2-3 in (5-7.5 cm) wide. Cultivars include 'Burning Daylight' (deep orange), 'Cartwheels' (yellow), 'Chicago Royal Robe' (deep purple, green throat), 'Golden Orchid' (golden yellow), 'Hyperion' (pure yellow), 'Kwanso Flore-Pleno' (double, dusky orange), 'Pink Damask' (pink, yellow throat), 'Stafford' (bronzy red), and 'Stella d'Oro' (dwarf, canary-yellow).

Hemerocallis lilioasphodelus (syn. *H. flava),* up to 3 ft (90 cm) high, has clear yellow scented flowers in early summer.

Cultivation

Plant in midfall or midspring in a sunny or lightly shaded spot in fertile soil. After planting, leave undisturbed. Cut the stems almost to ground level after flowering.

Propagation Divide and replant the tuberous roots, but only after 5-6 years, in midfall or early spring.

Pests/diseases Trouble free.

HEMP AGRIMONY — see *Eupatorium*

Hemerocallis 'Cartwheels'

Hemerocallis 'Golden Orchid'

Hesperis

dame's rocket, sweet rocket

Hesperis matronalis

- ❏ Height 2-3 ft (60-90 cm)
- ❏ Planting distance 1½ ft (45 cm)
- ❏ Flowers early summer to midsummer
- ❏ Moist soil
- ❏ Sunny or lightly shaded site
- ❏ Herbaceous
- ❏ Zones 3-8

Sweet rocket's long spikes of flowers lend a gentle fragrance to summer evenings. *Hesperis matronalis* is an extremely hardy, undemanding border perennial. Its branching stems are clothed with dark green narrow leaves and, from early summer, loose spikes of small cross-shaped flowers that vary in color from white to purple. Double-flowered forms are occasionally seen. The plants can be short-lived, but they self-seed freely.

Cultivation
Plant in groups of three in well-drained but moisture-retentive soil in midfall or midspring. It thrives in full sun. Cut stems back to near ground level in fall.
Propagation Sow seeds in an outdoor bed in midspring; prick out the seedlings when they are large enough to handle and move to permanent sites in fall.
Alternatively, divide and replant in fall or spring.
Pests/diseases Trouble free.

Heuchera

alumroot

Heuchera 'Red Spangles'

- ❏ Height 2-3 ft (60-90 cm)
- ❏ Planting distance 1 ft (30 cm)
- ❏ Flowers summer to fall
- ❏ Light, well-drained soil
- ❏ Sunny or partially shaded site
- ❏ Semievergreen
- ❏ Zones 3-8

Clusters of tiny bell-shaped flowers form a swath of pink, red, white, or greenish yellow on long, reddish stalks. Alumroot has a dense mat of rounded dark green leaves that are lobed and hairy.

Popular species
Heuchera cylindrica grows up to 3 ft (90 cm) high, with creamy white to greenish-yellow flowers. *Heuchera sanguinea,* up to 2 ft (60 cm) high, has bright coral-red flowers. The leaves are often marbled. Cultivars include 'Bressingham Hybrids' (mixed white, pinks, and reds) and 'Red Spangles' (crimson-scarlet).

Cultivation
Plant firmly in midfall or midspring in a sunny or partially shaded site in light, well-drained soil. If the crowns of old plants rise out of the soil, mulch them. Or lift, divide, and replant in fall.
Propagation Sow seeds in early spring to midspring in a cold frame. Prick out into flats and later into a nursery bed. Plant out in fall.
Pests/diseases Trouble free.

× Heucherella

heucherella

× Heucherella tiarelloides

- ❏ Height 1-1½ ft (30-45 cm)
- ❏ Planting distance 1-1½ ft (30-45 cm)
- ❏ Flowers late spring to midsummer
- ❏ Moist, well-drained soil
- ❏ Sunny or partially shaded site
- ❏ Herbaceous
- ❏ Zones 3-8

A hybrid of *Heuchera* and *Tiarella,* heucherella is rather similar in appearance to *Heuchera*. Its graceful sprays or spikes of tiny bell-shaped flowers come in shades of pink and are excellent for cutting. Dark or golden green rounded and lobed leaves form spreading ground cover.

Popular species
× *Heucherella* 'Bridget Bloom,' up to 1½ ft (45 cm) high, has compact dark green foliage and sprays of pink flowers in late spring to midsummer.
× *Heucherella tiarelloides* is up to 1½ ft (45 cm) high with spreading light-green leaves and spikes of salmon-pink flowers in spring.

Cultivation
Plant in midfall or midspring in sun or light shade in any moist, well-drained soil.
Propagation Divide and replant in midfall or midspring.
Pests/diseases Trouble free.

Hieracium

hawkweed

Hieracium villosum

- ❏ Height 1-2 ft (30-60 cm)
- ❏ Planting distance 1 ft (30 cm)
- ❏ Flowers early summer to midsummer
- ❏ Any ordinary soil
- ❏ Sunny or partially shaded site
- ❏ Ultrahardy; herbaceous
- ❏ Zones 3-9

Though not the most glamorous of perennials, hawkweed is a useful plant, growing in any soil, even a poor, dry one. Its yellow dandelionlike flowers rise on stiff stems from rosettes of hairy silvery leaves, which are sometimes spotted purple.

Popular species
Hieracium lanatum (syn. *H. tomentosum)* is grown for its densely silvered leaves, which provide a better display if the flowers are removed.
Hieracium maculatum (spotted hawkweed) has reddish flower stems and purple-spotted leaves.
Hieracium villosum (shaggy hawkweed) forms a clump of woolly grayish leaves.

Cultivation
Plant from midfall to midspring, in any ordinary soil and in sun or partial shade.
Propagation Divide and replant between fall and spring.
Pests/diseases Trouble free.

HIMALAYAN BLUE POPPY — see *Meconopsis*
HONESTY — see *Lunaria*

Hosta

hosta, plantain lily

Hosta 'Halcyon'

- ❏ Height 10-60 in (25-150 cm)
- ❏ Planting distance 10-30 in (25-75 cm)
- ❏ Flowers midsummer to fall
- ❏ Well-drained, rich, moisture-retentive soil
- ❏ Partially shaded site
- ❏ Herbaceous
- ❏ Zones 3-8

The outstanding feature of all hostas is their bold and textured foliage. The plants form mounds or clumps of splendid heart- or lance-shaped leaves, creating a lush display from late spring through summer and into fall.

The leaves are blue-green, gray-green, or mid- to dark green, often with yellow, white, or silvery markings. They are sometimes heavily veined or crinkled. In mid- to late summer spikes or clusters of bell- or funnel-shaped flowers, which may be white or shades of purple, rise over the leaves on straight stalks.

Provided the soil is kept moist, these reliable and adaptable plants provide excellent ground cover for borders, combining well with a wide range of foliage and flowering plants.

Popular species/hybrids
Hosta crispula grows up to 2 ft (60 cm) high and 1½ ft (45 cm) wide and has broad, long-pointed, waxy leaves about 8 in (20 cm) long, with prominent white edges. Deep lilac flowers appear in midsummer.
Hosta elata and *H. montana* are up to 3 ft (90 cm) high and 2½ ft (75 cm) wide. The wavy-edged dark green leaves, up to 10 in (25 cm) long, form glossy mounds. Loose clusters of white to deep lavender-blue flowers rise above the foliage on rigid stems in early summer to midsummer. The cultivar *H. montana* 'Aureamarginata' has leaves with wide yellow-cream edges.
Hosta fortunei, up to 2½ ft (75 cm) high and 2 ft (60 cm) wide, has gray to sage-green heart-shaped, pointed leaves that turn yellow in fall. About 5 in (13 cm) long, the leaves are deeply veined and long-stalked. Lilac flowers bloom in midsummer. Some cultivars are 'Albo-picta' (creamy yellow, edged and striped pale green, fading to cream), 'Aurea' (yellow to green), 'Aureo-marginata' (green, edged yellow), 'Marginato-alba' (syn. 'Albo-marginata'; green, edged with white, and green-gray beneath), and 'Obscura' (green, edged with creamy yellow).
Hosta hybrids, usually 2-3 ft (60-90 cm) high and 2 ft (60 cm) wide, offer still more choice of leaf form and color. They include 'Gold Standard' (upright, puckered blue-green leaves; broad gold-green center), 'Honeybells' (light green wavy leaves up to 1 ft/30 cm long; lilac flowers striped violet), 'Krossa Regal' (10 in/25 cm long grayish-green, slightly wavy-edged leaves arching outward; lavender flowers on 5 ft/1.5 m stems in late summer), 'Royal Standard' (heart-shaped, wavy and puckered green leaves; white flowers in late summer), and

Hosta sieboldiana

Hosta crispula

Hosta fortunei 'Albo-picta'

'Thomas Hogg' (glossy dark green 8 in/20 cm leaves, edged cream; pale lilac flowers in early summer).

Hosta lancifolia, up to 2 ft (60 cm) high and 1½ ft (45 cm) wide, forms a neat mound of narrow, lance-shaped glossy dark green leaves, about 5 in (13 cm) long. Pale lilac flowers appear in late summer.

Hosta rectifolia, up to 3 ft (90 cm) high and 1½ ft (45 cm) wide, has upright, lance-shaped dark green leaves, which may be as long as 1 ft (30 cm). Violet-blue flowers, 2 in (5 cm) long, appear on slender spikes in late summer.

Hosta sieboldiana (syn. *H. glauca),* forms a mound up to 2 ft (60 cm) high and wide. The glossy midgreen leaves are heavily veined and up to 16 in (40 cm) long. Off-white flowers with a purplish tinge appear in late summer. The best cultivar is 'Elegans' (blue-green leaves 1 ft/30 cm wide); other cultivars include 'Frances Williams' (mature leaves edged yellow) and 'Helen Doriot' (to 3 ft/90 cm; puckered blue-green leaves).

Hosta sieboldii (syn. *H. albomarginata),* up to 1½ ft (45 cm) high and wide, has narrow green

Hosta lancifolia

Hosta undulata

leaves, 6 in (15 cm) long, with a thin white edge. Funnel-shaped lilac flowers, striped violet, appear in mid- to late summer.

Hosta tardiana is a hybrid between *H. sieboldiana* 'Elegans' and *H. tardiflora*. It has bluish leaves and grows up to 16 in (40 cm) high and 10 in (25 cm) wide. The cultivar 'Halcyon' has silvery gray leaves and dense flower clusters of pale lilac.

Hosta tardiflora is up to 10 in (25 cm) high and wide. It forms a neat mound of glossy midgreen lance-shaped leaves, topped with purple flowers in early fall.

Hosta undulata is up to 2 ft (60 cm) high and wide, with mid-green wavy, oblong leaves with white or silvery markings and pale lilac flowers in late summer. Cultivars include 'Erromena' (to 4 ft/1.2 m; plain midgreen leaves and slightly darker flowers) and 'Medio-variegata' (1 ft/30 cm; light green leaves, center variegated yellow with spikes of purple flowers).

Hosta ventricosa (syn. *Hosta caerulea*) grows up to 3 ft (90 cm) high and 2 ft (60 cm) wide. This vigorous species has gray heart-shaped leaves, shiny underneath and about 8 in (20 cm) long. Violet-mauve flowers appear in mid- to late summer. One cultivar is 'Aureo-maculata' (syn. 'Variegata'; to 2½ ft/75 cm; leaves bordered yellow).

Cultivation

During suitable weather in mid-fall or early spring, plant hostas in light shade or dappled sun in any well-drained but moisture-retentive soil enriched with leaf mold or well-decayed compost. Variegated plants retain their coloring best when grown in light shade.

Propagation Divide and replant the crowns after 4-5 years as new growth emerges in early spring.

Pests/diseases Slugs and snails may devour leaves, often destroying whole plants.

Hosta lancifolia

HOUND'S TONGUE — see *Cynoglossum*

Incarvillea

hardy gloxinia

Incarvillea delavayi

❑ Height 2 ft (60 cm)
❑ Planting distance 1 ft (30 cm)
❑ Flowers late spring to early summer
❑ Rich, well-drained soil
❑ Sunny, open site
❑ Herbaceous
❑ Zones 5-7

Incarvillea delavayi is a beauty of the early-summer garden. Rich rose-pink flowers, shaped like funnels or trumpets, cluster on stout stalks. The first few blooms on each plant often appear before the tufts of deep green leaflets have fully developed.

Cultivation
Plant in early spring to midspring in rich, well-drained soil in a sunny, open site. Set the fleshy-rooted crowns 3 in (7.5 cm) deep.

Renewed growth begins in late spring. To protect the crowns from accidental damage, mark established plants with sticks when the dead foliage is removed in fall. A mulch of compost that is 1 in (2.5 cm) deep in fall is beneficial and also helps to indicate the whereabouts of old plants.

Propagation Divide established plants and replant them in spring immediately after flowering.

Alternatively, sow seeds thinly in a shallow furrow outdoors in early spring to midspring. Leave for a year, then transplant young plants to their final positions.

Pests/diseases Generally trouble free.

Inula

inula

Inula magnifica

❑ Height 2-6 ft (60-180 cm)
❑ Planting distance 1½-3 ft (45-90 cm)
❑ Flowers midspring to midfall
❑ Any moisture-retentive, fertile soil
❑ Sunny site
❑ Ultra-hardy; herbaceous
❑ Zones 3-8

Inulas are very hardy plants grown for their showy yellow, golden yellow, or greenish-yellow flowers set against midgreen leaves. The daisylike blooms have thin petals that give them a spidery appearance.

Popular species
Inula ensifolia, up to 2 ft (60 cm) high, forms a clump of narrow, pointed leaves with yellow flowers in midsummer.

Inula hookeri, up to 2 ft (60 cm) high and wide, has a bushy mass of hairy, oblong leaves and greenish-yellow flowers in late summer.

Inula magnifica grows up to 6 ft (1.8 m) tall, with large leaves that are hairy underneath, and yellow flowers that are 6 in (15 cm) wide in late summer. It is suitable for growing at the back of beds or in waterside gardens.

Inula royleana (Himalayan elecampane) is up to 2 ft (60 cm) high and wide, with oval leaves on unbranched stems and orange-yellow flowers in late summer and fall.

Cultivation
Plant in midfall or early spring in any moist, fertile soil.

Propagation Divide and replant in fall or spring.

Pests/diseases Trouble free.

JACOB'S LADDER — see *Polemonium*

JACOB'S ROD — see *Asphodeline*

JAPANESE ANEMONE — see *Anemone*

JOE PYE WEED — see *Eupatorium*

KING'S SPEAR — see *Asphodeline*

KNAPWEED — see *Centaurea*

Kniphofia
red-hot poker, torch lily

Midseason *Kniphofia*

Early-season *Kniphofia*

- ❏ Height 2-6 ft (60-180 cm)
- ❏ Planting distance 2 ft (60 cm)
- ❏ Flowers early summer to fall
- ❏ Any well-drained soil
- ❏ Sunny site
- ❏ Herbaceous or evergreen
- ❏ Zones 6-9

The unmistakable dense spikes of pendent tubular flowers, rising over clumps of grassy foliage, make red-hot pokers outstanding focal points for herbaceous and mixed beds.

Set on strong upright stems, the pokerlike flower spikes are traditionally yellow with hot red or orange tips. However, a wide range of hybrids is now available in colors that include cool creams, yellows, and greenish yellows.

The narrow leaves are mid- to bright green or gray-green. A few are evergreen, but the majority are herbaceous.

Kniphofia 'Royal Standard'

Popular species/hybrids
Early types, 2-3½ ft (60-105 cm) tall, bloom in early summer to midsummer. They include 'Earliest of All' (flame-red), 'Primrose Beauty' (soft yellow), and 'Vanilla' (pale yellow).

Midseason types, 3-5 ft (90-150 cm) tall, flower in midsummer to late summer. They include 'Gold Mine' (orange-yellow), 'Royal Standard' (vermilion and acid-yellow), 'Springtime' (yellow and coral), and 'Underway' (apricot-orange).

Late-season types flower in late summer to fall. They include *K. caulescens* (coral-red, fading to yellow; evergreen), *K. galpinii* (short, fat rusty-orange spikes, tipped pale yellow), 'Gold Mine' (deep yellow), 'Little Maid' 2 ft/60 cm; white), 'The Rocket' (coral-

red), *K. uvaria* (original red-hot poker; coarse evergreen leaves and bright red buds that open to orange to yellow flowers), and 'Wayside Flame' (deep orange-red).

Cultivation
Red-hot pokers like full sun and adapt to almost any well-drained

Lamium
dead nettle

Lamium maculatum 'Beacon Silver'

❏ Height ½-2 ft (15-60 cm)
❏ Planting distance 1-2 ft (30-60 cm)
❏ Flowers late spring to midsummer
❏ Any soil
❏ Partially shaded site
❏ Herbaceous or evergreen
❏ Zones 3-8

To many gardeners dead nettle is little more than a rampant weed, but several ornamental types are suitable for cultivation and are particularly useful for gardens that have poor soil. Some provide good shade-tolerant ground cover with their nettlelike green, silver, or golden leaves. The tubular, hooded flowers come in pretty shades of pink and yellow.

Popular species
Lamium galeobdolon (yellow archangel), up to 1½ ft (45 cm) high and 2 ft (60 cm) wide, is correctly known as *Lamiastrum galeobdolon* (syn. *Galeobdolon luteum*). It is suitable for wild gardens. 'Variegatum,' up to 1 ft (30 cm) high, has silver-flushed leaves, tinted bronze in winter, and spikes of yellow flowers in summer. Though rampant, it is useful for ground cover.
Lamium maculatum, up to 1 ft (30 cm) high and 2 ft (60 cm) wide, has midgreen leaves with a central silver stripe and pink flowers in late spring. Cultivars include 'Aureum' (semievergreen golden leaves) 'Beacon Silver' (a good carpeting plant with silvery leaves), and 'Chequers' (up to 8 in/20 cm high with smaller leaves).

Cultivation
Plant in any soil in a shady site in midfall or early spring. *Lamium maculatum* 'Aureum' needs a moist, rich soil.
Propagation Divide and replant the roots in midfall or early spring.
Pests/diseases Generally trouble free.

Kniphofia uvaria

Kniphofia 'Little Maid'

soil. Plant in early fall to midfall or in midspring in holes large enough to take the spread-out roots. Winter mulch heavy soils.
Propagation Divide in spring.
Pests/diseases Slugs may damage buds. Thrips may cause a fine mottling and discoloring of the leaves and flowers.

KNOTWEED — see *Polygonum*
LADY FERN — see *Athyrium*
LADY ORCHID — see *Dactlorrhiza*
LADY'S MANTLE — see *Alchemilla*
LAMB'S TAIL — see *Cotyledon*

Lamium maculatum 'Chequers'

Lathyrus

everlasting pea

Lathyrus latifolius 'White Pearl'

❏ Height 6-10 ft (1.8-3 m)
❏ Planting distance 1½ ft (45 cm)
❏ Flowers early summer to early fall
❏ Any fertile, well-drained soil
❏ Sunny site
❏ Herbaceous
❏ Zones 4-7

Perennial sweet pea or everlasting pea *(Lathyrus latifolius)* uses its clinging tendrils to scramble up trellises, wire fences, and shrubs, covering them with color.

Its flowers open in clusters on long stalks, against a background of dull green leaves divided into two slightly pointed oval leaflets.

'Pink Pearl' has pink flowers; 'White Pearl' is a good, profusely flowering white cultivar.

Cultivation

Plant in midfall or midspring in any fertile, well-drained soil in full sun. Support against fences, trellises, or pea sticks.

Deadhead unless seeds are required, and cut down the current year's growth to ground level in mid- to late fall.

Propagation Sow seeds in a cold frame in early spring. Prick out as soon as they are large enough to handle. Plant out in midfall.

Alternatively, divide and replant in fall or spring.

Pests/diseases Aphids may infest plants.

LENTEN ROSE — see *Helleborus*
LEOPARD'S-BANE — see *Doronicum*

Liatris

gayfeather, blazing star

Liatris spicata

❏ Height 2-6 ft (60-180 cm)
❏ Planting distance 1½ ft (45 cm)
❏ Flowers late summer to early fall
❏ Moist, well-drained soil
❏ Sunny, open site
❏ Herbaceous
❏ Zones 3-9

Gayfeather's bristly looking, almost thistlelike flower heads are borne in tall, dense spikes that weave in the breeze and provide vertical interest in herbaceous and mixed borders. The spikes, which open from the top downward, are excellent as long-lasting cut flowers. They come in white, pink, or purple shades and rise from clumps of narrow, grasslike midgreen leaves that arch gracefully.

Popular species

Liatris aspera is up to 6 ft (1.8 m) high. Cultivars include 'September Glory' (deep purple flowers) and 'White Spire' (up to 4 ft/1.2 m high, with white flowers).
Liatris graminifolia, up to 3 ft (90 cm) high, tolerates dry soil and has sparse narrow leaves and purple flower spikes.
Liatris spicata, up to 3 ft (90 cm) tall and spreading to 1½ ft (45 cm), is a particularly good species for poor soil. The fluffy

Liatris spicata 'Kobold'

flower spikes, borne on sturdy leafy stems, are lilac and up to 1 ft (30 cm) long. They are borne from midsummer to early fall. The cultivar 'Kobold' is a similar but smaller (2 ft/60 cm) plant.

Cultivation

Plant all species in early fall to midfall or in early spring to midspring, setting the tuberous roots in an open, sunny site. Most soils are suitable, provided they are moisture retentive, but heavy soil may cause the roots to rot. Mulch annually in spring to conserve moisture, and water well during prolonged spells of dry weather. The plants disappear completely below ground in winter; mark their positions to avoid damage during cultivation.

Propagation Divide and replant in spring every 3-4 years.

Sow seeds in early spring in a cold frame or greenhouse. Prick out and grow on in nursery rows until the fall of the following year, then move the young plants to their permanent positions.

Pests/diseases Slugs may eat young shoots.

Ligularia

golden ray

Ligularia dentata and *L.d.* 'Desdemona'

❏ Height 3-6 ft (90-180 cm)
❏ Planting distance 2½-3 ft (75-90 cm)
❏ Flowers midsummer to late summer
❏ Moist soil
❏ Partially shaded or sunny site
❏ Herbaceous
❏ Zones 5-8

Ligularia is a striking plant with a mound of large leaves and bright, showy flowers. These yellow or golden yellow blooms are either large and daisylike, held in sprays over the foliage, or packed into tall, upright spikes.

These perennials, formerly in the genus *Senecio*, thrive in moist or boggy soils, especially locations near water, but adapt readily to ordinary soils.

Popular species/cultivars

Ligularia dentata (syn. *Senecio clivorum*) is up to 5 ft (1.5 m) high. The glossy deep green heart-shaped leaves are sometimes flushed purple underneath. Branched stems carry sprays of yellow daisy flowers that are 3-4 in (7.5-10 cm) wide in midsummer to late summer. Cultivars include 'Desdemona' (orange-red flowers; leaves and stems heavily flushed purple), the hybrid 'Greynog Gold' (up to 6 ft/1.8 m high; huge spikes of orange flowers), and 'Othello' (orange-red flowers; stems and leaves strongly flushed with red-purple). *Ligularia (Senecio) przewalskii*, up to 6 ft (1.8 m) high, has irregularly toothed leaves that are roughly triangular. From midsummer to late summer purple-

Ligularia stenocephala 'The Rocket'

brown spikes, up to 2 ft (60 cm) high, hold ragged yellow flowers. *Ligularia stenocephala* 'The Rocket' has yellow flowers on black stems above large, toothed foliage.

Cultivation

Plant in midfall or midspring. Boggy soil is preferable, but the plants tolerate ordinary soil, provided it is kept moist.
Propagation Lift, divide, and replant in mid- to late spring.
Pests/diseases Slugs and snails may eat young plants.

LILYTURF — see *Liriope* and *Ophiopogon*

Limonium

sea lavender

Limonium latifolium

❏ Height 1½-2 ft (45-60 cm)
❏ Planting distance 2-3 ft (60-90 cm)
❏ Flowers midsummer to late summer
❏ Any ordinary well-drained soil
❏ Sunny site
❏ Evergreen
❏ Zones 3-9

Perennial sea lavender's stiff-looking, rounded heads of bell-shaped pinkish or lavender-blue flowers rise over clumps of pointed, narrow, oblong leaves. They are suitable as cut or dried flowers.

Popular species

Limonium latifolium, up to 2 ft (60 cm) high, has lavender-blue flowers with white sepals on wiry stems. Cultivars include 'Blue Cloud' (pale lavender-blue) and 'Violetta' (rich violet).

Cultivation

Plant in midspring in ordinary well-drained soil in a sunny site.
Propagation Sow seeds when temperatures rise to between 55-61° F (13-16° C). Prick out and harden off in a cold frame. Grow on until the fall of the next year.

Alternatively, take root cuttings in spring and root in a cold frame. When the cuttings have developed three or four leaves, set out in a nursery bed and grow on until fall of the next year.
Pests/diseases Botrytis (gray mold) may cause decay in the stems and flowers; powdery mildew appears as a white powdery coating.

Linaria

toadflax

Linaria purpurea

- ❏ Height 3-4 ft (90-120 cm)
- ❏ Planting distance 1½ ft (45 cm)
- ❏ Flowers early summer to early fall
- ❏ Any ordinary well-drained soil
- ❏ Sunny site
- ❏ Herbaceous
- ❏ Zones 4-9

The curious flowers of toadflax are said to resemble a dragon's open jaws. Held in sprays or on slender spikes, they may be pink, shades of purple, or yellow, and sometimes have patches of a contrasting color. The narrow leaves are gray or midgreen. The plants are often short-lived, but seed themselves freely.

Popular species

Linaria genistifolia dalmatica up to 4 ft (1.2 m) high and 1½ ft (45 cm) wide, has narrow, lance-shaped midgreen leaves and spikes of pale yellow flowers.
Linaria purpurea, up to 4 ft (1.2 m) high and 15 in (38 cm) wide, has gray to midgreen linear leaves and slender spikes of purple-blue flowers. 'Canon J. Went' has light pink flowers.
Linaria triornithophora, up to 3 ft (90 cm) high, has gray-green leaves and rosy-purple flowers and is less hardy than the other species.

Cultivation

Plant in midfall or early spring in any ordinary well-drained garden soil in sun. In colder climates protect *L. triornithophora* during the winter.
Propagation Sow seeds thinly in late winter to early spring in a cold frame. Prick out the seedlings and plant out in midspring to late spring.

Seeds may also be sown in the flowering site. Thin the seedlings to the necessary spacing.
Pests/diseases Trouble free.

Linaria triornithophora

Linum

flax

Linum flavum 'Compactum'

- ❏ Height 1-2 ft (30-60 cm)
- ❏ Planting distance 9-12 in (23-30 cm)
- ❏ Flowers late spring to late summer
- ❏ Any ordinary well-drained soil
- ❏ Full sun
- ❏ Herbaceous
- ❏ Zones 5-9

The wide-open, five-petaled flowers of perennial flax are lovely when the sun shines fully on them, bringing out their clear blues and yellows. Though the flowers are short-lived, they are produced in such profusion that the leaves are covered with blooms throughout the summer months.

Popular species

Linum flavum (golden flax), up to 1½ ft (45 cm) high and 9 in (23 cm) wide, is a hardy sub-shrubby border plant with lance- to spoon-shaped leaves that are blue-gray to green. Golden yellow flowers are in bloom from early to late summer. The cultivar 'Compactum' is smaller and neater than the rest of the species.
Linum narbonense, up to 2 ft (60 cm) high and 1 ft (30 cm) wide, is a hardy border plant and the most popular of the perennial species. It has narrow, lance-shaped gray-green leaves and bears loose sprays of rich blue flowers from early summer. In mild areas *L. narbonense* is sometimes evergreen.
Linum perenne, up to 1½ ft (45 cm) tall and 1 ft (30 cm) wide, is a hardy if short-lived, border plant.

Liriope

liriope, lilyturf

Liriope muscari

❑ Height 1-1½ ft (30-45 cm)
❑ Planting distance 12-15 in (30-38 cm)
❑ Flowers late summer to late fall
❑ Light, well-drained soil
❑ Sunny or partial shaded site
❑ Evergreen
❑ Zones 6-9

Linum narbonense

It bears narrow lance-shaped gray-green leaves as well as masses of sky-blue flowers throughout the summer.

Cultivation

Plant in midfall to late fall or early to midspring in any ordinary well-drained soil. An open site in full sun is necessary to obtain the maximum effect from the plant's brilliant flowers. Cut down all dead growth in midfall to late fall.

Propagation Perennial flax is a short-lived plant and requires frequent propagation. All species grow easily from seed, although named cultivars do not come completely true to type. Sow seeds in early to midspring in pots or flats in a sterilized seed-starting medium in a cold frame. Prick out the seedlings into nursery rows when they are large enough to handle. Grow on until midfall; then transplant to the flowering site.

Take cuttings of soft basal shoots that are 2 in (5 cm) long in late spring and root in a cold frame. Move the rooted cuttings to an outdoor nursery bed and grow on until midfall or the fol-

lowing spring before transferring them to their permanent positions.

Pests/diseases Generally trouble free.

LION'S-HEART — see
Physostegia

The closely packed, knobbly flower spikes of liriope rise on wiry stems from a clump of glossy, grasslike deep green leaves. The bell-shaped flowers are usually mauve to lilac; a few cultivars have white flowers and leaves variegated gold or yellow.

These late-flowering plants are suitable for the front of a bed.

Popular species

Liriope muscari, up to 1½ ft (45 cm) high, has violet flower spikes from late summer to late fall. Cultivars include 'Silvery Sunproof' (leaves variegated gold) and 'Variegata' (leaves striped with cream).

Liriope spicata (creeping lilyturf), up to 15 in (38 cm) high, has more upright leaves and bright lilac-mauve flowers from late summer to midfall.

Cultivation

Plant in early to midspring in any well-drained soil, ideally sandy loam, and in sun or partial shade. After flowering cut off the flower spikes; the leaves are attractive throughout the year.

Propagation Lift, divide, and replant the fibrous matted roots in early spring to midspring.

Pests/diseases Trouble free.

Lobelia

lobelia

Lobelia × gerardii

- ❏ Height 1-4 ft (30-120 cm)
- ❏ Planting distance 12-15 in (30-38 cm)
- ❏ Flowers midsummer to midfall
- ❏ Rich, moist soil
- ❏ Sheltered, partially shaded site
- ❏ Moderately to ultra-hardy; herbaceous
- ❏ Zones 4-8

The reds of perennial lobelias outshine other reds in an herbaceous bed. There are also lobelias with blue and purple flowers. Unlike the low-growing annual lobelias, the perennials carry distinctive tubular, lipped flowers on wand-like spikes, providing a vertical focal point for the middle of a bed.

The lance-shaped leaves grow at the base of the plant and on the flower stems; they sometimes have purplish tints.

Popular species

Lobelia cardinalis is up to 4 ft (1.2 m) high, usually short-lived, and not reliably hardy. The often purplish stems carry lance-shaped midgreen leaves, with brilliant scarlet flowers from midsummer to late summer.

Lobelia × gerardii, up to 4 ft (1.2 m) tall, has dark green leaves and spikes of purple trumpet-shaped blooms from late summer to midfall.

Lobelia × hybrida plants are generally hardy and 3-4 ft (90-120 cm) tall with reddish to copper-tinted leaves. Hybrids include 'Bees Scarlet' (moderately hardy; large vivid scarlet flowers) and 'Queen Victoria' (moderately hardy; deep plum-red leaves; vivid scarlet flowers).

Lobelia siphilitica, up to 3 ft

Lobelia splendens

(90 cm) high, is a hardy plant with light green leaves and spikes of clear blue flowers that are 2½ ft (75 cm) long in midsummer to late summer. 'Alba' is white.

Lobelia splendens is similar to *L. cardinalis,* but half-hardy. Flower spikes of bright scarlet rise on thick, branching stems above basal rosettes of purple, ovate, and toothed leaves. The spikes open in late summer and continue well into the fall.

Cultivation

Plant lobelias in midspring in rich, moist soil in a sheltered and partially shaded site. Taller plants, especially *L. × gerardii,* may need to be staked.

Moderately hardy lobelias need winter protection. Cover the roots with leaves or lift in late fall and store in boxes in a greenhouse or cold frame. When new growth begins in early spring to midspring,

separate the rosettes and pot them in potting soil. Plant out when renewed growth is well established.

Propagation Sow seeds in early spring at a temperature of 55-61° F (13-16° C), harden off, and prick out into a nursery bed. Lift *L. cardinalis* from the nursery bed and overwinter in a cold frame. Leave other species in the nursery bed and plant out the following midspring.

Alternatively, increase by division in early spring.

Pests/diseases Damping off and root rot are usually due to rhizoctonia, a fungus disease, causing the plants to collapse. Stem rot can show as pale spots on leaves.

LOOSESTRIFE — see *Lysimachia* and *Lythrum*

Lunaria

perennial honesty

Lunaria rediviva

❑ Height 3-3½ ft (90-105 cm)
❑ Planting distance 2 ft (60 cm)
❑ Flowers spring
❑ Light soil
❑ Partially shaded site
❑ Herbaceous
❑ Zones 4-8

Perennial honesty (*Lunaria rediviva*) looks quite lovely in spring with its branched clusters of four-petaled starry flowers in such a pale shade of purple that they seem white from a distance. The flowers are later replaced by papery lance-shaped seed heads, which should be picked at the end of summer if they are to be dried for winter decoration.

The large, sharply toothed midgreen leaves form a bushy mound about 3 ft (90 cm) high.

Cultivation

Lunaria grows best in light soil in a partially shaded site. Plant in early fall or early spring.

Propagation Sow seeds in midspring in a nursery bed. Thin out the seedlings, or transplant them, with 6 in (15 cm) spacing, and grow on. Plant out in early fall.

Alternatively, lift and divide in early spring.

Pests/diseases Club root may distort the roots, but the top growth is unaffected. No symptoms are seen until the plants are lifted. A virus disease causes white streaks on the flowers, which may also be distorted.

LUNGWORT — see *Pulmonaria*
LUPINE — see *Lupinus*

Lupinus

lupine

Lupinus 'Russell Hybrids'

❑ Height 2-4 ft (60-120 cm)
❑ Planting distance 2 ft (60 cm)
❑ Flowers early summer
❑ Well-drained, neutral or slightly acid soil
❑ Sun or light shade
❑ Herbaceous
❑ Zones 4-9

Lupines' colorful, knobbly flower columns have made them very popular. The pealike flowers, packed densely on strong, upright stems, come in shades of pink, blue, purple, yellow, orange, red, and white. They may be all one color (self), or the lower petal and upper petals may contrast in color (bicolored).

The midgreen leaves are deeply divided into a rough hand shape.

Popular types

'Russell Hybrids' (garden hybrids), derived primarily from *Lupinus polyphyllus,* are most often up to 4 ft (1.2 m) tall and 2 ft (60 cm) wide. Spikes, up to 2 ft (60 cm) long, are thickly packed in early summer with short-lived self or bicolored flowers in shades of white, yellow, orange, red-purple, and blue.

Cultivars include 'Chandelier' (yellow), 'Dwarf Lulu' (up to 2 ft/60 cm high; mixed colors), 'My Castle' (brick-red), 'Noble Maiden' (white-and-cream), 'The Chatelaine' (pink-and-white),

Lupinus 'Russell Hybrids' (bicolored)

'The Governor' (blue-and-white), and 'The Pages' (carmine-pink).

Cultivation
Plant in sun or light shade in midfall or early spring. Lupines like well-drained soil, either neutral or slightly acid.

Propagation Propagate lupine from cuttings. In early spring to midspring take 3-4 in (7.5-10 cm) long cuttings close to the rootstock, preferably with a small piece of rootstock attached. Root in sandy soil in a cold frame. Grow in pots or transfer to nursery rows in late spring to early summer. Plant out in midfall.

Propagate species from seed. Named varieties do not come true, and self-sown seedlings differ from the parents. Sow thinly in a cold frame in early spring. Prick out to 6 in (15 cm) apart in nursery rows and plant out in midfall. Remove the flower spikes for the first year to encourage well-rooted plants.

Pests/diseases Virus diseases cause symptoms such as mottled or yellowing leaves, light green spots turning brown in older leaves, upcurled or twisted leaflets, brown streaks on leaf stalks, or flowers with broken coloring. Aphids, slugs, and snails may attack the plants.

Modern seed strains are more resistant than 'Russell Hybrids.'

Lupinus 'Russell Hybrids' (bicolored)

Lupinus 'The Governor'

Lychnis
campion

Lychnis chalcedonica

Lychnis viscaria 'Splendens Flore Plena'

Lychnis coronaria 'Abbotswood Rose'

❑ Height 1-3 ft (30-90 cm)
❑ Planting distance 9-15 in (23-38 cm)
❑ Flowers late spring to early fall
❑ Any ordinary well-drained soil
❑ Sun
❑ Herbaceous
❑ Zones 4-8

Though the pretty, open flowers of campion are usually saucer-shaped, the plant has varying floral habits, giving the separate species quite different effects in bloom. The flowers may be held in sprays, clusters, or tightly packed heads resembling large, flattened drumsticks. The blooms come in shades of magenta, pink, red, orange, purple, and white. Campions are good border plants, with the shorter species sited at the front or as edging. All are excellent as cut flowers.

The leaves are usually lance-shaped and mid- to dark green, sometimes flushed purple, or silver-gray.

Popular species
Lychnis × arkwrightii, up to 1 ft (30 cm) high and wide, has mid-green, purple-flushed leaves. The scarlet-orange blossoms have toothed petals that open from early summer to late summer.
Lychnis chalcedonica (Maltese Cross or Jerusalem Cross), up to 3 ft (90 cm) high and 15 in (38 cm) wide, has midgreen leaves. Brilliant scarlet cross-shaped flowers are held in drumsticklike heads up to 5 in (13 cm) wide in midsummer to late summer.
Lychnis (Agrostemma) coronaria (rose campion or mullein pink) is up to 2 ft (60 cm) high and 1 ft (30 cm) wide with woolly, silvery-gray leaves. Sprays of magenta-pink flowers open from midsummer to early fall. This species does well in poor, dry soil, but is often short-lived. Some cultivars include 'Abbotswood Rose' (cerise-pink), 'Alba' (white), and 'Atrosanguinea' (deep red-pink).
Lychnis flos-jovis (flower-of-Jove) is a reliable border plant up to 2 ft (60 cm) high and 1 ft (30 cm) wide. The silvery or gray hairy leaves form a dense tuft; loose, rounded clusters of purple or red flowers appear from early summer to late summer. 'Alba' is a white-flowered cultivar.
Lychnis × haageana, up to 1 ft (30 cm) high and 8 in (20 cm) wide, has midgreen, occasionally purple-flushed, leaves and small clusters of orange or scarlet flowers in early summer to midsummer.
Lychnis viscaria, syn. *Lychnis (Viscaria) vulgaris* (German catchfly), is up to 1 ft (30 cm) high and 12-15 in (30-38 cm) wide. The leaves are tufted and grasslike and the dense oval clusters of carmine flowers open from late spring to early summer. Some cultivars include 'Alba' (white) and 'Splendens Pena'

(double carmine flowers and dark leaves).

Cultivation
Campions thrive in any ordinary well-drained garden soil in sun. Plant in midfall or early spring, or in late spring if raised from seed sown early in the year. Taller plants in exposed sites may need twiggy sticks for support. Dead-head all species, particularly *L. coronaria,* to prevent self-seeding. Remove dead stems in fall or spring and mulch annually in early spring with compost or organic material.
Propagation Sow seeds in a cold frame in late spring or early summer. Prick out seedlings into nursery rows and plant out in permanent positions from midfall.

Alternatively, increase species and specially named cultivars, from cuttings taken in midspring to late spring. Root basal cuttings that are 1½-3 in (38-75 mm) long in a cold frame.
Pests/diseases Aphids and spittlebugs may damage flowering shoots. A virus disease may cause mottling on the leaves of *L. chalcedonica. L. × haageana* is a favorite of slugs.

Lysimachia
loosestrife

Lysimachia punctata

Lysimachia clethroides

❏ Height 2-36 in (5-90 cm)
❏ Planting distance 9-18 in (23-45 cm)
❏ Flowers early summer to early fall
❏ Moist garden soil or water's edge
❏ Sun or partial shade
❏ Herbaceous or evergreen
❏ Zones 3-8

Lysimachia, one of many plants commonly called loosestrife, is an easy-to-grow plant. Its species vary in habit, though all are invasive. The three described below may all be grown in a flower bed; *L. nummularia* (moneywort or creeping Jenny) also thrives in waterside locations.

Popular species
Lysimachia clethroides, up to 3 ft (90 cm) high and 1½ ft (45 cm) wide, has lance-shaped midgreen leaves, which may turn orange or

Lysimachia nummularia

red in fall. Small white star-shaped flowers form arching spikes up to 6 in (15 cm) long from midsummer to early fall.
Lysimachia nummularia (moneywort or creeping Jenny) is an evergreen waterside plant, which will also grow in ordinary soil. The rounded midgreen leaves trail over an area up to 1½ ft (45 cm) wide; bright yellow cup-shaped flowers appear in early summer to midsummer. The species is good for ground cover. 'Aurea' has yellow leaves.
Lysimachia punctata (yellow loosestrife), up to 3 ft (90 cm) high and 1½ ft (45 cm) wide, has lance-shaped midgreen leaves and whorls of bright yellow cup-shaped flowers on spikes up to 8 in (20 cm) long in early summer to late summer.

Cultivation
Plant in midfall or midspring in any moist garden soil in sun or partial shade.
L. nummularia may also be grown at the edge of water, where it needs soil 2 in (5 cm) deep. Set the plant a few inches from the pool's rim with the shoots growing toward the water.
In rich soils the lower stems of tall species may need support.
Propagation Divide and replant in midfall or early spring.
Pests/diseases Generally trouble free.

Lythrum
loosestrife

Lythrum salicaria 'Robert'

❏ Height 2-5 ft (60-150 cm)
❏ Planting distance 1½ ft (45 cm)
❏ Flowers early summer to early fall
❏ Ordinary or wet soil
❏ Sun or semishade
❏ Ultra-hardy; herbaceous
❏ Zones 3-9

This tough plant, also known as loosestrife, looks handsome in beds or near water with its spires of purple, pink, or red flowers and lance-shaped midgreen leaves.

Popular species
Lythrum salicaria is up to 5 ft (1.5 m) tall with red-purple flowers. Some cultivars include 'Firecandle' (vivid rose red) and 'Robert' (rose-red).
Lythrum virgatum has narrower leaves than *L. salicaria* and violet-pink flowers. A cultivar is 'The Rocket' (deep rose-pink).

Cultivation
Lythrum grows well in ordinary garden soil but thrives in damp or wet soil. Plant in sun or semishade in midfall or from late winter to midspring.
Propagation Divide the roots of named cultivars in fall or spring. Sow seeds of the species in midspring in a greenhouse at a temperature of 61° F (16° C). Prick out when large enough to handle and grow in containers until the following fall.
Pests/diseases Trouble free.

Macleaya
plume poppy

Macleaya microcarpa

- ❏ Height 5-8 ft (150-240 cm)
- ❏ Planting distance 3 ft (90 cm)
- ❏ Flowers mid- to late summer
- ❏ Deep, rich soil
- ❏ Sunny, sheltered site
- ❏ Herbaceous
- ❏ Zones 4-10

Plume poppy needs plenty of space to spread its plumes of tiny pink or whitish-buff flowers. The bronze lobed leaves are 8 in (20 cm) wide and gray-white on the undersides.

Popular species
Macleaya cordata (syn. *Bocconia cordata*) grows up to 8 ft (2.4 m) tall, with pearly white flowers. *Macleaya microcarpa* (syn. *Bocconia microcarpa*) is similar, but with buff flowers. 'Coral Plume' is rich pink.

Cultivation
Plant from midfall to early spring in rich, deep soil in a sunny and sheltered site.
Propagation Divide and replant from midfall to early spring. Or detach outer shoots with root attached and replant.
Pests/diseases Trouble free.

MAIDENHAIR FERN — see *Adiantum*
MAIDENHAIR SPLEENWORT — see *Asplenium*
MALE FERN — see *Dryopteris*
MALTESE CROSS — see *Lychnis*

Malva
mallow

Malva alcea

- ❏ Height 2-4 ft (60-120 cm)
- ❏ Planting distance 1½-2 ft (45-60 cm)
- ❏ Flowers early summer to midfall
- ❏ Any garden soil
- ❏ Sun or partial shade
- ❏ Herbaceous
- ❏ Zones 3-10

Malva, related to the annual mallow of the genus *Lavatera*, has deep-cut foliage and five-petaled flowers and thrives in poor soils.

The leaves are light green to midgreen, and it bears purple to rose-pink or white funnel-shaped flowers on upright stems.

Popular species
Malva alcea, up to 4 ft (120 cm) high, has light green lobed, toothed leaves. Purple-pink flowers open from midsummer to midfall.
Malva moschata (musk mallow) is 3 ft (90 cm) high with deeply cut, lobed midgreen leaves, which give off a musky smell when crushed. Rose-pink flowers open from early summer to early fall.

Cultivation
Plant from midfall to early spring in sun or a partially shaded site in any kind of soil.
Propagation Sow seeds in early to midspring in a cold frame or greenhouse at a temperature of 61°F (16°C). Prick out the seed-

Malva moschata 'Alba'

lings and grow the young plants on in a nursery bed before planting out the following spring.

Alternatively, take cuttings 3 in (7.5 cm) long of basal shoots and insert them in sandy soil in a cold frame in midspring. Plant out the rooted cuttings in their flowering positions in fall or spring.
Pests/diseases Rust may appear as orange pustules containing spores. The pustules, which appear on leaves, stems, and fruits, later turn brown.

MARJORAM — see *Origanum*
MASTERWORT — see *Astrantia*

Matteuccia

ostrich fern, shuttlecock fern

Matteuccia struthiopteris

❏ Height 3-5 ft (90-150 cm)
❏ Planting distance 3 ft (90 cm)
❏ Foliage plant
❏ Any moisture-retentive soil
❏ Partial shade
❏ Herbaceous
❏ Zones 3-8

In spring the arching golden green fronds of the ostrich fern (*Matteuccia struthiopteris,* syn. *Struthiopteris germanica*) unfurl into the form of an elegant vase. Later, the fronds surround an inner shuttlecock-shaped circle of shorter, dark brown fronds, giving the plant one of its names.

This fern is at its best in late spring, as the fronds tend to turn brownish by late summer. Like most ferns, it prefers moist soil, and it does well even in boggy conditions, perhaps under trees.

Cultivation
Plant ostrich fern in midfall or midspring in any ordinary moisture-retentive soil; for free-draining soils, use large amounts of organic materials. The plant likes partial shade but tolerates sun. Give it plenty of space, preferably 3 ft (90 cm) or more for root development.
Propagation Remove offsets and replant in midspring.
Pests/diseases Trouble free.

MAYAPPLE — see *Podophyllum*
MEADOW CLARY — see *Salvia*
MEADOW RUE — see *Thalictrum*
MEADOWSWEET — see *Filipendula*

Meconopsis

meconopsis

Meconopsis × *sheldonii*

❏ Height 1-5 ft (30-150 cm)
❏ Planting distance 1-2 ft (30-60 cm)
❏ Flowers early summer to early fall
❏ Rich, well-drained but moist soil
❏ Semishaded, sheltered site
❏ Herbaceous
❏ Zones 6-9

Meconopsis is a beautiful hardy perennial. The species include the sky-blue Himalayan poppy, which some gardeners consider perfect in both color and form in spite of its temperamental nature; the easygoing yellow or orange Welsh poppy; and many others.

The frail-looking five-petaled blooms usually come in shades of blue, yellow, or orange with long golden anthers. They open from early summer to early fall. The midgreen leaves may be oblong, ferny, or deeply cut.

Some species are short-lived and a few are monocarpic (they die after flowering once), but these lovely plants are well worth regrowing every few years.

Popular species
Meconopsis betonicifolia, syn. *M. baileyi* (Himalayan blue poppy), is 3-5 ft (90-150 cm) high, with hairy oblong leaves. The beautiful sky-blue flowers, up to 2 in (5 cm) wide, are carried in small clusters

Meconopsis betonicifolia

Mentha
mint

Mentha × suaveolens 'Variegata'

- ❏ Height 1-4 ft (30-120 cm)
- ❏ Planting distance 2-4 ft (60-120 cm)
- ❏ Flowers midsummer to early fall
- ❏ Any moist soil
- ❏ Sunny or partially shaded site
- ❏ Herbaceous
- ❏ Zones 5-10

Meconopsis cambrica

at the top of the stems in early summer to midsummer. This species may be monocarpic if allowed to flower in its first year. 'Alba' is white.

Meconopsis cambrica (Welsh poppy), 1-2 ft (30-60 cm) high, has ferny, slightly hairy basal leaves and many lemon-yellow or orange flowers up to 2½ in (6 cm) wide. Although short-lived, it seeds itself freely.

Meconopsis regia grows 3-5 ft (90-150 cm) high and 2 ft (60 cm) wide and has a rosette of large, deeply cut leaves that are up to 20 in (50 cm) long and covered with bronze hairs. The cup-shaped golden yellow flowers are up to 4 in (10 cm) wide. This species is monocarpic.

Meconopsis × sheldonii, up to 4 ft (120 cm) high and 1½ ft (45 cm) wide, has rich blue flowers that sometimes measure over 4 in (10 cm) wide. Divide regularly to avoid deterioration.

Cultivation
Plant in early spring to midspring. In North America this plant flourishes only in regions with cool, moist summers and mild winters such as the Pacific Northwest. Most species need rich acid to neutral soil that is moist but quick draining, in a semishaded and sheltered site. *M. cambrica* does well in any garden soil and in any spot with protection from full, midday sun. Monocarpic species usually take 2-4 years before they flower and die.

Meconopsis needs plenty of water in summer, but as little as possible in winter. Deadhead regularly to prolong flowering.

Propagation Sow seeds as soon as they are mature in a cold frame or greenhouse in late summer or early fall. Prick out the seedlings into boxes and overwinter in a well-ventilated greenhouse or cold frame. Germination is slower in spring, but seeds may be sown in early spring to midspring at a temperature of 55-61°F (13-16°C). Prick out the seedlings and grow on in nursery rows. Then transfer the young plants to their permanent site in early fall to midfall. Cultivars do not come true to type.

Pests/diseases Downy mildew may show as furry gray patches on leaf undersurfaces.

Many people confine mint to the herb garden. But the genus has several types with ornamental, sometimes variegated foliage.

The pointed leaves are pale green, midgreen, or gray-green and are a broad lance shape. Popular varieties often have variegated leaves, with splashes of white or yellow. The hooded flowers, which are rather insignificant, are borne in short spikes and appear from midsummer to early fall. They come in shades of purple, pink, and white.

Mint is easy to grow in moist soil and useful in borders, rock gardens, and between paving stones. Some species are invasive, so they are best planted with the roots enclosed in a container.

Popular species
Mentha × gentilis (red or Scotch mint) is a hybrid of *M. arvensis* and *M. spicata*. Up to 2 ft (60 cm) high and 3 ft (90 cm) wide, it has red-purple stems and midgreen leaves. Spikes of pale purple tubular flowers appear from midsummer to early fall. The cultivar 'Variegata' (with yellow-splashed leaves) is the best ornamental form.

Mertensia

Virginia cowslip

Milium

Bowles' golden grass

Mentha x gentilis 'Variegata'

Mertensia virginica

Milium effusum aureum

Mentha longifolia (horsemint) is a variable plant up to 1-4 ft (30-120 cm) high and 2 ft (60 cm) wide. It has large gray-green aromatic leaves up to 3½ in (9 cm) long and 4 in (10 cm) spikes of pink, lilac, or white flowers in midsummer.

Mentha suaveolens (apple mint), sometimes sold under the name *Mentha × rotundifolia,* is considered to have the best flavor of the culinary mints. Up to 3 ft (90 cm) high and 4 ft (120 cm) wide, it has hairy, pale green, rounded aromatic leaves. 'Variegata' (pineapple mint) is an ornamental cultivar with aromatic leaves edged and splashed with white.

Cultivation
Ornamental mint likes a sunny or partially shaded site in any ordinary garden soil, preferably one that remains moist in summer. Plant in midfall or early spring with the roots restricted in containers.
Propagation Divide the roots at any time from midfall to early spring. Choose vigorous 6-9 in (15-23 cm) long rhizomes and replant them directly in their permanent positions.
Pests/diseases Mint rust — promoted by fertilization with uncomposted manures — may cause the shoots and leaves to become swollen and distorted.

❑ Height 1-2 ft (30-60 cm)
❑ Planting distance 1 ft (30 cm)
❑ Flowers late spring
❑ Rich, moist soil
❑ Shady site
❑ Herbaceous
❑ Zones 3-10

The pretty, easy-to-grow Virginia cowslip, or Virginia bluebells *(Mertensia virginica),* has loose clusters of drooping purple-blue bell-shaped flowers. Borne at the top of upright stems, which bend over slightly under their weight, the flowers are suitable for cutting. The blue-gray leaves are oval and sit in pairs along the stems. The floral display finishes by early summer, and the foliage dies down completely by midsummer. The cultivar 'Rubra' is pink.

Cultivation
Plant in midfall to late fall or early spring to midspring. A rich loamy soil in a moist shady site is ideal, but the plants can adapt.
Propagation Divide and replant from midfall to early spring.

Alternatively, sow seeds when mature or in mid-summer to late summer, in a cold frame or greenhouse. The next spring, prick the seedlings out into nursery rows.
Pests/diseases Trouble free.

MICHAELMAS DAISY— see *Aster*

❑ Height 1½-2 ft (45-60cm)
❑ Planting distance 1 ft (30 cm)
❑ Foliage plant
❑ Moisture-retentive soil
❑ Partial shade
❑ Herbaceous
❑ Zones 5-10

Bowles' golden grass *(Milium effusum aureum)* is a handsome foliage plant, brightening lightly shaded sites with its bright yellow, arching grassy leaves. Tufted but slender in habit, the grassy mounds are topped in summer with dainty oatlike flower plumes of pale yellow. They are suitable for drying. Golden grass is ideal for highlights in herbaceous and mixed borders and for edging by trees and shrubs.

Cultivation
Plant in midfall or early spring in any moisture-retentive soil and in light shade. Cut flower stems for drying before they begin to set seed and remove any remainder from the base in late fall.
Propagation Sow seeds in the open in early spring to midspring. Remove any unwanted seedlings while they are still small. The plant self-seeds freely and breeds true to type.
Pests/diseases Trouble free.

Mimulus
monkey flower

Mimulus guttatus

❏ Height 1-4 ft (30-120 cm)
❏ Planting distance 2 ft (60 cm)
❏ Flowers midspring to midfall
❏ Any moist soil
❏ Sun or light shade
❏ Herbaceous or evergreen
❏ Zones 6-10

Monkey flowers appeal to children with their cheerful flowers in bright shades of red, pink, yellow, orange, and white. These trumpet-shaped, lipped blooms often having striking blotches in contrasting colors and resemble snapdragon flowers. They usually appear in late spring, continuing until early fall.

The plants like moist, even boggy soil, bringing color to waterside settings. However, they will adapt to any moist soil.

Popular species
Mimulus aurantiacus, syn. *M. glutinosus* or *Diplacus glutinosus* (bush monkey flower), is a semi-hardy evergreen subshrub up to 1½ ft (45 cm) high and 15 in (38 cm) wide. The sticky lance-shaped leaves are mid- to dark green, and the flowers are orange, salmon, pale crimson, buff, or white, appearing in succession from midspring to midfall. This species may be grown as a pot plant indoors or in a cool greenhouse, where it will reach much larger proportions.
Mimulus cardinalis (scarlet monkey flower) is an herbaceous species up to 4 ft (120 cm) high and 2 ft (60 cm) wide. It has sticky,

Mimulus luteus

hairy, sharply toothed midgreen leaves and narrow scarlet to cerise, yellow-throated flowers with prominent stamens. This species tolerates dryish soil, but requires a sheltered position.
Mimulus guttatus (common monkey flower), a very hardy herbaceous species native from Alaska to Mexico, is up to 2 ft (60 cm) high and 1 ft (30 cm) wide, with yellow flowers that are blotched brown-purple.
Mimulus lewisii, up to 3 ft (90 cm) high and 1½ ft (45 cm) wide, is a very hardy, rather floppy plant with sticky, hairy grayish leaves and rose-pink flowers from midsummer to early fall.
Mimulus luteus (golden monkey flower) has a 1 ft (30 cm) tall mound of toothed, oval leaves. It bears golden flowers spotted red or brown in their throats.
Mimulus ringens (Allegheny monkey flower), up to 3 ft (90 cm) high and 1 ft (30 cm) wide, will grow in moist soil or water up to a depth of 6 in (15 cm). It has dark green narrow leaves and flowers from late summer to early fall.

Cultivation
Plant in spring in sun or partial shade in any ordinary moist garden soil or at water's edge. In cold regions it may be best grown as an annual.

Mimulus lewisii

Propagation Divide and replant in early spring to midspring. Alternatively, in midspring root 2 in (5 cm) cuttings in a cold frame in a well-drained, rich organic rooting medium.

Sow seeds in midspring to late spring under glass; prick out the seedlings singly into pots and grow in a cold frame or transplant to nursery rows before moving to permanent sites in spring.
Pest/diseases Trouble free.

MIND-YOUR-OWN-BUSINESS
— see *Soleirolia*
MINT — see *Mentha*

Miscanthus

silver grass

Miscanthus sinensis 'Variegatus'

Miscanthus sinensis 'Zebrinus'

❏ Height 3-10 ft (90-300cm)
❏ Planting distance 3 ft (90 cm)
❏ Foliage plant
❏ Any moist soil
❏ Sunny site
❏ Herbaceous
❏ Zones 5-10

Established silver grass grows at an astonishing rate, reaching up to 10 ft (300 cm) in one season, starting anew each year.

The slender, upright but arching midgreen leaves usually have a paler midrib. Cultivars offer a choice of yellow- or white-striped leaves and some have silky flower plumes.

Silver grass makes a good screen or windbreak, or it can provide shade for other plants. It thrives in moist soil and looks attractive when planted by water.

The plant is suitable for drying; cut it down in late summer for this purpose. Otherwise, leave the foliage on the plant, so it continues to provide a windbreak and foliage interest in the winter.

Popular species
Miscanthus floridulus (giant Miscanthus), up to 10 ft (300 cm) high, is coarsely textured, with pale green leaves and white flower plumes in the fall.

Miscanthus sacchariflorus (eulalia grass), 7-9 ft (210-270 cm) high, has narrow, arching midgreen toothed leaves with paler midribs.

Miscanthus sinensis, syn. *Eulalia japonica* (Japanese silver grass), is a very hardy species from 4-8 ft (120-240 cm) high. It forms a 3 ft (90 cm) wide clump of narrow blue-green leaves with a white midrib. The lower leaves are hairy underneath. Cultivars include 'Giganteus' (the highest cultivar for screening), 'Gracillimus' (to 5 ft/150 cm high, with very narrow leaves), 'Purpurascens' (red-tinted plumes turning purple in fall), 'Silver Feather' or 'Silberfeder' (to 7 ft /210 cm high, with arching sprays of silky flower plumes in fall), 'Variegatus' (to 5 ft/150 cm high, with leaves striped bright yellowish and silver-white), and 'Zebrinus' (zebra grass; to 7 ft/210 cm high, with striking yellow bands across its leaves).

Cultivation
Plant in early spring to mid-spring in any moist soil. Despite their height, these grasses do not need staking. If the foliage is left over winter, cut down all dead stems to ground level in late spring before new growth begins.
Propagation Divide and replant the roots in early spring to mid-spring.
Pests/diseases On lower leaves, powdery mildew may appear initially as white or brown patches of fungal growth. The leaves turn yellow and shrivel, and the trouble gradually spreads over the entire plant, leaving a gray-white coating on leaves and stems. Toward the end of the season, small black fruiting bodies develop on the diseased area.

MIST FLOWER — see
Eupatorium

Monarda
bergamot, Oswego tea

Monarda didyma 'Cambridge Scarlet'

❑ Height 2-3 ft (60-90 cm)
❑ Planting distance 1½ ft (45 cm)
❑ Flowers summer
❑ Moist soil
❑ Sun or partial shade
❑ Herbaceous
❑ Zones 4-10

Bergamot *(Monarda didyma)* has dense flowers of red, pink, purple or white. The hairy, aromatic midgreen leaves are lance-shaped and may be used as a tea.

Cultivars include 'Adam' (cerise-scarlet), 'Cambridge Scarlet' (red), 'Croftway Pink' (rose-pink), 'Prairie Night' (purple-violet), and 'Snow White' (white).

Cultivation
Plant groups of four to six in midfall or early spring to midspring.
Propagation Divide the roots in early spring every 2 or 3 years. Plant out tufts 2 in (5 cm) wide, discarding the center.
Pests/diseases It is prone to mildew, particularly in dry soils.

MONDO GRASS — see *Ophiopogon*
MONEYWORT — see *Lysimachia*
MONKEY FLOWER — see *Mimulus*
MONKSHOOD — see *Aconitum*
MOURNING WIDOW — see *Geranium*
MULLEIN — see *Verbascum*
MUSK MALLOW—see *Malva*
NEEDLE GRASS — see *Stipa*

Nepeta
catmint

Nepeta × *faassenii*

❑ Height 1-3 ft (30-90 cm)
❑ Planting distance 1-2 ft (30-60 cm)
❑ Flowers late spring to early fall
❑ Well-drained ordinary soil
❑ Sun or partial shade
❑ Herbaceous
❑ Zones 3-10

Old-fashioned catmint has been used for centuries as edging and ground cover. Its cloud of tiny blue to violet tubular, hooded flowers appears from late spring to fall. The often aromatic leaves may be gray-green or midgreen.

Popular species
Nepeta × *faassenii,* up to 2 ft (60 cm) high, has aromatic gray-green leaves and lavender-blue flowers from late spring.
Nepeta nervosa, up to 2 ft (60 cm) high, is a bushy plant with veined midgreen leaves, which are narrower than those of other species. Clear blue or sometimes yellow flowers appear from midsummer.
Nepeta sibirica (syn. *N. macrantha)* up to 3 ft (90 cm) high, has aromatic leaves and violet-blue flowers on upright stems. Some cultivars include 'Blue Beauty' (to 1½ ft/45 cm, with lavender-blue flowers).

Cultivation
Plant in a sunny or partially shaded spot in well-drained ordinary garden soil from midfall to early spring.
Propagation Divide and replant in early spring to midspring. Alternatively, increase *N. nervosa* and *N.* × *faassenii* in midspring from basal cuttings that are 2-3 in (5-7.5 cm) long. Root in a cold frame, pot, and plunge outside. Plant out the following spring.

Sow seeds of *N. nervosa* in early spring to midspring in a cold frame or greenhouse at a temperature of 61°F (16°C). Prick them out and grow on.
Pests/diseases Powdery mildew may cause a white powdery coating on the leaves.

NEW ZEALAND FLAX — see *Phormium*
OBEDIENT PLANT — see *Physostegia*

Oenothera
evening primrose, sundrops

Oenothera missouriensis

❑ Height 4-36 in (10-90 cm)
❑ Planting distance 9-24 in (23-60 cm)
❑ Flowers early summer to early fall
❑ Any well-drained garden soil
❑ Open, sunny site
❑ Herbaceous
❑ Zones 4-10

The faintly scented, gleaming cup-shaped blooms of evening primroses or sundrops look like numerous specks of sunlight shining against the foliage. Each flower may live for only one day, but so many are produced in succession that the display lasts throughout the summer months. Many species bloom during the evening, the flowers opening in late afternoon and closing again at dawn — although some, such as *Oenothera missouriensis,* leave their blossoms open for several days once they have unfolded their buds.

The leaves are generally narrow to lance-shaped, from pale to dark green. Most species are upright and ideal for borders, and the mat-forming *O. missouriensis* is suitable for edging the front of a flower bed.

Popular species
Oenothera fruticosa, ½-2 ft (15-60 cm) high, is an ultrahardy species with narrow midgreen leaves and yellow flowers 1-2 in (2.5-5 cm) wide from early to late summer.
Oenothera missouriensis (Ozark sundrops) is ½-1 ft (15-30 cm) high and forms a mat 1½ ft

Oenothera fruticosa

(45 cm) wide of narrow mid- to dark green leaves. Its beautiful short-stemmed, pale yellow flowers, up to 5 in (13 cm) wide, open in the evening and last for several days throughout the summer months.
Oenothera perennis, syn. *O. pumila* (nodding sundrops), is up to 2 ft (60 cm) high and 1½ ft (45 cm) wide, with pale to midgreen lance-shaped leaves and loose leafy spikes of 1 in (2.5 cm) wide yellow flowers in midsummer.
Oenothera tetragona (syn. *O. fruticosa youngii* or *O. youngii)* is an ultrahardy plant that grows up to 3 ft (90 cm) high and 1 ft (30 cm) wide. It has dark green leaves and spikes of clear yellow flowers up to 2 in (5 cm) wide throughout the summer. Some cultivars, usually growing up to 2 ft (60 cm) tall and forming a neat mound, include 'Fireworks' (golden yellow), 'Highlight' (bright yellow),

and 'Yellow River' (rich yellow).

Cultivation
Plant in midfall or midspring in any well-drained ordinary garden soil in an open, sunny site. Water well in dry weather. Cut faded flower spikes back to ground level in midfall.
Propagation Sow seeds in a cold frame in midspring. Prick out the seedlings and grow on in nursery rows. Plant in permanent positions in midfall.

Cultivars do not come true from seed. Divide and replant the roots in early spring to midspring.
Pests/diseases Powdery mildew appears as a powdery white coating on the leaves. Root rot may occur in heavy, wet soils.

Onoclea

sensitive fern

Onoclea sensibilis

❏ Height 1-2 ft (30-60 cm)
❏ Planting distance 3 ft (90 cm)
❏ Foliage plant
❏ Moist soil
❏ Shaded site or sun
❏ Herbaceous
❏ Zone 4

The long-stemmed, pale blue-green fronds of the sensitive fern *(Onoclea sensibilis)* wither and turn brown at the first touch of frost in fall. In spring large sterile fronds with mainly triangular scalloped leaflets unfurl from fat red buds. Then in late summer narrow fertile fronds that resemble strings of beads appear and last through winter.

The sensitive fern spreads rapidly through underground runners and is ideal as ground cover for boggy banks and streamsides.

Cultivation
Plant in midspring, setting the rhizomes just below the surface of any permanently moist soil. An open, shaded site is ideal, but this fern tolerates full sun if moisture is abundant.
Propagation Divide the rhizomes in midspring, making sure that each piece contains a growing point before planting them at least 3 ft (90 cm) apart.
Pests/diseases Trouble free.

Ophiopogon

lilyturf, mondo grass

Ophiopogon planiscapus 'Nigrescens'

❏ Height ½-2 ft (15-60 cm)
❏ Planting distance ½-2 ft (15-60 cm)
❏ Flowers midsummer
❏ Fertile, well-drained but moisture-retentive soil
❏ Light shade
❏ Evergreen
❏ Zones 7-10

Lilyturf, a year-round ground cover with dark green grassy leaves, has bell-shaped white, purple, or purple-pink flowers on short spikes; blue berries follow.

Popular species
Ophiopogon jaburan, up to 2 ft (60 cm) high and wide, is clump forming, with whitish flowers and violet-blue berries.
Ophiopogon japonicus (mondo grass), up to 1 ft (30 cm) high and 1½ ft (45 cm) wide, spreads using stolons.
Ophiopogon planiscapus, ½-1 ft (15-30 cm) tall and up to 1½ ft (45 cm) wide, has white or purplish-pink flowers. The low-growing 'Nigrescens' has purple-black leaves and white to violet flowers.

Cultivation
Plant in spring in fertile, well-drained but moist soil, in a sheltered, lightly shaded site.
Propagation Lift, divide, and replant the fibrous roots.
Pests/diseases Slugs and snails attack foliage.

ORCHIS — see *Dactylorhiza*

Origanum

common or wild marjoram

Origanum vulgare 'Aureum'

❏ Height 1½-3 ft (45-90 cm)
❏ Planting distance 1-1½ ft (30-45 cm)
❏ Flowers midsummer
❏ Well-drained ordinary soil
❏ Sunny spot
❏ Herbaceous
❏ Zones 3-10

Though the fragrant-leaved common marjoram *(Origanum vulgare)* is most often grown as a culinary herb, the ornamental cultivar *O. v.* 'Aureum' is more than suitable for decorative use in borders or for edging. Rounded leaves, yellow when young and turning green later, grow in whorls on wiry stems, with clusters of rosy purple flowers in midsummer.

Cultivation
Plant in early spring to midspring in a sunny spot in well-drained ordinary soil.
Propagation Lift and divide in midfall or early spring.
Alternatively, take 1-2 in (2.5-5 cm) cuttings of nonflowering basal shoots from midsummer to early fall and root in a cold frame. Pot and overwinter in the frame. Plant out the following early spring to midspring.
Pests/diseases Generally trouble free.

ORNAMENTAL RHUBARB — see *Rheum*

Osmunda
royal fern

Osmunda regalis in spring

Osmunda regalis in summer

❏ Height 3-6 ft (90-180 cm)
❏ Planting distance 4-6 ft (120-180 cm)
❏ Foliage plant
❏ Moist, acid, humus-rich soil
❏ Sun or partial shade
❏ Herbaceous
❏ Zones 3-9

The imposing royal fern *(Osmunda regalis)* is a giant among native ferns and looks magnificent when grown in moist or boggy soils. Coppery young fronds unfurl from straight stalks in the spring, turning a fresh green as the season progresses and the stalks blacken. The fertile fronds resemble dried flowers or dead astilbe blooms. In fall the plant turns a rich brown.

Cultivation
Plant in early spring to midspring in sun or partial shade in moist, acid, humus-rich soil. Place the crowns at soil level. Top-dress with humus or compost in spring.
Propagation Sow fresh spores during summer in a greenhouse.

Alternatively, lift and divide well-separated crowns in spring.
Pests/diseases Trouble free.

Osmunda regalis in fall

OSTRICH FERN— see
Matteuccia
OSWEGO TEA—see *Monarda*

Paeonia
peony

Paeonia arietina

❏ Height 1-3 ft (30-90 cm)
❏ Planting distance 2-3 ft (60-90 cm)
❏ Flowers late spring to midsummer
❏ Any moist, well-drained garden soil
❏ Sun or partial shade
❏ Herbaceous
❏ Zones 2-8

When the peony's huge, often fragrant flowers first start to open, it is a sign that summer is near. These magnificent plants, one of the best-loved and oldest genera of hardy perennials, are invaluable for early summer color in herbaceous and mixed borders. After planting, they may take 3-4 seasons before they flower, but once established and thriving, they will survive for 50 years or more.

The blooms, from the cup-shaped single flowers of the species to the bowl-shaped mass of petals of double-flowered cultivars, measure 2½-6 in (6-15 cm) wide and come in a vast range of colors. They are set on long stems against a neat bush of glossy midgreen, dark green, or gray-green foliage, attractive enough to hold its own in the border once the flowers have disappeared, usually before midsummer. The deeply cut leaves, often tinted red in spring, occasionally develop crimson tints in fall. Unlike many herbaceous perennials, the foliage remains neat even after the flowers fade. Some species have colorful seed heads in fall.

Paeonia lactiflora

Paeonia lactiflora 'Edulis Superba'

Paeonia mlokosewitschii

Paeonia lactiflora 'Great Lady'

Paeonia cambessedesii

Paeonia lactiflora 'White Wings'

Paeonia 'Monsieur Jules Elie'

Popular species

Paeonia anomala, up to 2 ft (60 cm) high and wide, has finely divided dark green leaves and crimson flowers that are 3-4 in (7.5-10 cm) wide, with yellow stamens, from late spring.

Paeonia arietina, up to 2½ ft (75 cm) high and 3 ft (90 cm) wide, has midgreen to grayish-green, finely divided leaves, which are hairy underneath. Hairy stems carry fragrant rose to magenta-pink flowers up to 5 in (13 cm) wide in late spring and early summer.

Paeonia cambessedessii, which requires protection from hard freezes, is up to 1½ ft (45 cm) high and wide. The leathery leaves are purple underneath. Deep rose-pink flowers, 2½-4 in (6-10 cm) wide, with red stamens and purple pistils, blossom from late spring onward.

Paeonia daurica, hardy to zone 3, is 1-2 ft (30-60 cm) high. It has wavy-edged leaves that are hairy underneath and in late spring, simple cups of rose-red petals.

Paeonia emodi, hardy to zone 3, up to 3 ft (90 cm) high and wide, has dark green leaves that are paler underneath, and fragrant, pure white, 3-4 in (7.5-10 cm) wide flowers with yellow stamens from late spring to early summer.

Paeonia lactiflora, syn. *P. albiflora* (Chinese peony), is now rarely grown but is the main parent of hundreds of cultivars and hybrids. These are generally 2½-3 ft (75-90 cm) high, with 4-6 in (10-15 cm) wide flowers which appear in late spring or early summer. The flowers may be single, semidouble, or fully double.

Single cultivars, usually with golden or yellow stamens, include 'Claire de Lune' (yellow), 'Great Lady' (deep shining pink), 'Krinkled White' (large, crepelike white petals), 'Scarlett O'Hara' (red), and 'Sea Shell' (pink).

Semidouble "Japanese" and anemone-flowered cultivars include 'Bowl of Beauty' (fragrant, deep pink with creamy white center), 'Chocolate Soldier' (fragrant scent, purple-red with mottled-yellow center), 'Doreen' (fuchsia-pink with a gold center), 'Montezuma' (bright crimson with yellow center), 'Pink Lemonade' (strongly fragrant, pink with a pink, yellow, and cream center), and 'Prairie Moon' (soft yellow).

Double cultivars include 'Angel Cheeks' (fragrant, red-striped soft pink petals), 'Border Gem' (white, with deep pink outer petals), 'Dawn Pink' (dark to medium rose-pink), 'Dinner Plate' (fragrant, shell-pink), 'Edulis Superba' (fragrant, rosy lilac), 'Festiva Maxima' (fragrant, white flecked with crimson), 'Honey Gold' (white petals around yellow), 'Monsieur Jules Elie' (fragrant, silvery rose-pink), 'Monsieur Martin Cahuzac' (dark crimson-maroon), 'Phillip Rivoire' (rose-scented, crimson), and 'Sarah Bernhardt' (fragrant, apple-blossom pink).

Paeonia mlokosewitschii, a very hardy species up to 2 ft (60 cm) high and 3 ft (90 cm) wide, has soft gray-green leaves with downy undersides. Lemon-yellow flowers are 3-4 in (7.5-10 cm) wide, with golden stamens in mid- to

Paeonia officinalis 'Rubra Plena'

late spring. The red seedpods are particularly striking in fall.

Paeonia officinalis has been superseded by its cultivars, which are generally up to 2½ ft (75 cm) high and 3 ft (90 cm) wide. They include 'Alba Plena' (double, white), 'Rosea Superba' (double, bright pink), and 'Rubra Plena' (double, deep crimson).

Paeonia peregrina (syn. *P. lobata)* is a very hardy, spreading species up to 2 ft (60 cm) high and wide. The deeply cut leaves are shiny and midgreen above, and grayish green and slightly hairy underneath. Cup-shaped, deep red flowers, up to 4 in (10 cm) wide, appear from late spring to early summer. Cultivars include 'Sunshine' (salmon-scarlet).

Paeonia × smouthii, up to 2 ft (60 cm) high and wide, has finely

Paeonia lactiflora 'Festiva Maxima'

Paeonia lactiflora 'Dawn Pink'

Paeonia anomala

Paeonia mlokosewitschii (seedpods)

dissected dark green leaves and crimson flowers, 3 in (7.5 cm) wide, from late spring on.

Paeonia tenuifolia (fernleaf peony), grows up to 1½ ft (45 cm) high and wide. It has dense, very finely cut fernlike foliage, and shiny, deep crimson flowers up to 3 in (7.5 cm) wide with golden stamens. A cultivar is 'Plena' (double).

Cultivation

Grow peonies in any moist, well-drained soil in sun or partial shade. The site should be shaded from early-morning sun.

Plant them 1-2 in (2.5-5 cm) deep in mild weather in early fall or early spring — in the South, before new growth begins. After planting, lightly fork a handful of bonemeal into the soil.

Water well during dry weather and mulch annually in light soils. Avoid disturbing the plants unless it is absolutely necessary. Deadhead the flowers as they begin to fade, unless the plant is being grown for its seed heads.

Cut down the foliage in late fall.

Peonies may need support, particularly in exposed positions; use twiggy sticks, metal-link stakes, or wire-ring supports.

When cutting flowers, take only a few stems from each plant. To prevent the petals from dropping, cut the blooms as they begin to open and lay them flat in a cool, dry place for 24 hours. Then trim ½ in (12 mm) from the stems and place in deep water.

Propagation All peonies can be raised from seed, although cultivars and hybrids do not come true. Sow seeds in early fall in a cold frame and prick out into a nursery bed the following late spring. Grow on for 3-4 years, then plant out in early fall or early spring. Alternatively, divide and replant in early fall. Cut the tough crowns with a sharp knife, ensuring that each piece has roots and dormant buds.

Pests/diseases Japanese beetles attack the flowers of late-blooming types.

Peony wilt may cause foliage

and shoots to collapse during blooming season.

Leaf spots of various sizes and colors are caused by a number of fungi but may be controlled by removing all leaves and stems in late fall and spraying with an approved fungicide several times during the growing season.

A gray velvety fungal growth may appear on the flower buds and stem bases. When similar symptoms occur late in the season, they are often caused by gray mold fungus.

A physiological disorder, causing the flower buds to remain small and hard and fail to open, may be due to frost damage, overdry soil, malnutrition, too deep planting, or root disturbance.

A virus disease appears as a yellow mosaic of irregularly shaped patches or rings on the leaves.

PAMPAS GRASS — see
Cortaderia

Papaver

oriental poppy

Papaver orientale 'Harvest Moon'

P. orientale 'Helen Elizabeth'

- ❏ Height 2-4 ft (60-120 cm)
- ❏ Planting distance 2-3 ft (60-90 cm)
- ❏ Flowers late spring to early summer
- ❏ Well-drained ordinary soil
- ❏ Sunny site
- ❏ Ultrahardy; herbaceous
- ❏ Zones 3-7

Despite the delicate crepe-paper appearance of its flowers, Oriental poppy *(Papaver orientale)* is an ultrahardy plant that thrives in full sun.

The spectacular flowers appear at the very end of spring or the beginning of summer. The typical poppy bloom has five thin, slightly overlapping petals of bright scarlet, with prominent black stamens in the center, and usually a large black blotch at the base of each petal. The large seedpods are suitable for drying.

Cultivars of the Oriental poppy (some are listed at right) measure up to 5 in (13 cm) wide and come in scarlet, orange, red, and shades of pink as well as pure white. Some have ruffled or frilled petals, and a few are semidouble.

The flowers of all types are short-lived, but with regular deadheading there is sometimes a second flush later in the season. Blooms are borne singly on rather hairy stems, which are usually floppy and need staking. The flowers rise above spreading clumps of deeply cut, coarse and hairy, mid- to deep green leaves, which die down by midsummer.

These plants provide a colorful early-season display for beds and are charming in a wild garden.

Popular cultivars
'Beauty of Livermore' bears bright red blossoms with unusually long stems.
'Bonfire' has ruffled scarlet petals with black centers.
'China Boy' has ruffled apricot flowers with white centers.
'Curlilocks' is semierect with serrated, frilly vermilion petals with black throats.
'Glowing Embers' is a strong grower of upright habit, more than 3½ ft (105 cm) tall, with ruffled orange-red blooms.
'Glowing Rose' is an early bloomer with large watermelon-pink flowers.
'Harvest Moon' has deep orange semidouble flowers that tend to fade in strong sun.
'Helen Elizabeth' is an early bloomer, with ruffled flowers of light salmon-pink.
'Lavender Glory' bears lavender flowers with black throats.
'Mrs. Perry' bears salmon-pink flowers.
'Perry's White' has off-white flowers.
'Raspberry Queen' bears raspberry-colored petals touched with black at the base.
'Salmon Glow' has rich salmon-pink double flowers.
'Springtime' bears white flowers edged with pink.
'Turkish Delight' has flesh-pink flowers.
'White King' is an early bloomer with large, substantial flowers of pure white petals touched with

Papaver orientale 'China Boy'

Papaver orientale 'Perry's White'

black at the base of the blossom.

Cultivation
Plant in midfall or early spring to midspring in well-drained ordinary soil in a sunny spot. Stake the plants as they grow. Deadhead after flowering.

In mild weather Oriental poppy and its cultivars may produce a few more flowers in fall if the first flower stems are cut down.

Propagation Divide and replant the roots in early spring to midspring. Or take root cuttings and root in a cold frame in winter.

Alternatively, sow seeds in pots or pans of seed compost and place in a cold frame or greenhouse in midspring. Prick out in nursery rows when the plants are big enough to handle, and plant out from midfall to midspring.

Cultivars do not come true from seed.

Pests/diseases Yellow blotches on the leaves are caused by downy mildew.

PEARLY EVERLASTING — see *Anaphalis*

Peltiphyllum

umbrella plant

Peltiphyllum peltatum

- ❑ Height 2-4 ft (60-120 cm)
- ❑ Planting distance 3 ft (90 cm)
- ❑ Flowers early spring
- ❑ Moist soil
- ❑ Sun or semishade
- ❑ Herbaceous
- ❑ Zones 5-7

The umbrella plant *(Peltiphyllum peltatum)* is named for its elegant leaves — bright green circular disks, up to 1 ft (30 cm) wide, which have lobed edges and are held on long stalks. In fall the foliage turns an eye-catching bronze. In early spring, before the leaves begin to unfold, thick, bare flower stems push up through the ground and are topped with large rounded heads of white or pink flowers.

Grown primarily for its foliage, the umbrella plant provides handsome ground cover for moist banks or by pools and streams, but it is invasive and not recommended for small gardens.

Cultivation

Plant the rhizomes in midfall, in rich and permanently moist soil in full sun or light shade. Get rid of dead leaves on the site during winter.

Propagation Lift, divide, and replant rhizomes, 3 ft (90 cm) apart, during suitable weather in summer or fall.

Pests/diseases Trouble free.

Pennisetum

fountain grass

Pennisetum villosum

- ❑ Height 1-3 ft (30-90 cm)
- ❑ Planting distance 1-2 ft (30-60 cm)
- ❑ Flowers early summer to midfall
- ❑ Well-drained ordinary garden soil
- ❑ Sunny, sheltered spot
- ❑ Hardiness varies; herbaceous
- ❑ Zones 5-9

Pennisetum's graceful narrow leaves and feathery flower plumes tremble and waver in the slightest breeze, giving the grass a delicate, misty look.

The arching leaves are midgreen, gray-green, or blue-gray. They surround narrow-stalked, cylindrical flower plumes, which may be yellow, purple, pink, and brown, or white. Use the plumes in fresh arrangements or dry them for winter decoration.

Pennisetum alopecuroides may be grown as a specimen plant. *P. orientale* and *P. villosum* look lovely planted in clusters.

Popular species

Pennisetum alopecuroides (Chinese pennisetum, or rose fountain grass) is a good specimen plant, up to 3 ft (90 cm) high and 2 ft (60 cm) wide. It has gray-green leaves and tawny yellow or purplish flower plumes in fall. The hardiest of these plants, this species overwinters to zone 5.

Pennisetum orientale, up to 1½ ft (45 cm) high and 1 ft (30 cm) wide, has hairy blue-gray leaves and bristly brown-green or silvery pink flower spikes. It may be grown as an annual.

Pennisetum villosum (feathertop), up to 2 ft (60 cm) high and 1 ft (30 cm) wide, has arching midgreen leaves and white or brownish-purple flower spikes. This species is usually grown as an annual north of zone 9.

Cultivation

Plant in midspring in any well-drained ordinary garden soil in a sunny, sheltered spot. In warm, sheltered areas, protect the plants during winter with evergreen boughs, coarse sand, or weathered ashes. In colder areas, lift the plants in midfall and overwinter in pots in a cool greenhouse. Plant out in spring, after the last frost.

Cut flower plumes for winter decoration when fully developed; hang them upside down to dry.

Propagation Divide and replant perennial species in midspring.

Germinate seeds of species to be treated as annuals in early spring to midspring under glass at a temperature of 59-63°F (15-17°C). When the seedlings are large enough to handle, prick them out into flats; plant out in late spring after the last frost.

Pests/diseases Trouble free.

Penstemon

penstemon

Penstemon fruticosus

P. × gloxinioides 'Sour Grapes'

Penstemon digitalis

❏ Height 1½-4 ft (45-120 cm)
❏ Planting distance 1½-2 ft (45-60 cm)
❏ Flowers late spring to fall
❏ Well-drained soil
❏ Sunny site
❏ Hardiness varies (most intolerant of wet weather); herbaceous
❏ Zones 3-10

Penstemon's bright spikes of long-lasting snapdragonlike flowers fill the border with color from early summer and bloom repeatedly until fall when deadheaded regularly.

The trumpet-shaped flowers come in shades of pink, red, blue, and purple and sometimes white. The leaves are usually lance-shaped and may be midgreen or gray-green.

Popular species

Penstemon barbatus (syn. *Chelone barbata*) is an ultrahardy (zones 3-9) species up to 3 ft (90 cm) high and 2 ft (60 cm) wide. It has midgreen leaves and spikes of rosy red flowers, 1 in (2.5 cm) long, with bearded lips. Cultivars come in various shades of pink, scarlet, purple, or white; the cultivar 'Bashful' bears orange blossoms.

Penstemon digitalis flourishes in the eastern and central United States from zones 3-9. It produces 2-4 ft (60-120 cm) tall spikes of white blooms that are sometimes flushed with purple in late spring and early summer.

Penstemon fruticosus is a hardy subshrubby border species that grows up to 2 ft (60 cm) high and 15 in (38 cm) wide. It has profuse lavender-purple flowers. The cultivar 'Holly' has hollylike leaves.

Penstemon × gloxinioides (syn. *P. × hybridus)*, a group of hybrids of varied parentage, flourish only on the Pacific Coast in zones 9-10 and are best treated as half-hardy annuals elsewhere. They grow up to 3 ft (90 cm) high and 1½ ft (45 cm) wide with densely set spikes of 2 in (5 cm) long flowers and midgreen leaves. Cultivars include 'Firebird' (bright red), 'Garnet' (deep red), 'Holly's White' (white with a pink blush), 'Mesa' (deep lavender blue), 'Midnight' (deep purple), and 'Sour Grapes' (purple).

Penstemon hartwegii is a border species up to 2 ft (60 cm) high and 16 in (40 cm) wide. It has rich green leaves and bright scarlet flowers, 2 in (5 cm) long. The blooms of 'Scarlet Queen' are exceptionally brilliant.

Penstemon heterophyllus (zones 5-10), is a subshrubby species up to 2 ft (60 cm) high and 1½ ft (45 cm) wide. It has narrow gray-green leaves on rather woody stems and blue, pink-flushed flowers in short spikes. 'Blue Bedder' has flowers of clear blue. Both the species and the cultivar are suitable for the front of sunny, sheltered flower beds.

Cultivation

Penstemons thrive in full sun and require a very well-drained garden soil — these plants will not tolerate wet conditions around the roots and prefer the humidity-free air of the western states. Plant perennial species in early spring to midspring. Cut them down to ground level after flowering and protect the crowns of moderately hardy types with a deep mulch in winter. Do not fertilize.

Propagation Take cuttings of nonflowering side shoots that are 3 in (7.5 cm) long in late summer to early fall and root in a cold frame. Plant out the following spring when all danger of frost has passed.

Cultivars do not come true from seed, but several good strains of mixed colors are available. In late winter to early spring, germinate seeds under glass at a temperature of 55-64°F (13-18°C). Prick out into flats and harden the seedlings off in a cold frame. Plant out in late spring.

Pests/diseases Trouble free.

PEONY — see *Paeonia*
PERENNIAL PEA — see *Lathyrus*

Perovskia

Russian sage

Perovskia atriplicifolia

- ❏ Height 3-5 ft (90-150 cm)
- ❏ Planting distance 1½-2 ft (45-60 cm)
- ❏ Flowers late summer to early fall
- ❏ Any light well-drained soil
- ❏ Sun
- ❏ Herbaceous
- ❏ Zones 5-10

Russian sage *(Perovskia atriplici-folia)* is a very hardy perennial of shrubby habit that does especially well in seaside gardens. The downy branching stems have small gray-green, coarsely toothed leaves, which smell of sage. In late summer and early fall, the plant has daintily branched flower spikes bearing tubular violet-blue flowers. The cultivar 'Blue Haze' bears light blue flowers and leaves almost uncut; 'Blue Spire' has blooms of a richer blue than the species and finely lobed leaves.

Cultivation

Plant from late fall to midspring in any light and well-drained soil; Russian sage does particularly well in alkaline soils and needs full sun. Leave the faded stems to overwinter on the plant, before cutting them back to about 1½ ft (45 cm) in early spring.

Propagation Take cuttings, 3 in (7.5 cm) long, from side shoots in midsummer and root in a cold frame. Plant the rooted cuttings in their permanent sites the following spring.

Pests/diseases Trouble free.

Phalaris

gardener's garters, ribbon grass

Phalaris arundinacea 'Picta'

- ❏ Height 2-5 ft (60-150 cm)
- ❏ Planting distance 2 ft (60 cm)
- ❏ Flowers early summer to midsummer
- ❏ Any well-drained ordinary garden soil
- ❏ Sun or partial shade
- ❏ Herbaceous
- ❏ Zones 4-9

Gardener's garters *(Phalaris arundinacea* 'Picta') is a handsome grass that retains its appearance year-round.

The spearlike leaves, vertically striped green and cream-white, are brightest in spring. In early summer to midsummer there is a profuse, but insignificant, display of green or purple flower plumes. The leaves turn yellow in fall.

In rich, moist soil the plant grows to 5 ft (150 cm) high and can be invasive. In drier soils it may reach only half that height but is more manageable.

Cultivation

Plant in midfall or midspring, as weather permits, in any well-drained ordinary garden soil in a sunny or partially shaded site. Restrict the spreading rhizomes by replanting every 2-3 years, or plant the roots in a pot and sink into the ground. Alternatively, surround the plant with vertical slates.

Propagation Divide and replant the roots from midfall to mid-spring during suitable weather.

Pests/diseases Trouble free.

Phlomis

phlomis

Phlomis samia

- ❏ Height 2-6 ft (60-180 cm)
- ❏ Planting distance 2-3 ft (60-90 cm)
- ❏ Flowers late spring to midsummer
- ❏ Any ordinary soil
- ❏ Sun
- ❏ Herbaceous
- ❏ Zones 3-10

Phlomis species are excellent border plants, valued for their bushy growth habit and abundance of attractive oval to heart-shaped, downy leaves. The perennial species are related to Jerusalem sage, an evergreen shrub, but they are generally hardier and less fussy about soil as long as they are grown in full sun. The erect flower stems are set at regular intervals with densely packed whorls of tubular and hooded flowers, each 1 in (2.5 cm) or more long.

Popular species

Phlomis russeliana (syn. *P. viscosa*) grows 2½-4 ft (75-120 cm) high and bears large, wrinkled, ovate midgreen leaves. In early summer and midsummer the sturdy stems are studded with tiers of clear yellow flowers.

Phlomis samia, 2-3 ft (60-90 cm) tall, has heart-shaped leaves that are midgreen above and gray and woolly on the undersides. Whorls of creamy yellow flowers appear from late spring to early summer, with faint green and pink markings inside.

Phlomis tuberosa, an ultrahardy

Phlomis russeliana

species (to zone 3), grows 4-6 ft (120-180 cm) tall from tuberous roots. It blooms in summer with pink to rose-purple flowers.

Cultivation
Plant in a sunny spot in any kind of soil in midfall or midspring, as weather permits. Cut the faded stems back to near-ground level in midfall.
Propagation Divide and replant the roots of established plants in midfall or early spring.

Alternatively, sow seeds in midspring in a cold frame or on a sunny windowsill at a temperature of 59-64°F (15-18°C). Prick out the seedlings into individual pots of sterilized potting soil when they are large enough to handle. Plant out in permanent sites in fall; in cold areas, overwinter young plants in a cold frame and set them out during midspring.
Pests/diseases Generally trouble free.

Phlox
phlox

Phlox paniculata 'Eva Cullum'

❏ Height 1-4 ft (30-120 cm)
❏ Planting distance 1½ ft (45 cm)
❏ Flowers early summer to early fall
❏ Any well-drained fertile garden soil
❏ Sun or partial shade
❏ Herbaceous
❏ Zones 3-9

One of the great beauties of the flower garden, phlox provides elegant and indispensable features for the back of herbaceous flower beds. It carries massed heads of blooms on upright, leafy stems. Excellent as cut flowers, the blooms range in color from pastel shades of pink, blue, mauve, and white to richer shades of salmon-pink and violet. The lance-shaped leaves are usually midgreen.

Popular species
Phlox divaricata, syn. *P. canadensis* (wild blue phlox), is a spreading border species up to 1 ft (30 cm) high and 1½ ft (45 cm) wide. Violet-blue to lavender and pink or white flowers are borne in loose heads in early summer. This species is suitable for edging. The cultivar 'Laphamii' has deep blue flowers; 'Fuller's White' is pure white. Hybrids, which are all free flowering, include 'Anja' (reddish purple), 'Hilda' (lavender with a pink eye), and 'Susanne' (white with a red eye).
Phlox maculata, a border species up to 3 ft (90 cm) high and 1½ ft (45 cm) wide, has midgreen leaves and purple-spotted stems. Slightly tapering heads of fragrant purple-pink flowers appear from midsummer to early fall. Cultivars include 'Alpha' (rose-pink) and 'Omega' (white, tinged violet).
Phlox paniculata (garden phlox) has dense oval heads of scented flowers. The species has been superseded by numerous cultivars, usually up to 4 ft (120 cm) high, with white, pink, red, or

P. paniculata 'Dodo Hanbury Forbes'

Phlox paniculata 'Mt. Fuji'

Phlox paniculata

purple flowers, sometimes with contrasting eyes, from midsummer to late summer. They include 'Blue Ice' (white with a pinkish eye), 'Border Gem' (violet-blue), 'Bright Eyes' (pale pink with a crimson eye), 'Cherry Pink' (bright carmine-rose), 'Dodo Hanbury Forbes' (large, clear light pink blossoms), 'Dresden China' (shell-pink), 'Eva Cullum' (pink with a red eye), 'Franz Schubert' (lilac), 'Harlequin' (violet-purple with cream-variegated leaves), 'Mt. Fuji' (white), 'Orange Perfection' (orange-salmon), 'Pinafore Pink' (pale pink with a crimson eye; dwarf: to 1 ft/30 cm tall), 'Prince of Orange' (orange-salmon), 'Pro-

gress' (violet with a darker eye), 'Sir John Falstaff' (salmon-pink), 'Starfire' (deep red), and 'White Admiral' (pure white).

Cultivation
Plant in groups of three or five, in a sunny or partially shaded position in midfall, late winter, or early spring. The soil should be fertile and moist but well drained, and the location should have good air circulation. Water copiously during prolonged dry spells. Mulch annually in spring with compost.

Older perennial phlox plants produce numerous shoots. Thin out the weaker ones in spring to leave about six healthy shoots on each plant. In exposed sites, support the plants with pea sticks. In midfall cut all flower stems down to ground level.

Propagation Divide healthy old clumps in midfall or early spring; replant only sections from the sides of the clump and discard the old wooden center. Or, in late winter or early spring, slice off the crown, leaving only the roots in the soil. In spring or early summer, dig up and replant the young plantlets that appear from the roots.

Alternatively, take 3-4 in (7.5-10 cm) base stem cuttings in early spring and root in a frost-free frame or tray of rooting medium. When cuttings have

Phormium

flax lily, New Zealand flax

Phormium tenax 'Variegatum'

Phlox paniculata 'Cherry Pink'

rooted and danger of frost is past, harden off and plant out in nursery rows. Plant in permanent positions after 18 months.

Pests/diseases Phlox may be affected by several pests and diseases.

Red spider mites attack all sorts, especially in hot, dry weather, causing stippling and later yellowing of leaves. Treat by spraying plants with a recommended miticide.

Nematodes (soil-borne eelworms) may invade young shoots causing distortion of developing leaves and stunting. Dig up, bag, and dispose of affected plants. Avoid planting phlox in the same spot for several years.

Powdery mildew may spread across foliage in midsummer as a white feltlike growth; spray promptly with an approved fungicide.

❏ Height 3-12 ft (90-360 cm)
❏ Planting distance 2-5 ft (60-150 cm)
❏ Flowers midsummer to early fall
❏ Deep, moist soil
❏ Sunny site
❏ Evergreen
❏ Zones 8-10

With its bold clump of large strap-shaped leaves, the flax lily is a striking and dominant specimen plant for a lawn or a strong centerpiece for a bed of annuals.

Although it is grown mainly for its foliage, the plant sometimes produces tall spikes of tubular flowers, which shoot up over the foliage in summer. They are followed by seedpods, which are curved in shape, looking much like scimitars.

Popular species

Phormium colensoi is up to 7 ft (230 cm) high and 3 ft (90 cm) wide, with yellow flowers and twisted, nodding seedpods. The arching green leaves are more lax than those of *P. tenax*.

Phormium tenax (New Zealand flax) is up to 12 ft (360 cm) high

and 5 ft (150 cm) wide, with stiff, rough and leathery olive-green leaves. In late summer, it has rusty red flowers with purple stems. These are followed by thick seedpods that are held erect. Cultivars, grown for their foliage, include 'Bronze Baby' (bronze leaves; semidwarf), 'Purpureum' (bronze-purple leaves), and 'Variegatum' (dark green leaves, striped yellow).

Cultivation

Plant in late spring in deep, moist soil in a sunny site. Protect the plants in winter with straw. Remove all dead flower stems from late summer onward.

Propagation Germinate seeds in spring when the temperature is 59-64°F (15-18°C). Prick out into flats when the seedlings are large enough to handle, then harden off. Transplant to a protected nursery bed until spring of the following year.

Cultivars do not breed true. Increase by division in mid- to late spring.

Pests/diseases Trouble free.

Phygelius
phygelius

Phygelius aequalis

❑ Height 2-3 ft (60-90 cm)
❑ Planting distance 2 ft (60 cm)
❑ Flowers midsummer to midfall
❑ Light soil
❑ Sunny, sheltered site
❑ Herbaceous
❑ Zones 6-10

Phygelius, a colorful and attractive evergreen shrub from South Africa, is treated in northern climates as an herbaceous perennial that is hardy in average winters.

The narrow tubular flowers, in shades of pink and creamy yellow or white, dangle prettily from the sparse branches. They are like Christmas tree ornaments, providing valuable late-season color.

Popular species
Phygelius aequalis, up to 2½ ft (75 cm) high, has toothed, lance-shaped midgreen leaves and panicles up to 9 in (23 cm) long of buff-red flowers. A cultivar is 'Yellow Trumpet' (yellow).
Phygelius capensis, up to 3 ft (90 cm) high, has mid- to dark green oval leaves and 1 ft (30 cm) long panicles of coral-red flowers. It may also be grown as a climber, in which case it can reach a height of 6 ft (180 cm) or more.

Cultivation
Plant in midspring in a sunny, sheltered spot, preferably in light soil. Trim to ground level in spring.

Phygelius does not need staking if it is grown as a bed plant, though *P. capensis* should be secured to a trellis or similar support if it is to be trained up a wall.
Propagation Divide and replant the roots in early spring to midspring. Sow seeds in a cold frame in midspring. Prick out seedlings when they are large enough to handle. Pot on or plant out in nursery rows until midfall. Overwinter the plants in a cold frame and then plant out the following spring.
Pests/diseases Trouble free.

Physalis
Chinese lantern

Physalis alkekengi

❑ Height 1-2 ft (30-60 cm)
❑ Planting distance 1½ ft (45 cm)
❑ Fruits late summer to early fall
❑ Any well-drained ordinary garden soil
❑ Sunny or semishaded site
❑ Herbaceous
❑ Zones 3-10

Chinese lantern *(Physalis alkekengi)* is grown for its bright orange, swollen seed cases.

Unbranched stems carry midgreen oval leaves; insignificant white flowers are followed by papery lantern-shaped seed cases, which are often dried for winter decoration.

Cultivation
Plant in early spring to midspring in a sunny or semishaded site in well-drained ordinary garden soil. The plants' invasive underground runners should be dug out and cut off in fall.
Propagation In early spring to midspring, lift and divide, then replant.

Sow seeds in midspring and transplant the seedlings to a nursery bed when large enough to handle. Set out in fall.
Pests/diseases Trouble free.

Physostegia
obedient plant, lion's-heart

Physostegia virginiana 'Vivid'

- ❏ Height 1-4 ft (30-120 cm)
- ❏ Planting distance 2 ft (60 cm)
- ❏ Flowers midsummer to early fall
- ❏ Ordinary garden soil
- ❏ Sun or partial shade
- ❏ Herbaceous
- ❏ Zones 3-9

Physostegia virginiana was given the name "obedient plant" because if a flower is pushed to one side, it stays where it is put.

The tubular, lipped purplish-pink flowers are closely set on upright, leafy spikes from midsummer to early fall. The lance-shaped leaves are midgreen.

Good border cultivars are 'Bouquet Rose' (pink), 'Summer Snow' (white), and 'Vivid' (up to 20 in/50 cm; rose-pink flowers, appearing later than the others).

Cultivation
Plant in midfall or spring in ordinary garden soil in sun or partial shade. Mulch in spring and keep moist in dry weather.
Propagation Divide in midfall or early spring. Replant only the vigorous outer roots.

Alternatively, take 2-3 in (5-7.5 cm) cuttings of young shoots in early spring to midspring. Root in a cold frame and plant out in midfall.
Pests/diseases Trouble free.

Phytolacca
poke, pokeweed

Phytolacca americana

- ❏ Height 3-12 ft (90-360 cm)
- ❏ Planting distance 3 ft (90 cm)
- ❏ Flowers summer
- ❏ Moisture-retentive soil
- ❏ Sun or partial shade
- ❏ Herbaceous
- ❏ Zones 3-9

Although it is considered a weed throughout much of North America, poke's colorful fall foliage and berries can make it an asset in the garden.

The stems are sparsely set with midgreen ovate leaves, 8 in (20 cm) or more long, taking on red and purple tints in fall. From early summer onward, tiny flowers, starlike and greenish white, are borne in dense upright spikes; they mature to a reddish brown and are followed by poisonous blue-black berries.

Cultivation
Plant in midfall or midspring in any moisture-retentive soil and in sun or light shade.
Propagation Divide and replant the fleshy roots in fall or spring. Or sow seeds outdoors in midspring. Prick out the seedlings into a nursery row and plant out the following fall.
Pests/diseases Trouble free.

PIGGY BACK PLANT — see *Tolmiea*
PINCUSHION FLOWER — see *Scabiosa*
PINK — see *Dianthus*
PLANTAIN LILY — see *Hosta*

Platycodon
balloon flower

Platycodon grandiflorus 'Apoyama'

- ❏ Height 1-2½ ft (30-75 cm)
- ❏ Planting distance 15 in (38 cm)
- ❏ Flowers early to late summer
- ❏ Well-drained ordinary soil
- ❏ Sunny to semishaded position
- ❏ Herbaceous
- ❏ Zones 3-10

The clustered swollen buds of *Platycodon grandiflorus,* which comes from China, are held at the tops of leafy stems like bunches of balloons. Set against a clump of toothed, grayish oval leaves, the buds open in early summer into pale blue saucer-shaped flowers with pointed petals.

A long-lived plant, balloon flower is suitable for the front of beds. The species itself is rarely grown, having been superseded by numerous cultivars, including 'Albus' (pure white), 'Apoyama' (deep mauve), 'Double Blue' (bright blue double flowers), and 'Mother of Pearl' (pale pink semi-double flowers).

Cultivation
Plant in midfall or early spring in well-drained ordinary soil in a sunny to semishaded site. The fleshy roots resent disturbance.
Propagation In early spring, divide and replant any plants over 3 or 4 years old. They are slow to reestablish, and propagation by seed is preferable. Sow indoors in early spring and prick out the fragile seedlings carefully. Grow on until planting out the following spring.
Pests/diseases Trouble free.

Podophyllum
podophyllum

Podophyllum hexandrum

❏ Height 1-1½ ft (30-45 cm)
❏ Planting distance 1½ ft (45 cm)
❏ Flowers late spring to early summer
❏ Rich, moist soil
❏ Partial shade
❏ Ultrahardy; herbaceous
❏ Zones 3-9

Podophyllums are useful, if poisonous, plants for shady moist borders and woodland areas, where the creeping rootstocks form attractive ground cover. The flowering season is comparatively short, but the foliage holds interest for many months. The near-circular leaves are lobed and often sharply toothed. The five-petaled, saucer-shaped, waxy flowers are followed by conspicuous fruits.

Popular species
Podophyllum hexandrum (syn. *P. emodi*) grows 1 ft (30 cm) high and has midgreen lobed leaves, which are marbled with coppery brown when young. The white flowers, with golden stamens, appear in early summer and are followed by bright red fruits, up to 2 in (5 cm) long. The variety *P. hexandrum chinensis* is smaller, with more boldly patterned leaves and flowers delicately flushed with pink. The white-flowered hybrid 'Majus' grows to 1½ ft (45 cm) tall.
Podophyllum peltatum (mayapple) is ultrahardy (to zone 3) and 1½ ft (45 cm) high and wide. The lobed leaves, as much as 1 ft (30 cm) in diameter, are bright

green. Creamy white flowers are borne during late spring and early summer; the lemon-shaped fruits are golden yellow.

Cultivation
Plant in early spring to mid-spring, setting the rhizomes just below ground level, in moist soil containing plenty of humus. A partially shaded site is preferred.
Propagation Divide the rhizomes of established plants in spring, replanting at a distance of 1½ ft (45 cm). Sow seeds in early spring from fruits harvested in summer. Prick out the seedlings when large enough to handle and grow on in a nursery bed before planting out a couple of years later. Hybrid cultivars do not come true to type.
Pests/diseases Trouble free.

POKEWEED — see *Phytolacca*

Podophyllum hexandrum chinensis

Polemonium
Jacob's ladder

Polemonium foliosissimum

❏ Height 1½-3 ft (45-90 cm)
❏ Planting distance 1-2 ft (30-60 cm)
❏ Flowers midspring to early fall
❏ Any ordinary soil
❏ Partial to full shade; tolerates full sun only where summers are temperate
❏ Herbaceous
❏ Zones 3-9

Jacob's ladder is a colorful, light-textured plant. Its long-lasting flowers form a cloud of color over the finely divided ferny leaves.

The flowers, which grow in loose clusters, are cup- or saucer-shaped and come in shades of blue, lavender, and pink, with some white and yellow cultivars.

The midgreen or dark green leaves are deeply divided into lance-shaped leaflets, arranged in pairs on a long midrib. They are borne upright on arching stems or form tufted mounds.

Intolerant of humid heat, Jacob's ladder does not thrive in the Southeast. But in more temperate climates, such as the Northwest, it is a useful, easy-to-grow plant. Though it adapts well to any ordinary soil, it flowers profusely in rich, moist soils.

Popular species
Polemonium caeruleum, up to 3 ft (90 cm) high and 1½ ft (45 cm) wide, has tufts of arching midgreen leaves. Loose clusters of lavender-blue flowers appear on upright, branched stems from midspring to midsummer or later. This species, which is also known as Greek valerian, self-seeds readily. 'Album' is white.
Polemonium carneum is a species

Polemonium caeruleum 'Album'

that is moderately hardy (zones 5-9) and about 1½ ft (45 cm) high and wide. The spreading, many-branched stems form a dome of midgreen leaves. A profusion of pink cup-shaped flowers appear from midspring to midsummer. Cultivars offer purplish-pink, yellow, and blue flowers.

Polemonium foliosissimum, up to 2½ ft (75 cm) high and 2 ft (60 cm) wide, has dark green leaves on upright stems and clusters of cup-shaped lavender-blue flowers with yellow centers from early summer to early fall. A long-lived species, it seldom self-seeds.

Cultivation

Plant in midfall or early spring or midspring in partial to full shade. Jacob's ladder grows in any soil but flowers profusely in deep, rich loamy soil, as the fibrous roots quickly exhaust the soil. Cut back faded flower stems to basal leaf growth as soon as flowering is over. On exposed sites, support the plants with canes or pea sticks. Mulch light soils annually in spring.

Propagation Divide and replant older plants in midfall or early spring. Or sow seeds in spring; prick out the seedlings when large enough to handle and grow on in a nursery bed before transplanting the following spring.

Pests/diseases Generally trouble free.

POLYANTHUS — see *Primula*

Polygonatum

Solomon's seal

Polygonatum odoratum 'Variegatum'

❏ Height 2-6 ft (60-180 cm)
❏ Planting distance 1-2½ ft (30-75 cm)
❏ Flowers late spring to early summer
❏ Any well-drained but moisture-retentive, rich soil
❏ Partial to full shade
❏ Herbaceous
❏ Zones 4-9

The slender, graceful stems of Solomon's seal arch away from the plant's center, carrying pairs of upward-curving leaves and, from late spring, small clusters of hanging, narrow bell-shaped flowers. The oval leaves are pale green to midgreen and the berries blue or black. These plants enjoy dappled shade and leafy soil.

Popular species

Polygonatum commutatum (great Solomon's seal) grows up to 6 ft (180 cm) high in rich, moist soil. It has narrow oblong leaves.
Polygonatum × hybridum (syn. *P. multiflorum*) is about 3 ft (90 cm) tall and has glossy oblong leaves on arching stems that bear pendent flowers in early summer.
Polygonatum odoratum is up to 2 ft (60 cm) high. 'Variegatum' has white-edged leaves.

Polygonatum × hybridum

Cultivation

Plant in early fall or early spring in well-drained, but moisture-retentive, humus-rich soil in partial to full shade. Mulch annually in spring.

Propagation Divide and replant in midfall or early spring. Sow seeds, which may take 18 months to germinate, in a cold frame or protected bed before midfall.

Pests/diseases Sawflies damage the leaves.

Polygonum

knotweed

Polygonum amplexicaule 'Atrosanguineum'

Polygonum bistorta 'Superbum'

P. affine 'Donald Lowndes'

❏ Height ½-5 ft (15-150 cm)
❏ Planting distance 2-4 ft (30-120 cm)
❏ Flowers early to late summer
❏ Moist soil
❏ Sun or partial shade
❏ Herbaceous
❏ Zones 3-8

With its dense flower spikes rising firmly over strong clumps of foliage, knotweed is a bold, striking plant for borders, ground cover, and trailing over walls.

The tiny pink to dark red or white flowers are bell-shaped and borne in succession throughout the summer.

Popular species

Polygonum affine, up to 9 in (23 cm) high, forms a mat up to 1½ ft (45 cm) wide. The lance-shaped leaves are rusty brown in winter. Cultivars include 'Darjeeling Red' (deep pink with dark green leaves), 'Dimity' (dwarf; light pink with bright green leaves), and 'Donald Lowndes' (rose-red).

Polygonum amplexicaule, up to 5 ft (150 cm) high and 4 ft (120 cm) wide, has deep green heart-shaped leaves. Cultivars include 'Atrosanguineum' (crimson) and 'Firetail' (scarlet).

Polygonum bistorta 'Superbum' (snakeweed) grows up to 3 ft (90 cm) high and 2 ft (60 cm) wide. It forms a mat of light green leaves and 6 in (15 cm) spikes of clear pink flowers.

Polygonum campanulatum, up to 3 ft (90 cm) high and 2½ ft (75 cm) wide, is bushy and spreading, with pointed midgreen leaves and loose heads of pink flowers.

Polygonum japonicum compactum, up to 3 ft (90 cm) tall and wide, bears pink flowers that mature to a deep rose and then give way to crimson seeds.

Cultivation

Plant in midfall or early spring in moist soil in sun or partial shade. *P. campanulatum* is best grown in light shade. Pinch back ground cover plants two or three times during summer to encourage side branches.

Propagation Divide and replant in early spring or midfall.

Pests/diseases Trouble free.

Polypodium

common polypody

Polypodium vulgare

❑ Height 6-15 in (15-38 cm)
❑ Planting distance 15 in (38 cm)
❑ Foliage plant
❑ Humus-rich, well-drained soil
❑ Partial shade or sun
❑ Very hardy; evergreen
❑ Zones 3-7

A creeping fern, common polypody *(Polypodium vulgare)* spreads over the ground, forming a thick evergreen carpet of elegantly drooping midgreen fronds.

New growth starts in mid- to late spring, and the plant retains its fresh color until late winter.

Common polypody is exceptionally hardy and easy to grow in dry, stony soil and wall crevices. It provides year-round foliage interest on tree trunks and on banks in alkaline areas.

Popular cultivars include 'Bifidum' (soft green fronds with divided stipe or stem), 'Cornubiense' (lacy, golden green fronds), and 'Cristatum' (crested fronds).

Cultivation

Plant in partial shade or sun in mid- to late spring when the new fronds begin to appear. Humus-enriched soil containing plenty of stones is best. Set the rhizomes (creeping rootstocks) just beneath the surface of the soil and anchor with stones or staples of bent wire.

Propagation Divide and replant in mid- to late spring.

Pests/diseases Rust may appear as scattered or loosely grouped brown spore pustules on the undersurface of the fronds.

Polystichum

shield fern

Polystichum setiferum

❑ Height 2-3 ft (60-90 cm)
❑ Planting distance 1-5 ft (30-150 cm)
❑ Foliage plant
❑ Humus-rich, moist soil
❑ Shady site
❑ Evergreen or semievergreen
❑ Zones 4-9

Shield fern is a popular woodland fern that thrives in alkaline or limy soil, provided it is moist and rich in humus.

Polystichum includes several hardy garden ferns and others suited for indoors. The stiff and leathery leaf fronds, glossy and dainty in some species, are popular in flower arrangements.

Popular species

Polystichum acrostichoides (Christmas fern), a hardy plant, grows 1-2 ft (60-90 cm) tall and up to 2 ft (60 cm) wide. It bears somewhat coarse but glossy evergreen fronds.

Polystichum setiferum 'Herenhausen'

Potentilla

potentilla, cinquefoil

Polystichum aculeatum

Polystichum aculeatum (prickly or hard shield fern), up to 3 ft (90 cm) high and 2½ ft (75 cm) wide, is an evergreen fern with deep green glossy and leathery fronds. The stalks and midribs are covered with brown scales. It is hardy only to zone 6.

Polystichum setiferum (soft shield or hedge fern), up to 3 ft (90 cm) high and 5 ft (150 cm) wide, is evergreen in mild winters. It has gently arching midgreen fronds with scaly stems. Popular cultivars include 'Divisilobum' (finely divided fronds), 'Herenhausen' (slightly glossy), 'Plumosa' (semiprostrate, with dense, feathery fronds), and 'Plumoso-divisilobum' (finely divided, overlapping fronds).

Cultivation

Plant in early spring to midspring in a shady site in humus-rich, moist soil.

Propagation Sow spores in early spring at a temperature of 50°F (10°C).

Divide the multiple crowns in early spring to midspring. Or detach the fronds bearing bulblets (small pealike bulbs on the undersurface of the fronds) in early fall to midfall. Fill flats with an organic-enriched potting soil and peg the fronds onto the surface. Pot the young plants when they are well developed.

Pests/diseases Trouble free.

POPPY — see *Papaver*

Potentilla atrosanguinea 'Gibson's Scarlet'

- ❏ Height 1½-24 in (4-60 cm)
- ❏ Planting distance 6-24 in (15-60 cm)
- ❏ Flowers late spring to early fall
- ❏ Well-drained ordinary garden soil
- ❏ Full sun
- ❏ Herbaceous
- ❏ Zones 5-10

Potentillas are delightful plants with brightly colored saucer-shaped flowers held above attractive foliage.

The flowers are generally in shades of red, pink, and bright yellow and may be single, semidouble, or double.

The taller types are suitable for herbaceous and mixed beds, while the mat-forming and creeping types make excellent ground cover in sunny sites. Potentillas can also be grown in raised beds and rock gardens.

Popular species

Potentilla atrosanguinea is the main parent of many hybrids. Usually 1½-2 ft (45-60 cm) high and wide, the hybrids have gray-green strawberrylike leaves. Profuse flowers 1½-2 in (4-5 cm) wide are borne in loose sprays from early summer to early fall. Hybrids include 'Firedance' (up to 15 in/38 cm; salmon-orange blooms with red centers), 'Gibson's Scarlet' (to 1½ ft/45 cm; single, brilliant scarlet), 'Glory of Nancy' (semidouble, orange-

Potentilla atrosanguinea 'Yellow Queen'

brown and coral-red), 'Red' (to 2 ft/60 cm; purplish red), 'William Rollison' (semidouble, orange-red, yellow reverse), and 'Yellow Queen' (to 16 in/40 cm; semidouble, bright yellow; early).

Potentilla aurea forms a carpet 2-6 in (5-15 cm) high and 1 ft (30 cm) wide. It has bright green silky leaves and clusters of bright yellow flowers ¼-¾ in (1-2 cm) wide. It is suitable for edging.

Potentilla cinerea, up to 3 in (7.5 cm) high and 1½ ft (45 cm) wide, is a spreading plant with small, in-cut gray-green leaves and bright yellow flowers that bloom in summer.

Potentilla cinerea

Potentilla atrosanguinea 'William Rollison'

Potentilla crantzii (syn. *P. alpestris)* is up to 6 in (15 cm) high and wide, with tufted deep green leaves and yellow, blotched orange flowers 1 in (2.5 cm) wide. *Potentilla nepalensis,* up to 2 ft (60 cm) high and 16 in (40 cm) wide, has deep green toothed leaves and very profuse branching sprays of rose-red flowers up to 1½ in (4 cm) wide. Hybrids include 'Miss Wilmott' (cherry pink with darker shading) and 'Roxana' (pink to rosy orange). *P. nitida* forms a mat up to 3 in (7.5 cm) high and 1 ft (30 cm) wide. It has silvery hairy leaves and 1 in (2.5 cm) wide pale pink flowers in mid- and late summer. *Potentilla tabernaemontani* (syn. *P. verna)* forms a mat up to 8 in (20 cm) high and 2 ft (60 cm) wide. The leaves are dark green and divided; the flowers are yellow and appear in late spring.

Cultivation
Plant in midfall or early spring in well-drained ordinary soil and full sun. *P. nepalensis* and its cultivars are short-lived and exhaust themselves with profuse flowering. Cut them back hard after flowering and replace them every 3-4 years.
Propagation Divide and replant cultivars in midfall or early spring.
   Sow seeds of the species in early spring to midspring. When the seedlings are large enough to handle, prick them out and later transplant to a nursery bed. Plant out in midfall.
   Alternatively, take 2-3 in (5-7.5 cm) basal cuttings in midspring and root in a cold frame. Treat the same as seedlings.
Pests/diseases Trouble free.

Potentilla nepalensis 'Roxana'

PRIMROSE—see *Primula*

Primula

primula

Primula sieboldii

Primula nutans

- ❏ Height 3-48 in (7.5-120 cm)
- ❏ Planting distance 6-15 in (15-38 cm)
- ❏ Flowers midwinter to midsummer (depending on species and climate)
- ❏ Moist or well-drained fertile soil
- ❏ Sun or partial shade
- ❏ Herbaceous
- ❏ Zones 3-10

With its soft yellow flowers and dense clusters of leaves, the English primrose *(Primula vulgaris)* is one of the first signs that the dull days of winter are over.

Other primulas have many different flower types, from the perfectly round heads of the drumstick primula to the nodding bell-shaped flowers of the sikkimensis types and the profuse single blooms of the *P. juliae* hybrids. The five-petaled flowers range in color from white to yellow, orange, red, cerise, pink, purple, and even blue. The leaves may be held in ground-hugging rosettes or loose clusters.

Most species prefer moist soil and look their best in the informal setting of a woodland or spring bulb planting. The low-growing alpine primulas are suitable for edging beds and for growing in rock gardens. Border primulas require more moisture than alpine types, and many thrive by the waterside, notably the candelabra primulas.

Alpine types

Auricula primulas have rounded clusters of flowers in spring and fleshy, often farinose (coated with a white mealy powder) leaves.

Primula auricula (auricula) is 6 in (15 cm) high and wide with pale to gray-green, often farinose leaves and bright yellow scented flowers. Cultivars include 'Dale's Red' (brick red with yellow centers), 'Rapp Purple' (large, rich purple flowers), 'Red Dusty Miller' (farinose leaves; red flowers), and 'Yellow Dusty Miller' (farinose leaves; yellow flowers).

Primula marginata, up to 4 in (10 cm) high and 9 in (23 cm) wide, has farinose, gray-green, silver-edged, toothed leaves. The scented flowers are pale lavender to violet.

Primula × *pubescens* is usually 4 in (10 cm) high and 6 in (15 cm) wide, with midgreen farinose leaves. Cultivars include 'Bewerley White' (creamy white) and 'Mrs. J. H. Wilson' (violet with a white eye).

Cortusoid types have clusters of flowers above lobed and toothed, crinkled and hairy leaves. They need moist, but well-drained, humus-rich soil in partial shade.

Primula sieboldii, up to 9 in (23 cm) high and 1 ft (30 cm) wide, has tufts of pale green, prominently lobed and toothed leaves and white, red, or purple flowers in late spring to early summer. It is the best species for gardens in northeastern states.

Farinose types have clusters of dainty flowers in early spring to

Primula × *pubescens*

midspring and rosettes of farinose leaves. They like cool, moist soil in partial shade.

Primula farinosa (bird's-eye primrose) is up to 6 in (15 cm) high and wide, with rosettes of silvery leaves and yellow-eyed, pink, rosy lilac, or purple flowers. *Primula frondosa* is similar to *P. farinosa,* but sturdier. The larger flower clusters are rose-lilac.

Primula rosea is a showy species, up to 1 ft (30 cm) high, that prefers boggy soil. It has tufts of green, toothed leaves. The flowers are an intense rose-pink. Cultivars include 'Grandiflora' (very large deep pink flowers) and 'Peter Klein' (rose-pink).

Muscarioid primulas include *P. vialii* (syn. *P. littoniana),* which is up to 1 ft (30 cm) high and has dense spikes of flowers and tufted, slightly powdery pale green leaves. The early-summer flowers

Primula denticulata

Primula florindae

are lavender-blue, but crimson in bud. It likes limy soil and a well-drained, dryish spot in a rock crevice or cool, partial shade.

Nivalis types have clusters of flowers on tallish stems and strap-shaped leathery leaves. They thrive in very well drained, moist soil in cool semishade.

Primula chionantha is about 1 ft (30 cm) high with white, yellow-eyed flowers in late spring.

Petiolaris primulas have tight clusters of flowers in spring, held on very short stems and set among dense rosettes of leaves. They need protection from winter wetness and thrive in well-drained, rich soil in cool shade.

Soldanelloid primulas have tight heads of bell-shaped, usually pendent flowers and soft, hairy leaves. Acid, gritty, moist soil in cool semishade is best.

Primula nutans, up to 1 ft (30 cm) high and wide, has rosettes of rather upright, gray-green velvety leaves that are up to 8 in (20 cm) long. Its scented lavender to violet flowers bloom in early summer.

Vernalis types have single primrose flowers borne in profusion. The leaves are often crinkled and hairy. They thrive in cool, humus-rich soil in light shade and need to be divided regularly.

Primula juliae and its hybrids are 3-6 in (7.5-15 cm) high with midgreen leaves and flowers of various colors from midwinter to spring. Cultivars include 'Alba' (white), 'Dorothy' (light yellow), 'Garryarde Guinevere' (sometimes sold as *P. × garryarde;* bronze leaves and soft pink flowers), 'Jay Jay' (cerise), 'Kinlough Beauty' (salmon-pink, striped cream), and 'Wanda' (wine-red).

Primula vulgaris, syn. *P. acaulis* (English primrose), is up to 6 in (15 cm) high with rosettes of bright green leaves and profuse pale yellow flowers with darker centers in early spring. Outstanding among its cultivars is the 'Barnhaven Doubles' strain in various shades.

Border types

Candelabra primulas display tiered whorls of flowering blooms in summer on tall stems above generally upright toothed leaves up to 1 ft (30 cm) long.

Primula beesiana, up to 2 ft (60 cm) high and 1 ft (30 cm) wide, has light green, rough-tex-

tured and slightly farinose leaves and lilac flowers with yellow eyes. *Primula bulleyana,* up to 2½ ft (75 cm) high and 1 ft (30 cm) wide, has dark green leaves with reddish midribs and golden yellow to light orange-red flowers.

Primula japonica (Japanese primrose), up to 2½ ft (75 cm) high and 1 ft (30 cm) wide, has reddish-purple flowers with yellow eyes from late spring to midsummer. Cultivars include 'Alba' (white), 'Carminea' (carmine), 'Miller's Crimson' (crimson), and 'Postford's White' (white with a yellow eye).

Primula pulverulenta, up to 2 ft (60 cm) high and 1 ft (30 cm) wide, has pale green wrinkled leaves and wine-red to crimson flowers with darker eyes on farinose stems.

Drumstick primulas include *Primula denticulata,* which produces compact ball-shaped clusters of flowers on upright stalks from early to late spring, with rosettes of leathery leaves thinly coated with farina (white powder). The flowers are pale lilac to deep purple, and the leaves are up to 8 in (20 cm) long. This species may also be annual or biennial.

Primula japonica

Primula obconica

Primula vialii

German primulas all belong to a single species, *P. obconica*. Hardy in zones 8-10, they thrive in shade. They have clusters of pink, red, or lavender blooms atop upright 1 ft (30 cm) stems.

Sikkimensis primulas have long-stalked leaves and clusters of nodding bell-shaped flowers on tall stems in midsummer.

Primula florindae (giant cowslip), up to 4 ft (120 cm) high and 15 in (38 cm) wide, has clumps of heart-shaped midgreen leaves, each up to 10 in (25 cm) long. The scented flowers are pale yellow or occasionally orange to blood-red. It thrives in shallow water.

Primula sikkimensis (Himalayan cowslip) is up to 2 ft (60 cm) high and 1 ft (30 cm) wide, with pale green wrinkled leaves and fragrant pale yellow flowers.

Cultivation

These plants adapt well to temperate northern gardens. Many primulas originated at high altitudes on misty, cool mountains, and most do not flourish in heat and drought. Primulas must not be allowed to dry out in summertime, and waterlogging in winter is equally fatal in most cases. The exceptions are the border primulas, which tolerate even boggy soil at the edge of a pond or stream. In general, though, success with primulas depends on good drainage and attentive watering.

A soil enriched with compost or leaf mold is beneficial. Primulas

Primula frondosa

typically respond best to a semi-shaded position and a summer mulch, especially toward the southern edge of their range. Plant in early fall or early spring, as weather permits.

Propagation Divide most primulas after flowering. Increase dwarf, tufted, or mat-forming species in summer from cuttings that are 1-2 in (2.5-5 cm) long. Root in a cold frame; pot on and plant out the next spring or fall.

Alternatively, sow seeds in a cold frame or in a sheltered spot in the garden as soon as mature (usually from late spring to early fall). Keep the soil moist and prick out the seedlings into individual pots. Plunge outdoors and plant out in fall or the next spring.

Pests/diseases Aphids may cripple flowering shoots.

Slugs and snails may eat the leaves.

Cutworms and vine weevils may attack the roots, causing collapse of the plants.

Red spider mites attack during hot, dry weather, stippling leaves, then causing them to yellow.

Crown rot and root rot may blacken and rot the underground tissues.

Viral diseases cause problems such as stunted plants, mottled and distorted leaves, and inferior, white-flecked flowers. Remove and destroy affected plants.

Bacteria and fungi may cause spotting of the leaves. Controlling the aphids and leafhoppers that spread the diseases will assist in their control. Avoid as much as possible splashing foliage with water, and treat with a recommended fungicide.

Primula vulgaris

Pulmonaria
lungwort

Pulmonaria officinalis

❑ Height 1 ft (30 cm)
❑ Planting distance 1½ ft (45 cm)
❑ Flowers early to late spring
❑ Any ordinary garden soil
❑ Partially to fully shaded site
❑ Herbaceous or evergreen
❑ Zones 3-8

Grown for its superb foliage, as well as its flowers, lungwort forms an ornamental leafy carpet, often beautifully spotted or marbled. It makes a good ground cover in shady sites.

In spring the plant has tubular flowers carried in small clusters. Their color changes from pink to blue as they age, and depends on the soil type. As the flowers die down, the foliage thickens and spreads out, developing its full beauty. The leaves are oval or lance-shaped and plain midgreen or marked with silver or white spots or marbling.

Pulmonarias are evergreen in mild climates, but are herbaceous perennials in the North.

Popular species
Pulmonaria angustifolia (blue-eyed cowslip) has unspotted lance-shaped leaves and sky-blue flowers in midspring. 'Azurea' has clear blue flowers, and 'Johnson's Blue' has deep blue blooms.
Pulmonaria officinalis is known as Jerusalem cowslip. It has narrow, oval green leaves with white spots and purple-blue flowers in midspring to late spring.
Pulmonaria saccharata (Bethlehem sage) has narrow oval leaves with dense silver marbling. The flowers, which appear in early

Pulmonaria saccharata

spring to midspring, are pink when they open, changing to sky-blue. Cultivars are 'Argentea' (silvery white leaves), 'Margery Fish' (leaves mottled silver and green), 'Pink Dawn' (pink flowers), 'Roy Davidson' (sky-blue flowers and white-mottled leaves), and 'Sissinghurst White' (white flowers and green leaves).

Cultivation
Plant in midfall or early spring in any ordinary garden soil in a partially to fully shaded site. Keep the roots cool and moist during the growing season by watering and mulching.
Propagation Divide and replant the roots in midfall or early spring. Seeds may be sown outdoors in midspring, but they often produce inferior plants.
Pests/diseases Slugs may eat the leaves.

Pyrethrum
pyrethrum, painted daisy

Pyrethrum 'Double White'

❑ Height 2½-3 ft (75-90 cm)
❑ Planting distance 15-18 in (38-45 cm)
❑ Flowers early summer to midsummer
❑ Light, well-drained soil
❑ Open, sunny site
❑ Herbaceous
❑ Zones 4-10

With their simple daisy flowers in many clear, bright colors, pyrethrums *(Tanacetum coccineum,* formerly *Pyrethrum roseum)* are cheerful additions to a sunny bed or border.

The flowers, which appear in early summer, may be single or double and measure 2-3 in (5-7.5 cm) wide. They are borne on upright stems, in a range of reds and pinks, as well as white, all with gold centers. The feathery foliage is bright green.

Pyrethrums have a cottage-garden charm, and the flowers are excellent for cutting.

Popular cultivars
Single cultivars include 'Atrosanguineum' (red), 'Evenglow' (salmon), 'James Kelway' (crimson), 'May Robinson' (clear pink), and 'Robinson's Giant Singles' (mixed colors).

Double cultivars include 'Double Hybrids' (mixed colors), 'Park's Prize' (mixed colors), 'Princess Mary' (deep pink), 'Robinson's Doubles' (mixed colors), and 'Snowball' (white).

Cultivation
Plant pyrethrums in early spring in any light and well-drained soil in an open, sunny site. Stake

Ranunculus
buttercup

Ranunculus acris 'Flore Pleno'

with pea sticks in midspring to late spring.

Water well during the growing season, and cut back all stems as soon as the flowers are finished. Young plants may flower again in early fall.

Propagation Leave pyrethrums undisturbed for 3-4 years before increasing them.

Divide more mature roots in early spring or midsummer, after flowering, when new basal growth has started. Discard old woody root portions before replanting the divided rootstock.

Sow seeds in early spring indoors at a temperature of 61°F (16°C). Seedlings seldom come true to type.

Pests/diseases Generally trouble free.

❏ Height ½-3 ft (15-90 cm)
❏ Planting distance 1-2½ ft (30-75 cm)
❏ Flowers late spring to late summer
❏ Any moist ordinary garden soil
❏ Sun or partial shade
❏ Herbaceous
❏ Zones 4-9

The yellow or white flowers of buttercups shine out against the green foliage, making them attractive early-summer plants for borders.

The flowers vary from the wild six-petaled species to double-flowered forms and pompons.

Popular species
Ranunculus aconitifolius 'Flore Pleno,' up to 3 ft (90 cm) high and 2½ ft (75 cm) wide, has midgreen palmate leaves with deeply toothed lobes and bears profuse double, shining white flowers from late spring to early summer.

Ranunculus acris 'Flore Pleno,' up to 3 ft (90 cm) high and 1½ ft (45 cm) wide, is the double form of common meadow buttercup. It has deeply cut, lobed palmate leaves. The double flowers are bright yellow and shiny from early to late summer.

Ranunculus gramineus, a compact plant up to 1 ft (30 cm) high and 1 ft (30 cm) wide, has grassy leaves and sprays of glistening yellow flowers in late spring.

Ranunculus montanus, a creeper, reaches a height of only 6 in (15 cm) but spreads as much as 1 ft (30 cm). This yellow-flowered species makes an effective ground cover. 'Molten Gold' bears larger flowers than the species.

Cultivation
Plant in early fall or midspring in moist ordinary soil in sun or partial shade.

Propagation Divide and replant in midfall or early spring. Sow seeds of *R. gramineus* in late winter or early spring in a protected bed or cold frame. When the seedlings are large enough to handle, prick them out. Pot and plunge outside. Plant out in its permanent site in midfall or early spring.

Pests/diseases Trouble free.

RED-HOT POKER — see *Kniphofia*
RED VALERIAN — see *Centranthus*

Pyrethrum roseum

Ranunculus aconitifolius 'Flore Pleno'

Pyrethrum roseum 'Eileen May Robinson'

Rheum

ornamental rhubarb

Rheum palmatum

Rheum palmatum 'Atrosanguineum'

❏ Height 3-10 ft (90-300 cm)
❏ Planting distance 2-4ft (60-120 cm)
❏ Flowers late spring to early summer
❏ Rich, moist soil
❏ Sunny or partially shaded site
❏ Herbaceous
❏ Zones 5-7

Ornamental rhubarb is a striking, unusual, and very large specimen plant that thrives in waterside gardens and sunny borders where the soil is rich and moist.

Great glossy leaves unfurl in spring to form a huge round clump. Tall spikes carry loose sprays of beadlike flowers, which are sometimes concealed by large papery bracts.

Bear in mind that the stems of ornamental rhubarb are not edible. The leaves, like those of rhubarb, are poisonous.

Popular species

Rheum alexandrae, up to 4 ft (120 cm) high, has midgreen leaves and cream bracts that resemble long, drooping tongues. It flourishes only in cool, moist climates.

Rheum palmatum, up to 10 ft (300 cm) high, has deeply cut purple-red leaves, which turn green when the pinkish-red flowers have finished. The cultivar 'Atrosanguineum' (syn. 'Rubrum') has cerise-crimson flowers and exceptionally vivid red young leaves.

Cultivation

Plant in early spring, in sun or partial shade. Ornamental rhubarb gives a good display of leaves in ordinary garden soil, but the plants flower best in rich, moist soil. Water thoroughly in summer, especially in a drought, and feed occasionally with liquid fertilizer. Cut off the flower spikes when flowering has finished.

Propagation Lift and carefully divide old plants in late fall or early spring (as weather permits), ensuring that each division has a dormant crown bud.

Sow seeds outdoors in early spring to midspring. Prick out the seedlings when they are large enough to handle, grow on in a nursery bed, and plant out in the permanent site in late fall of the following year.

Pests/diseases Trouble free.

Rheum alexandrae

RIBBON GRASS — see *Phalaris*

Rodgersia
rodgersia

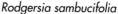
Rodgersia sambucifolia

Rodgersia pinnata 'Superba'

❏ Height 3-6 ft (90-180 cm)
❏ Planting distance 2-3 ft (60-90 cm)
❏ Flowers early summer to midsummer
❏ Moist soil
❏ Sunny or partially shaded site,
   sheltered from wind
❏ Herbaceous
❏ Zones 4-9

Rodgersia is a striking flower bed plant with large clumps of outstanding foliage, often tinted bronze, and strong, upright plumes of numerous tiny creamy or pink flowers, rising gracefully to a height of up to 6 ft (180 cm).

The midgreen to deep green leaves may be held in a fan, much like horse chestnut foliage, or divided into a string of leaflets. Rodgersias grow from rhizomatous roots and may take a couple of years to become established. Once growing strongly, they make superb specimen plants in the right situation and are ideal in the moist, semishaded and sheltered setting of an informal poolside or streamside planting.

Popular species
Rodgersia aesculifolia grows up to 6 ft (180 cm) high and has glossy, bronze, toothed horse-chestnut-like leaves, with each leaflet almost 1 ft (30 cm) long. The showy erect and much-branched plumes of star-shaped white or pink flowers are 1½ ft (45 cm) tall. Reddish seed heads follow the midsummer blooms. *Rodgersia pinnata,* up to 4 ft (120 cm) high, has deep green, sometimes bronzed leaves divided into leaflets that are prominently veined. It bears white to pink-red flower plumes, 1 ft (30 cm) long. Cultivars include 'Alba' (white), 'Elegans' (rose-pink), and 'Superba' (bronze-purple leaves and pink flowers in plumes up to 20 in /50 cm long).
Rodgersia podophylla, up to 4 ft (120 cm) high, has heavily veined, lobe-tipped horse-chestnut-like leaves that are bronzed when young, turning midgreen in summer and then coppery. The branched, loose flower sprays, up to 1½ ft (45 cm) long, are pale buff to creamy white.
Rodgersia sambucifolia, up to 3 ft (90 cm) high, is compact of habit, with leaves divided into leaflets; the flat-topped flower heads are creamy white.
Rodgersia tabularis (syn. *Astilboides tabularis)* is up to 3 ft (90 cm) high. It has long-stalked and scalloped bright green leaves in an almost circular umbrella-like shape up to 3 ft (90 cm) wide. The creamy white flower plumes are about 10 in (25 cm) long and feathery.

Cultivation
Rodgersias like a spot sheltered from the wind, partially shaded or sunny but moist. Plant the fleshy roots 1 in (2.5 cm) deep in moist soil containing decayed vegetable matter in early spring to midspring. Rodgersias will also grow in ordinary soil in wide herbaceous and mixed borders, though their height will be less than in moist conditions. Water well during the growing season; cut faded flower stems unless you want the seed heads for drying.
Propagation Division is the most reliable method of increase. Dig up the roots of established plants in early spring to midspring, just as new growth begins to show. Cut the rhizomes into sections, each with a growing point, and replant 1 in (2.5 cm) below the soil surface.

Sow seeds in early spring in a cold frame or sheltered bed, and prick out the seedlings as soon as they are large enough to handle. Set out in a nursery bed when the danger of frost has passed, and plant out in the permanent site in spring 2 years later. Cultivars do not come true to type and are best propagated by division.
Pests/diseases Trouble free.

Rodgersia podophylla

Romneya

tree poppy

Romneya coulteri

❑ Height 3-8 ft (90-240 cm)
❑ Planting distance 3-4 ft (90-120 cm)
❑ Flowers late spring to early summer
❑ Well-drained, humus-rich soil
❑ Sunny, sheltered site
❑ Herbaceous
❑ Zones 6-10

Tree poppies are subshrubby perennials that die back to the ground in late fall. They can be invasive, spreading through underground runners, but are reliably hardy only in mild-wintered, humidity-free regions.

The brilliant white flowers, with pleated petals surrounding a prominent center of golden stamens, resemble poppies. They are up to 6 in (15 cm) wide. Although short-lived, they bloom in succession over several months. Tree poppies are suitable for the back of borders or as specimen plants in sheltered sites.

Popular species

Roymneya coulteri grows 3-8 ft (90-240 cm) tall and wide. It bears blue-green, broadly ovate and deeply lobed leaves and pure white flowers. The variety *R. c. trichocalyx* bears rounded bristly buds and blossoms with pleated petals.

Cultivation

Romneyas resent any root distur-bance. In mid- to late spring set out young pot-grown plants, with the root ball intact, in deep rich soil that is well drained. A sunny spot sheltered from strong winds is essential. In mid- to late fall cut all stems down to just above ground level and apply a protective winter mulch or weathered ashes over the base of the plants.

Propagation Romneyas can be increased from seed or root cut-tings taken in fall, but the latter method may involve permanent damage to the parent plant. Seed propagation is preferable. Sow seeds in late winter or early spring when the temperature is 55-61°F (13-16°C). Once planted, cover with 1 in (2.5 cm) of hay or pine needles and burn. Prick out the seedlings into small pots of well-drained potting soil and keep them in a warm, sheltered loca-tion until roots fill the pots. Repot the young plants and overwinter in a frost-free spot before plant-ing in permanent sites the follow-ing late spring.

Alternatively, in late spring dig up and replant any well-grown suckers that have appeared a good distance from the parent.

Pests/diseases Wilting shoots and yellowing leaves are usually caused by unsuitable growing conditions.

Roscoea

roscoea

Roscoea cautleoides

❑ Height 1-1½ ft (30-45 cm)
❑ Planting distance 1 ft (30 cm)
❑ Flowers early to late summer
❑ Any moisture-retentive ordinary soil
❑ Sun or partial shade
❑ Herbaceous
❑ Zones 8-9

In areas of mild winters and cool summers, roscoea lies dormant until late spring, when its lance-like leaves suddenly appear, quickly followed by a fine show of elegant orchidlike flowers.

The leaves, up to 8 in (20 cm) long, are mid- to bright green. The flowers, held on strong, upright stems, appear in shades of yellow and purple.

Popular species

Roscoea cautleoides, up to 1 ft (30 cm) high, has soft yellow flow-ers in early summer.
Roscoea purpurea, up to 1½ ft (45 cm) high, is rich purple.

Cultivation

Plant in early spring in any mois-ture-retentive soil in sun or par-tial shade. Set the fleshy roots 3-4 in (7.5-10 cm) deep.
Propagation Roscoea may be di-vided and replanted in early spring. Alternatively, sow seeds in a cold frame in late summer to early fall. Prick out the seedlings when they are large enough to handle and grow on in a nursery bed for 2 seasons.
Pests/diseases Trouble free.

ROYAL FERN — see *Osmunda*

Rudbeckia
coneflower

Rudbeckia nitida 'Goldquelle'

❏ Height 2-7 ft (60-210 cm)
❏ Planting distance 1½-2 ft (45-60 cm)
❏ Flowers midsummer to late fall
❏ Any good, well-drained garden soil
❏ Open, sunny site
❏ Herbaceous
❏ Zones 3-10

Famous for their brilliant golden yellow blooms, coneflowers are excellent long-lasting perennials for both borders and cut flowers. In rich soils, they often spread to form wide clumps.

The species have an open leafy form, bearing numerous daisylike flowers, each with a prominent central black, brown, or greenish cone. The midgreen leaves are oblong, lance-shaped, deeply cut or divided into leaflets.

Single and double cultivars come in yellows and oranges.

Popular species
Rudbeckia fulgida, up to 2½ ft (75 cm) high, is a bushy species with midgreen leaves. Yellow to orange-brown flowers with purple-brown cones appear from midsummer to late fall. The species has been replaced by cultivars, usually with flowers that are 3-4 in (7.5-10 cm) wide. A cultivar is 'Goldsturm' (narrow-petaled, yellow).
Rudbeckia laciniata grows up to 7 ft (210 cm) high and has deeply divided leaves and yellow flowers with greenish cones from late summer to early fall. An example is the double-flowered lemon-yellow 'Golden Glow.'
Rudbeckia nitida is similar to *R. laciniata* but shorter, up to 4 ft (120 cm) with more prominent cones. Some cultivars include 'Goldquelle' (up to 2½ ft/75 cm;

Rudbeckia fulgida 'Deamii'

double) and 'Herbstsonne,' or 'Autumn Sun' (green cone).
Rudbeckia subtomentosa, with a height of 3 ft (90 cm) and a spread of 1½ ft (45 cm), has oval midgreen leaves that are finely covered in gray hairs. Its yellow flowers, 3 in (7.5 cm) wide, appear from midsummer to early fall; each has a buttonlike disk, rather than a cone, at its center.

Cultivation
Plant in midfall or early spring to midspring in any well-cultivated, well-drained garden soil in a sunny, open site. The plants need staking in exposed positions. In dry soils, mulch with compost in early spring, unless height restriction of taller plants is required.
Propagation Sow seeds in early spring to midspring or in late summer to early fall in a cold frame or on a cool windowsill. Prick out the seedlings when they are large enough to handle, grow on in a nursery bed, and plant out in midfall.

Cultivars grown from seed do not come true to type. Divide and replant the roots in midfall or early spring, replanting only the strong outer shoots.
Pests/diseases Slugs and snails may be troublesome. Control leaf miners and mildew with recommended pesticides.

RUSSIAN SAGE — see *Perovskia*
SAGE — see *Salvia*

Salvia
sage, clary

Salvia fulgens

❏ Height 1-6 ft (30-180 cm)
❏ Planting distance 1½-3 ft (45-90 cm)
❏ Flowers spring to midfall
❏ Any fertile, well-drained garden soil
❏ Sunny site
❏ Moderately or very hardy; herbaceous
❏ Zones 7-10, some to 3, 4, or 5

Planted in groups, perhaps in a long swath at the front of a bed, sage is a spectacular sight. The lower third of the strong upright stem is covered in a bushy mass of leaves, while the upper section carries dense, richly colored spikes of flowers in shades of purple, red, and pink. They bloom successively for a long time.

Popular species/hybrids
Salvia azurea (blue sage) is an upright plant reaching 6 ft (180 cm) with clear blue flowers from summer into fall. A southeastern native, it tolerates the humid heat of zone 10 and the winter cold of zone 5.
Salvia coccinea and *S. fulgens* are two southwestern natives that bear hairy leaves and vivid scarlet flowers in spring, summer, and fall. Both are hardy only in zones 8-10, and should have their crowns protected with a deep winter mulch at the northern end of their ranges. *S. coccinea* cultivars include 'Alba' (white), 'Bicolor' (white and red), and 'Lady in Red' (crimson).
Salvia farinacea (mealy cup sage), up to 3 ft (90 cm) tall, is somewhat hardier (to zone 7).

Salvia × superba

Sanguisorba
burnet

Sanguisorba obtusa 'Albiflora'

❏ Height 3-6 ft (90-180 cm)
❏ Planting distance 2-2½ ft (60-75 cm)
❏ Flowers early summer to fall
❏ Any moist soil
❏ Sun or partial shade
❏ Herbaceous
❏ Zones 3-9

Salvia pratensis (meadow clary) is an ultrahardy (zones 3-9) perennial, 1-3 ft (30-90 cm) high and 2 ft (60 cm) wide. Clump forming, with aromatic leaves up to 6 in (15 cm) long, it bears branched spikes of pink, lavender, blue, or violet flowers in early summer.

Salvia × superba is a very hardy hybrid (zones 4-7), often sold incorrectly as *S. nemorosa*. It is a bushy plant, up to 4 ft (120 cm) high and 3 ft (90 cm) wide, with aromatic gray-green, narrow oval leaves and spikes of violet-blue flowers with crimson-purple bracts in midsummer to fall. Cultivars and hybrids include 'East Friesland' (to 2½ ft/75 cm),

'Indigo Spires' (to 3½ ft/105 cm; deep blue, branching spikes), 'Lubeca' (to 2½ ft/75 cm), and 'May Night' (to 16 in/40 cm; violet; very early flowering).

Salvia uliginosa (bog sage) is a less hardy (only to zone 8) species, up to 5 ft (150 cm) high and 1½ ft (45 cm) wide, with branching spikes of sky-blue flowers in fall. This species thrives in moist soil and needs support.

Cultivation
Plant in midfall or early spring in any well-drained garden soil, preferably enriched with compost. A sunny site is best, with shelter for *S. fulgens*.

S. *pratensis* and S. *uliginosa* need staking with twiggy sticks or canes. Cut down all plants to ground level in late fall.

Propagation Divide and replant S. × *superba* from early fall to early spring. Other species are best raised from seed. Sow seeds in a sterilized seed-starting mix in midspring. When the seedlings are large enough to handle, prick them out into flats and then into nursery rows. Plant out in their permanent sites from fall to spring.

Pests/diseases Yellowed foliage and stunted growth on young plants are due to a physiological disorder, caused by too low temperatures.

Burnets are easy, long-lived, and accommodating plants suitable for borders with moisture-retentive soil and ideal for waterside planting. The bottlebrushlike flowers are good for cutting.

Burnet's elegant and abundant foliage is divided into many fine leaflets, which may have toothed or ragged edges.

Popular species
Sanguisorba canadensis grows 6 ft (180 cm) tall and spreads to about 2 ft (60 cm). The erect stems are clothed with pale green leaves and topped, from late summer into fall, with white flower spikes, 3-8 in (7.5-20 cm) tall.

Sanguisorba obtusa (Japanese burnet) is about 4 ft (120 cm) tall and has pale green, finely divided leaves up to 1½ ft (45 cm) long, with blue-green undersides. The wiry stems bear arching rose-pink flower spikes from early to late summer; the extraordinary long stamens give the flowers a fluffy appearance. The cultivar 'Albiflora' bears white flowers.

Sanguisobra tenuifolia, up to 4 ft (120 cm) high, resembles S. *canadensis* but has shorter red, sometimes white, flower spikes that

Salvia pratensis

Saponaria
bouncing Bet, soapwort

Scabiosa
scabious, pincushion flower

Scabiosa caucasica 'Clive Greaves'

❑ Height 1½-2½ ft (45-75 cm)
❑ Planting distance 1½-2 ft (45-60 cm)
❑ Flowers early summer to early fall
❑ Any well-drained, neutral to alkaline soil
❑ Full sun
❑ Herbaceous or evergreen
❑ Zones 3-10

Saponaria officinalis 'Rosea Plena'

❑ Height 1-3 ft (30-90 cm)
❑ Planting distance 2 ft (60 cm)
❑ Flowers summer
❑ Any fertile garden soil
❑ Sun or light shade
❑ Herbaceous
❑ Zones 3-10

Sanguisorba canadensis

are produced in early summer and midsummer.

Cultivation
Plant burnets in midfall or early spring in any kind of soil, provided it does not dry out. Choose a sunny or lightly shaded site and provide stakes or twiggy supports for the taller-growing species. Water thoroughly during the growing season and cut all stems back to ground level in late fall.
Propagation Divide and replant the roots in early spring or midspring. Alternatively, sow seeds in spring in a cold frame. Prick out the seedlings, when large enough to handle, into flats or pots and grow on in the open. Transplant the young plants to permanent sites in midfall of the following year.
Pests/diseases Trouble free.

Related to the popular creeping and trailing soapworts of rock gardens, the taller bouncing Bet *(Saponaria officinalis)* is suitable for beds and semiwild gardens. It grows up to 3 ft (90 cm) high, spreading to 2 ft (60 cm) or more wide, often becoming invasive. The erect stems bear pale green, narrowly lance-shaped leaves.

The species itself has small clusters of single, five-petaled flowers. It has been superseded by double-flowered forms, such as 'Alba Plena' (white) and 'Rosea Plena' (pink).

Cultivation
Plant saponaria in early fall or early spring in any fertile soil in sun or light shade. Pinch in late spring to encourage flower formation. Deadhead to prolong bloom and shear hard afterward to contain sprawling growth. Cut all stems down to ground level in late fall. During winter dig out spreading underground runners.
Propagation Divide and replant the roots from midfall to early spring. Seeds may be sown in spring, but seedlings seldom come true to type.
Pests/diseases Trouble free.

Related to the wild scabious that flourishes in alkaline soils and limestone grassland, garden forms of the perennial scabious have for centuries been valued for their charm and ease of cultivation. Daisy-type flowers, with overlapping and frilled petals surrounding a prominent yellow-green pincushionlike center, are produced over several months and are ideal for cutting. The silky seed heads can be dried for winter arrangements.

Suitable for herbaceous and mixed beds, scabious thrives in limy soil but is just as happy in neutral soil if it is given good drainage.

Popular species
Scabiosa caucasica, the most popular of perennial species, grows 1½-2½ ft (45-75 cm) high and forms a ground-hugging clump of herbaceous, midgreen lance-shaped leaves, deeply divided into narrow segments. Leafless flower stems rise above the leaf mounds from early summer onward, bearing clear lavender-blue flowers, 3 in (7.5 cm) or more wide. The species itself is rarely seen, having been superseded by numerous cultivars including the popular 'Clive Greaves' (rich lavender-blue), 'Compliment' (dark lavender), 'Issac House Hybrids' (mixed white and blue shades), and 'Miss Willmott' (white).

Sedum

sedum, stonecrop

Sedum roseum

❏ Height 10-24 in (25-60 cm)
❏ Planting distance 1-2 ft (30-60 cm)
❏ Flowers spring to midfall
❏ Any well-drained ordinary soil
❏ Full sun or partial shade
❏ Herbaceous or evergreen
❏ Zones 4-10

Well known for their dense heads of flowers in shades of rust to red, pink and yellow, or white, sedums are outstanding garden plants.

The numerous species, cultivars, and hybrids include hardy and half-hardy annuals as well as herbaceous or evergreen perennials. Some are too tender for growing outdoors, while the hardy but small mat-forming types are best grown in rock gardens, on walls, or in paving crevices. Those described here are all suitable for borders or beds where the shapes, textures, and colors of the fleshy foliage add contrast to softer-leaved all-green plants.

Popular species/hybrids

Sedum aizoon, up to 1½ ft (45 cm) high and wide, has lance-shaped shiny midgreen, coarsely toothed leaves and golden yellow flower heads in early summer to midsummer.

Sedum 'Autumn Joy' is an herbaceous hybrid with a height and spread of 2 ft (60 cm). It has ovate pale gray-green leaves. The flower heads, up to 8 in (20 cm) wide, are borne on thick, fleshy stems; they are pink when they first open in late summer or early fall, deepening to copper-red by midfall.

Sedum maximum has been superseded by cultivars. 'Atropurpureum' is up to 2 ft (60 cm) high, with purple-red stems and leaves; the pink flower heads,

Scabiosa (mixed)

Scabiosa columbaria, up to 2 ft (60 cm) tall, has evergreen basal leaves that are gray-green and lance-shaped, while the stem leaves are finely divided. Lilac-blue flowers with dark purple bristly centers are borne on hairy stems in summer to early fall.

Scabiosa ochroleuca is 2½ ft (75 cm) tall with erect flower stems rising from evergreen clumps of deeply divided, hairy silver leaves. The flowers, up to 4 in (10 cm) wide, are pale yellow. This species self-seeds freely.

Cultivation

Plant in early spring to midspring in full sun in fertile, well-drained, neutral to alkaline soil; adjust pH of acid soils by adding lime. Scabious thrives in coastal gardens but may need staking on windy sites. Deadheading ensures a continuous floral display. Cut all stems down to ground level in late fall.

Propagation While you can increase by sowing seeds in an outdoor bed in spring, seedlings do not come true to type. Division in midspring is preferable. It is a good idea to divide and replant large clumps every 3 or 4 years.

Pests/diseases Slugs and snails feed on young basal leaves. In poorly drained soils, root rot may lead to the collapse of plants. Very dry soils can encourage powdery mildew, which appears as a white coating on the leaves.

SEA HOLLY — see *Eryngium*
SEA KALE — see *Crambe*
SEA LAVENDER — see *Limonium*
SEDGE — see *Carex*

Sedum 'Autumn Joy'

Sidalcea

prairie mallow

Sidalcea malviflora

❏ Height 2-4½ ft (60-135 cm)
❏ Planting distance 1½-2 ft (45-60 cm)
❏ Flowers early to late summer
❏ Ordinary garden soil
❏ Sunny to partially shaded site
❏ Herbaceous
❏ Zones 5-10 in West, 5-7 in East

up to 6 in (15 cm) wide, appear in midsummer to late summer.

Sedum rosea, syn. *S. rhodiola* or *Rhodiola rosea* (rose-root), is up to 1 ft (30 cm) high and wide, with strap-shaped, closely packed blue-gray leaves on thick stems. Its pale yellow flower heads, 3 in (7.5 cm) wide, open from coppery buds from midspring through late spring. The roots have a rose scent when dry.

Sedum 'Ruby Glow' is up to 10 in (25 cm) high and 1 ft (30 cm) wide. Suitable for the front of a border, it has blue-green ovate leaves and bright ruby-red flower heads up to 4 in (10 cm) wide in midsummer to late summer.

*Sedum spectabile (*syn. *Hylotelephium spectabile*), up to 2 ft (60 cm) high and wide, has pale gray-green leaves and fluffy pink flower heads up to 6 in (15 cm) wide from early fall to midfall. Some cultivars are 'Brilliant' (deep rose-pink), 'Carmen' (bright carmine-pink), and 'Meteor' (carmine-red).

Sedum 'Vera Jameson,' up to 10 in (25 cm) high and 1 ft (30 cm) wide, has arching stems with deep purple leaves and dusty-pink flower heads in midsummer.

Cultivation

Plant sedums in full sun to partial shade in midfall or midspring.

S. maximum needs moisture-retentive soil. All other species thrive in any well-drained ordinary garden soil and are generally drought resistant.

Propagation Sow seeds in a cold frame or a protected bed in early spring to midspring. When the seedlings are large enough to handle, prick them out and later pot them singly. Plunge outside until midfall, then plant out. Named cultivars do not come true from seed.

All species may be divided and replanted in midfall or early spring.

Or take stem cuttings 1-3 in (2.5-7.5 cm) long from early spring to midsummer and root outdoors.

Pests/diseases Aphids may eat stems and leaves, making them sticky and sooty. Slugs may eat leaves and stems and check early growth. Crown or root rot may occur in overwet soil.

SENSITIVE FERN — see *Onoclea*
SHASTA DAISY — see *Chrysanthemum maximum*
SHIELD FERN — see *Polystichum*
SHUTTLECOCK FERN — see *Matteuccia*
SIBERIAN BUGLOSS — see *Brunnera*

Prairie mallow (*Sidalcea malviflora*) is a graceful plant with tall, branching spikes of silky flowers rising from clumps of leaves throughout summer. The funnel-shaped flowers come in shades of pink, and the leaves are midgreen. The lower leaves are rounded; the stem leaves are lobed and divided into segments.

Cultivars, generally up to 2½ ft (75 cm) high, include 'Brilliant' (deep rose), 'Elsie Heugh' (pale pink fringed flowers), 'Sussex Beauty' (clear pink), and 'William Smith' (salmon-pink).

Cultivation

Plant in midfall or early spring in ordinary garden soil in a sunny or lightly shaded spot. After flowering, cut the stems down to 1 ft (30 cm) to encourage rebloom.

Propagation Lift, divide, and replant in fall or early spring, discarding the center of the clump.

Sow seeds in a cold frame or protected bed in early spring, though cultivars do not come true to type. Prick out the seedlings and grow on in a nursery bed. Set out in midfall.

Pests/diseases Trouble free.

SILVER GRASS — see *Miscanthus*

Sisyrinchium

sisyrinchium

Sisyrinchium striatum

Sisyrinchium californicum

- ❑ Height 10-30 in (25-75 cm)
- ❑ Planting distance 1 ft (30 cm)
- ❑ Flowers early spring to early fall
- ❑ Well-drained, humus-rich soil
- ❑ Sunny site
- ❑ Herbaceous or evergreen
- ❑ Zones 4-10

More than 60 species of these relatives of the iris flourish as wildflowers across North America. Beautiful as they are, gardeners have brought only a few into domestication. Those described appear in perennial nurseries and are excellent choices for the front of sunny herbaceous borders. They bear erect spikes of satiny flowers, rising over a clump of grassy leaves. The flowers, usually star-shaped, come in shades of yellow to cream or blue to violet.

Popular species

Sisyrinchium angustifolium, syn. *S. gramineum* (blue-eyed grass), grows up to 1 ft (30 cm) high and 9 in (23 cm) wide. It bears violet-blue flowers from late spring until early fall.

Sisyrinchium bellum, 1-1½ ft (30-45 cm) tall, bears springtime clusters of violet-blue.

Sisyrinchium californicum (golden-eyed grass), up to 1 ft (30 cm) high and 6 in (15 cm) wide, is herbaceous. It has yellow flowers from late spring to early summer.

Sisyrinchium douglasii, syn. *S. grandiflorum* (grass widow), is up to 10 in (25 cm) high and 6 in (15 cm) wide. It has nodding, bell-shaped purple flowers with a satiny sheen in early spring.

Sisyrinchium striatum, an evergreen up to 2½ ft (75 cm) high and 1 ft (30 cm) wide, has gray-green sword-shaped leaves and pale or cream-yellow flowers from early summer to early fall. The cultivar 'Variegatum' has leaves striped cream and green, and needs some protection from bright sun. The species and its cultivar may be short-lived unless divided every 3 years, but the plants often self-seed.

Cultivation

Grow sisyrinchiums in well-drained soil containing plenty of humus. Plant in a sunny site in early fall or early spring. Remove faded flower stems and dead leaves in fall.

Propagation Sisyrinchiums often self-seed. Otherwise, germinate seeds in a cold frame or protected bed in fall or early spring. Prick out the seedlings, when large enough to handle, into flats and later transfer them to an outdoor nursery bed. Grow on for a year before moving them to their permanent flowering sites.

Alternatively, divide and replant established clumps in early fall or spring. Some of the species resent root disturbance and may take a couple of years to recover.

Pests/diseases Generally trouble free.

SCULPTURAL PLANTS

Bold leaves, architectural shapes, and unusual textures are spectacular qualities that add a new dimension to the garden.

Striking foliage is important in the appearance of a garden. Foliage displays can be achieved with small-scale plants such as ferns or herbs. At the other end of the scale are dramatically shaped plants that are impressive as isolated specimens. In between are plants that give a sense of form and structure against gently bobbing border perennials and provide a background for low-growing plants.

Many fine foliage plants thrive in shade — notably the hostas, whose bold leaves are as striking in texture as in shape, color, and size. Some, such as the arching clumps of 'Blue Umbrellas' or the ruffled golden blades of 'Piedmont Gold,' merit a focal position of their own.

Also good for semishade are the gigantic ornamental rhubarbs. They have a sculptural beauty, with their great glossy leaves unfurling to green and purple-red and their cerise-on-cream flower spikes majestically rising several yards in height.

Graceful grasses, elegant bamboos, the bold shapes of many euphorbias, and the velvety leaf candelabras of some verbascums are just some of the choices that add a sculptural dimension to the garden picture, creating lasting pleasure for those who see it.

▼ **Heart-shaped hosta** A recent American introduction, *Hosta* 'Francee' is an outstanding specimen plant for sun or shade. The broad and quilted, rich green leaves are edged with white to complement the white to pale lavender flower spikes.

▶ **Ornamental rhubarb** As a specimen feature on a large expanse of lawn or in the shelter of tall trees, few plants can rival the imposing *Rheum palmatum*. The furled leaves push up in spring and unfold into giant jagged-edged umbrellas as much as 3 ft (90 cm) wide. They are flushed with red, but turn bright green around the time the enormous stems branch into fluffy clusters of crimson.

▼ **Moisture lovers** In rich soil with plenty of moisture at the roots, two majestic foliage plants, *Rheum palmatum* (ornamental rhubarb) and the horse-chestnutlike *Rodgersia* (left), create a decorative leaf canopy in early summer. In its dappled shade thrive primulas and the golden orbs of *Trollius* (globeflower).

▲ **New Zealand flax** The plant called New Zealand flax (*Phormium tenax*) does not look at all like a flax. It forms a striking clump, up to 12 ft (360 cm) high, of stiff, sword-shaped leaves. Creating a truly sculptural effect, the yellow and pale green stripes of the variegated specimen shine against the red blades of its companion 'Purpureum' and a footing of cranesbill (*Geranium endressii*).

◄ **Giant reed** An elegant tall and sturdy grass, the giant reed (*Arundo donax*) flourishes in a sheltered site at the edge of water. It will grow over 8 ft (240 cm) high, bearing broad gray-green leaves and producing silky flower plumes that unfold red in late summer, fade to buff-white in fall, and last throughout winter.

Primeval spurge The evergreen *Euphorbia characias wulfenii* bears huge clublike flower panicles.

Smilacina
false Solomon's seal

Smilacina racemosa

❏ Height 1½-3 ft (45-90 cm)
❏ Planting distance 1½-2 ft (45-60 cm)
❏ Flowers early to late spring
❏ Deep, rich, moist soil
❏ Partially shaded site
❏ Herbaceous
❏ Zones 3-9

An unusual and elegant woodland plant, false Solomon's seal has graceful arching stems with double rows of glossy, broadly lance-shaped leaves and fluffy plumes of cream or white flowers, followed later by red berries.

Popular species
Smilacina racemosa (false spikenard), up to 3 ft (90 cm) high and 1½ ft (45 cm) wide, has closely set, light green leaves. It bears dense sprays of fragrant cream-white flowers and red berries.
Smilacina stellata (star-flowered lily of the valley), up to 2 ft (60 cm) high and 1 ft (30 cm) wide, has sprays of white starry flowers and dark red berries.

Cultivation
Plant in midfall or early spring in deep, rich soil in a partially shaded, moist site. The rhizomatous roots spread slowly and should not be disturbed for several years after planting.
Propagation Lift and divide old plants in midfall.
Pests/diseases Trouble free.

SNAKEWEED — see *Polygonum*
SNEEZEWEED — see *Achillea* and *Helenium*

Soleirolia
mind-your-own business

Soleirolia soleirolii

❏ Height 1-3 in (2.5-7.5 cm)
❏ Planting distance 2 ft (60 cm)
❏ Foliage plant
❏ Light, well-drained, humus-rich soil
❏ Cool, moist shade
❏ Evergreen
❏ Zone 10

Mind-your-own-business *(Soleirolia soleirolii,* syn. *Helxine soleirolii),* also known as baby's tears, forms a carpet of tiny leaves, each no more than ¼ in (6 mm) wide.

The flowers are insignificant, and the plant is grown solely for its bright green rounded leaves. These provide foliage interest throughout the year, unless a frost cuts them back.

Mind-your-own-business self-roots, spreading quickly to form low ground cover; it is particularly easy to propagate, though it can be invasive. It looks good growing in cool, moist shade, perhaps carpeting the ground underneath trees or shrubs.

Cultivation
Plant in spring in light, well-drained, humus-rich soil in a cool, moist, shady spot.
Propagation Detach portions of the parent and replant.
Pests/diseases Generally trouble free.

Solidago
golden rod

Solidago 'Goldenmosa'

Solidago 'Golden Dwarf'

❑ Height 1-6 ft (30-180 cm)
❑ Planting distance 15-36 in (38-90 cm)
❑ Flowers midsummer to midfall
❑ Ordinary garden soil
❑ Sun or partial shade
❑ Herbaceous
❑ Zones 3-10

Goldenrods grow wild in North America. Europeans have created a range of hybrids and cultivars that are far less invasive than their wild ancestors, and far more showy, too.

Popular species/hybrids
Solidago canadensis, 3-6 ft (90-180 cm) high and up to 3 ft (90 cm) wide, is a vigorous upright species with sharply serrated midgreen leaves and broad yellow flower plumes. It is suited to meadow and wild gardens. A cultivar is 'Golden Wings.'
Solidago × hybrida (syn. *S. × arendsii*) covers a group of noninvasive hybrids with golden green leaves and plumes or horizontally spreading sprays of flowers. They include 'Cloth of Gold' (to 2 ft/60 cm; deep yellow), 'Crown of Rays' (to 1½ ft/45 cm; yellow),

'Golden Dwarf' (to 1 ft/30 cm), 'Goldenmosa' (to 3 ft/90 cm; fluffy flower sprays), 'Golden Thumb' ('Queenie'; to 1 ft/30 cm; golden yellow), and 'Peter Pan' (to 5 ft/150 cm; bright yellow).

Cultivation
Plant in midfall or early spring in ordinary soil in sun or partial shade.
Propagation Goldenrods quickly exhaust the soil and should be divided and replanted regularly, from midfall to early spring.
Pests/diseases Caterpillars may spin the leaves together and eat them. Powdery mildew appears as a white coating.

SOLOMON'S SEAL — see *Polygonatum*
SOUTHERNWOOD — see *Artemisia*
SPEEDWELL — see *Veronica*
SPIDERWORT — see *Tradescantia*
SPLEENWORT—see *Asplenium*
SPURGE—see *Euphorbia*

Stachys

betony

Stachys byzantina 'Silver Carpet'

❏ Height 1-2 ft (30-60 cm)
❏ Planting distance 1-1½ ft (30-45 cm)
❏ Flowers late spring to late summer
❏ Well-drained ordinary garden soil
❏ Sun or partial shade
❏ Herbaceous or evergreen
❏ Zones 4-10

Betony is an outstanding ground-cover plant. Its flower spikes rise in shades of purple and pink over a dense, leafy, silver or mid- to bright green carpet. The species described below are herbaceous unless otherwise stated.

Popular species

Stachys byzantina, syn. *S. olympica* (lamb's ears, lamb's tongue, woolly betony), is an evergray species grown primarily for its foliage. It is up to 1½ ft (45 cm) high and 1 ft (30 cm) wide and

Stachys byzantina in flower

forms a mat of tongue-shaped, pale silvery green, woolly leaves. Spikes of purple flowers appear in midsummer, but since these are not especially attractive and detract from the effect of the foliage, gardeners often choose to clip them as they appear. A popular cultivar is 'Silver Carpet,' which is naturally flowerless.

Stachys macrantha, syn. *S. grandiflora* (woundwort), is up to 2 ft (60 cm) high and 1 ft (30 cm) wide. Mat forming, it has rosettes of broad, corrugated, mid- to dark green leaves and whorls of purple flowers. Cultivars include 'Alba' (white), 'Rosea' (rose), and 'Superba' (rich rose-purple).

Stachys spicata, up to 1½ ft (45 cm) high and wide, has bright green puckered leaves and bright pink flowers throughout summer.

Cultivation

Plant in early fall or midspring in well-drained ordinary garden soil in sun or partial shade. Remove flower stems in late fall.

Propagation All species and cultivars spread rapidly by underground runners, and many also self-seed. If necessary, divide and replant the roots from midfall to midspring.

Pests/diseases Trouble free.

STAR-FLOWERED LILY OF THE VALLEY — see *Smilacina*
STINKING HELLEBORE — see *Helleborus*

Stipa

feather or needle grass

Stipa pennata

❏ Height 3-6 ft (90-180 cm)
❏ Planting distance 1½-2 ft (45-60 cm)
❏ Flowers early summer to early fall
❏ Well-drained fertile soil
❏ Full sun
❏ Herbaceous or evergreen
❏ Zones 5-7

Feather grass, a light, airy plant, forms a clump of narrow mid- to gray-green leaves and has handsome feathery flower plumes, which can be dried for winter arrangements.

Popular species

Stipa calamagrostis, up to 4 ft (120 cm) high, has compact tufts of gray-green leaves and silvery to brown flower plumes.

Stipa gigantea, a near-evergreen up to 6 ft (180 cm) high, has a clump of gray-green leaves and silvery buff-violet flower plumes.

Stipa pennata, up to 3 ft (90 cm) high, is an herbaceous grass with midgreen leaves; its silvery-yellow flower plumes may be dried.

Cultivation

Plant in early spring to midspring in well-drained fertile soil in full sun.

Propagation Divide and replant in early spring to midspring.

Sow seeds outdoors in midspring. Transplant the seedlings to their permanent positions in late spring to early summer.

Pests/diseases Trouble free.

STOKES' ASTER — see *Stokesia*

Stokesia

Stokes' aster

Stokesia laevis

❑ Height 1-2 ft (30-60 cm)
❑ Planting distance 1½ ft (45 cm)
❑ Flowers late summer to midfall
❑ Well-drained soil
❑ Sun or light shade
❑ Herbaceous
❑ Zones 5-10

Despite its showy flowers composed of notched florets in shades of blue, lilac, pink, or white, Stokes' aster *(Stokesia laevis,* syn. *S. cyanea)* is not a well-known plant.

The individual blooms are up to 3 in (7.5 cm) wide and appear in succession over several months; the lance-shaped leaves are midgreen.

Stokes' aster is easy to care for and provides a long-lasting display. Cultivars include 'Alba' (to 1 ft/30 cm; white), 'Blue Danube' (light blue), 'Blue Star' (to 1 ft/ 30 cm; light blue), and 'Wyoming' (to 16 in/40 cm; deep blue).

Cultivation

Plant in midspring in any well-drained soil in sun or light shade. Support with stakes and twine or twiggy sticks.
Propagation Divide and replant in midspring.

Sow seeds in early spring. When the seedlings are large enough to handle, prick out into flats. Grow on in nursery rows and plant out the following midspring. Hybrid plants raised from seed seldom come true, but may give good color forms, which should be propagated by division.
Pests/diseases Trouble free.

Stylophorum

celandine poppy, wood poppy

Stylophorum diphyllum

❑ Height 1-1½ ft (30-45 cm)
❑ Planting distance 1 ft (30 cm)
❑ Flowers late spring to early summer
❑ Rich, moist soil
❑ Partial shade
❑ Herbaceous
❑ Zones 4-9

The celandine poppy *(Stylophorum diphyllum)* is charming in partial shade with its clusters of gleaming yellow poppylike blooms and downy lobed leaves.

The flowers, which measure up to 2 in (5 cm) wide and appear from late spring to early summer, are followed by silvery seedpods.

Cultivation

Plant from fall to spring in rich, moist soil in partial shade.
Propagation Divide and replant the roots in fall or spring.

Or sow seeds in a cold frame or protected bed in early spring. Prick the seedlings out into nursery rows and grow on until fall or spring, then plant them out.
Pests/diseases Trouble free.

STONECROP — see *Sedum*
STRAWFLOWER — see *Helichrysum*
SUNDROPS — see *Oenothera*
SUNFLOWER — see *Helianthus*
SWEET BERGAMOT — see *Monarda*
SWEET ROCKET —see *Hesperis*
SWEET WOODRUFF — see *Galium*

Symphytum

comfrey

Symphytum grandiflorum 'Hidcote Pink'

❑ Height 8-48 in (20-120 cm)
❑ Planting distance 15-48 in (38-120cm)
❑ Flowers early spring to late summer
❑ Moist ordinary or rich soil
❑ Sun or shade
❑ Herbaceous
❑ Zones 3-8

With its coarse-textured leaves and pretty tubular flowers in purple-blue and pink or white, comfrey is an excellent ground cover for moist beds or serves as a specimen plant near water.

The hairy midgreen leaves are usually broadly lance-shaped, and the flowers are held in sprays on branching stems.

Popular species

Symphytum caucasicum (blue comfrey), up to 2 ft (60 cm) high and 1½ ft (45 cm) wide, is suitable for wild gardens, where it flourishes in semishade. The drooping bell-shaped flowers are pink when they open, changing later to blue. They appear from mid-spring to early summer.
Symphytum grandiflorum, up to 15 in (38 cm) high and 2 ft (60 cm) wide, spreads rapidly as ground cover. The short-lived drooping sprays of white flowers appear from early spring to mid-spring. The cultivar 'Hidcote

Tellima

fringecup

Tellima grandiflora

- ❏ Height 1½-2 ft (45-60 cm)
- ❏ Planting distance 1½ ft (45 cm)
- ❏ Flowers late spring to early summer
- ❏ Moist, humus-rich soil
- ❏ Partial to full shade
- ❏ Semievergreen
- ❏ Zones 4-9

An effective ground-cover plant, fringecup *(Tellima grandiflora)* is grown mainly for its broad maple-like foliage, which forms a thick mat close to the ground, topped from late spring with spikes of numerous bell-shaped flowers.

The hairy lobed leaves are bright green and 4 in (10 cm) wide. The flowers are greenish white to green-yellow, turning reddish as they age. The leaves of 'Purpurea' turn purplish in winter.

Cultivation
Plant from early fall to early spring as weather permits. Fringecup prefers partial to full shade and a moist, humus-rich soil; add lots of peat or compost at planting time. Cut off the flower spikes after flowering unless seeds are required.

Propagation Divide and replant from early fall to early spring.

Sow seeds when mature or in early spring in a cold frame. The purple-leaved form does not come true from seed.

Pests/diseases Generally trouble free.

Thalictrum

meadow rue

Thalictrum aquilegifolium

- ❏ Height 2½-6 ft (75-180 cm)
- ❏ Planting distance 2 ft (60 cm)
- ❏ Flowers midspring to early fall
- ❏ Any ordinary or rich, moist soil
- ❏ Sun or partial shade
- ❏ Herbaceous
- ❏ Zones 3-10

The deeply divided leaves and fluffy flower sprays of meadow rue make it a lovely soft-textured plant for borders, and it is much sought after by flower arrangers.

The leaves vary from midgreen to blue or gray-green and are often divided into numerous small leaflets like maidenhair fern. The sprays of tiny flowers, which have no true petals, come in shades of pink, purple, and yellow.

Popular species
Thalictrum aquilegifolium, up to 3 ft (90 cm) high and 1½ ft (45 cm) wide, has finely divided, glossy gray-blue leaves. Sprays of fluffy mauve or purple flowers appear from late spring to midsummer. Cultivars include 'Album' (up to 3 ft/90 cm; white), 'Purpureum' (4 ft/120 cm; pale purple), and 'Thundercloud' (deep purple).

Thalictrum delavayi (often sold as *T. dipterocarpum*) is up to 5 ft (150 cm) high and 2 ft (60 cm) wide. It has dainty midgreen and slightly glossy leaves and large loose panicles of lilac-mauve flowers with yellow stamens. It flowers from early to late summer. Some cultivars include 'Album' (to 3 ft/90 cm; white) and 'Hewitt's Double' (to 3 ft/90 cm; mauve double flowers; likes shade and rich soil).

Symphytum rubrum

Pink' has pale pink flowers opening from maroon buds.

Symphytum officinale (common comfrey, boneset) grows up to 4 ft (120 cm) high and 2 ft (60 cm) wide. This coarse plant is suitable for wild or very informal gardens. It has yellowish-white, pink, or purple flowers in early summer.

Symphytum rubrum, up to 15 in (38 cm) high, has finer leaves than the other species and sprays of deep red flowers from late spring to late summer.

Symphytum × uplandicum 'Variegatum,' up to 4 ft (120 cm) high and wide, has hairy, white-edged gray-green leaves and purplish-pink flowers in summer.

Cultivation
Plant in midfall to late fall or early spring to midspring in ordinary garden soil in sun or shade. *S. rubrum* prefers rich, moist soil in partial shade. *S. caucasicum* occasionally requires staking. After flowering, cut back all flowering stems to basal growth.

Propagation Divide and replant the fleshy roots in early spring.

Pests/diseases Trouble free.

Thalictrum delavayi

Thalictrum minus (often sold as *T. adiantifolium*) is an ultrahardy species (zones 3-10), up to 3 ft (90 cm) high and 1 ft (30 cm) wide. It has gray-green leaves divided into numerous small leaflets and rather insignificant and loose sprays of purple-green flowers in midsummer.

Thalictrum rochebrunianum (often spelled *rocquebrunianum*) is an erect species reaching a height of 4-6 ft (120-180 cm) and width of 2 ft (60 cm). It has fernlike leaves on purple-blue stems and loose sprays of rose-lavender flowers with yellow stamens from summer to early fall. It is often sold under the name 'Lavender Mist.'

Thalictrum speciosissimum (frequently listed as *T. glaucum* or *T. flavum glaucum*) is up to 5 ft (150 cm) high and 2 ft (60 cm) wide. It has deeply divided blue-gray foliage and sprays of fluffy yellow flowers from mid- to late summer.

Cultivation
Plant in early spring to midspring in sun or partial shade; some shade and a summertime mulch are essential in hot climates. Any ordinary garden soil is suitable, but it thrives in rich, moist soil.
Propagation Divide and replant the roots in early spring to midspring. Divided plants are slow to become established. Apart from the double forms, which are infertile, meadow rue is best propagated from seed.

Sow seeds in early spring in a cold frame or protected bed. When they are large enough to handle, prick out the seedlings. Grow on in a nursery bed until the following early spring to midspring.
Pests/diseases Trouble free.

Thalictrum aquilegifolium 'Album'

Thelypteris
thelypteris

Thelypteris phegopteris

❏ Height 1-2 ft (30-60 cm)
❏ Planting distance 1½-2 ft (45-60 cm)
❏ Foliage plant
❏ Moist acid or neutral soil
❏ Partial shade or sun (in very moist soil)
❏ Hardiness varies with species; herbaceous
❏ Zones 3 or 4-9

Thelypteris is an ideal fern for the smaller garden with acid soil, and it looks lovely by the waterside. It forms a clump of light green, midgreen, or yellow-green fronds, often deeply cut.

Popular species
Thelypteris (Phegopteris) hexagonoptera (broad beech fern), up to 1½ ft (45 cm) high and wide, has midgreen fronds and tolerates some sun and dryness.
Thelypteris (Parathelypteris) noveboracensis (New York fern), up to 2 ft (60 cm) high and wide, has yellow-green fronds and tolerates sun in moist situations.
Thelypteris palustris, syn. *Dryopteris thelypteris* (marsh fern), is up to 2 ft (60 cm) tall with yellow-green fronds. This species likes moist soil, not too acid, near a pond.
Thelypteris phegopteris, syn. *Phegopteris connectii* (beech fern), is up to 2 ft (60 cm) high and wide, with light green flimsy fronds. It can be invasive.

Cultivation
Plant in midfall or early spring in moist acid soil in partial shade. *T. palustris* likes neutral boggy soil.
Propagation Sow the dustlike spores in early spring. Or lift and divide the rhizomes in midfall to early spring.
Pests/diseases Trouble free.

Tiarella

foamflower, tiarella

Tiarella cordifolia

❏ Height 1-2 ft (30-60 cm)
❏ Planting distance 1 ft (30 cm)
❏ Flowers late spring to early summer
❏ Moist or well-drained, acid or ordinary soil
❏ Cool, shady site
❏ Semievergreen
❏ Zones 3-9

With its mat of lobed, light green to midgreen leaves, topped with spikes of foamy cream to white flowers, tiarella makes excellent ground cover in cool, moist soil.

Popular species

Tiarella cordifolia, up to 1½ ft (45 cm) high, has maplelike, pale green to midgreen leaves, which turn bronze in winter. Cream-white flowers appear on spikes about 6 in (15cm) high from late spring to early summer. This species spreads through surface runners.

Tiarella wherryi is similar to *T. cordifolia* but taller, a clump former rather than a creeper, and more heat tolerant.

Cultivation

Plant in midfall or early spring to midspring in a shady, cool site and in acid to neutral soil that is moisture retentive. *T. cordifolia* in particular needs moist soil and is apt to die back if the ground dries out. Young outside growths may be replanted in early fall to midfall to fill in gaps.

Propagation Divide and replant the roots of tiarella in midfall or midspring.

Sow seeds in a cold frame or a protected bed in early spring. When the seedlings are large enough to handle, prick out into flats and then into a nursery bed. Plant out in a permanent site the following early spring.

Pests/diseases Generally trouble free.

TICKSEED — see *Coreopsis*
TOADFLAX — see *Linaria*
TOAD LILY — see *Tricyrtis*

Tolmiea

piggyback plant

Tolmiea menziesii 'Variegata'

❏ Height ½-2 ft (15-60 cm)
❏ Planting distance 15 in (38 cm)
❏ Flowers early summer
❏ Well-drained, humus-rich soil
❏ Partial shade or sun
❏ Evergreen
❏ Zones 7-10

Piggyback plant (*Tolmiea menziesii*) makes a good ground cover for rich soils in mild winter regions. Its common name refers to the plantlets that are produced on the backs of the leaves.

It spreads by rhizomes, forming tufts of hairy, midgreen maplelike leaves. In early summer slender branching stems with spires of insignificant green-white, red-flushed tubular flowers rise up to 2 ft (60 cm) over the foliage.

The cultivar 'Variegata' has yellow marbling on the leaves.

Cultivation

Plant in midfall or early spring in well-drained, humus-rich soil. Partial shade is ideal, but the plant tolerates sun.

Propagation Detach any leaves bearing well-developed plantlets and root in seed trays or pots.

Alternatively, peg leaves bearing immature plantlets on the soil, where they will root readily. Then lift and replant.

Pests/diseases Generally trouble free.

TORCH LILY — see *Kniphofia*

Tradescantia
spiderwort

Tradescantia × andersoniana 'Isis'

- ❏ Height 1½-2 ft (45-60 cm)
- ❏ Planting distance 2 ft (60 cm)
- ❏ Flowers early summer to early fall
- ❏ Well-drained moisture-retentive soil
- ❏ Sun or partial shade
- ❏ Herbaceous
- ❏ Zones 5-10

The garden varieties of spiderwort are hardy relatives of the well-known house plants. Their main parent is *Tradescantia virginiana*, a bed plant with pointed, strap-shaped dull green leaves. Unusual three-petaled flowers in shades of blue, purple, red, pink, and white appear throughout the summer and are up to 1½ in (4 cm) wide.

Hybrids, correctly listed under the name *T. × andersoniana* but sometimes sold as *T. virginiana*, include 'Blue Stone' (deep blue), 'Isis' (rich royal purple), 'Osprey' (white with fluffy blue centers), 'Purple Dome' (purple), and 'Red Cloud' (dark magenta).

Cultivation
Plant in midfall or early spring in sun or partial shade in any well-drained but moisture-retentive soil. Support with stakes or twiggy sticks in exposed sites.

Tradescantia 'Osprey'

Propagation Divide the roots every 3-4 years in early spring or fall.

Seeds may be sown in a cold frame or other protected bed in early spring, but named cultivars do not come true. When the seedlings are large enough to handle, prick out into flats. Grow on in a nursery bed and plant out in midfall.

Pests/diseases Slugs may eat shoots.

TREE POPPY — see *Romneya*

Tricyrtis
toad lily

Tricyrtis formosana

- ❏ Height 2-3 ft (60-90 cm)
- ❏ Planting distance 1½-2 ft (45-60 cm)
- ❏ Flowers early fall
- ❏ Rich, moist soil
- ❏ Partial to full shade
- ❏ Herbaceous
- ❏ Zones 5-9

Toad lily is a striking upright plant with white funnel-shaped flowers heavily spotted with mauve or purple. The blooms appear in early fall in loose, branched clusters at the top of leafy stems and have prominent stamens. They are excellent for cutting. The oval, pointed leaves are up to 6 in (15 cm) long.

Popular species
Tricyrtis formosana, up to 3 ft (90 cm) high, has mauve-spotted flowers and deep green leaves. The variety *T. f. stolonifera* has a spreading growth habit.
Tricyrtis hirta, up to 3 ft (90 cm) high, has hairy leaves and lilac-spotted flowers.

Cultivation
Plant in midspring in rich, moist soil in partial or full shade. Allow more sun in northern regions to ensure good flowering.
Propagation Divide and replant the rhizomatous roots in spring.

Or germinate seeds in midspring in a cold frame. Prick out and grow on indoors until the following midspring, then plant out in the final site.
Pests/diseases Slugs and snails may eat the leaves.

Trollius

globeflower

Trollius chinensis

Trollius europaeus

❏ Height 1½-2½ ft (45-75 cm)
❏ Planting distance 15-18 in (38-45 cm)
❏ Flowers late spring to early summer
❏ Ordinary, preferably moist garden soil
❏ Sun or partial shade
❏ Herbaceous
❏ Zones 3-10

The gleaming yellow to orange blooms of globeflower rise like diminutive suns against a mass of lobed leaves — a delightful sight by the waterside, the plant's favorite habitat.

Globeflower has mid- to deep green leaves that are round to oval and deeply cleft into toothed lobes. The blooms resemble large incurved buttercups up to 2½ in (6 cm) wide and are carried on stems 2½ ft (75 cm) high.

This plant, which is poisonous,

likes partial shade or sun, provided its roots are kept moist.

Popular species

Trollius chinensis (often sold as *T. ledebourii*) is up to 2½ ft (75 cm) high and 15 in (38 cm) wide, with open-petaled golden orange flowers up to 2½ in (6 cm) wide. The centers are filled with long, prominent stamens. The cultivar 'Golden Queen' bears deep orange flowers.

Trollius × cultorum, up to 2½ ft (75 cm) high, has flowers up to 2½ in (6 cm) wide. Hybrids include 'Canary Bird' (pale yellow), 'Earliest of All' (medium yellow), 'Etna' (dark orange), 'Fire Globe' (deep orange-yellow), 'Goldquelle' (very large midyellow flowers), 'Lemon Queen'

(pale yellow), 'Prichard's Giant' (tall, medium yellow), and 'Salamander' (fiery orange).

Trollius europaeus (common globeflower) is up to 2 ft (60 cm) high and 1½ ft (45 cm) wide; its flowers are lemon-yellow.

Cultivation

Plant in midfall or midspring in ordinary, preferably moist soil in sun or partial shade. Water thoroughly during dry weather. Cut the flower stems back to the base after flowering to encourage a second flush of blooms.

Propagation Divide and replant the fibrous roots in early fall to midfall or midspring.

Sow seeds in a cold frame as soon as mature or in early fall or midspring. Old seeds may take over a year to germinate, and the rate of success with these is very low. When the seedlings are large enough to handle, prick them out into nursery rows. Plant out in midfall to midspring of the following year.

Pests/diseases Generally trouble free.

TURTLEHEAD — see *Chelone*
UMBRELLA PLANT — see *Peltiphyllum*
VALERIAN — see *Centranthus* and *Valeriana*

Valeriana

valerian

Valeriana phu 'Aurea'

❏ Height 3-5 ft (90-150 cm)
❏ Planting distance 2-5 ft (60-150 cm)
❏ Flowers late spring to late summer
❏ Ordinary garden soil
❏ Full sun to partial shade
❏ Herbaceous
❏ Zones 5-10

The hardy perennial valerians include many species that are either short-lived or weeds, but the following are easily grown long-lived plants suitable for sunny herbaceous beds. They are erect plants with dense leaf clumps and tall flower stems topped with loosely branched clusters.

Popular species

Valeriana officinalis (common or cat's valerian), up to 5 ft (150 cm) high and 3 ft (90 cm) wide, forms a basal clump of leaves divided into lance-shaped leaflets and bears loose, flattened clusters of white, pink, or purple flowers, which have an unpleasant scent if bruised. Cultivars include 'Alba' (white flowers) and 'Coccinea' (red).

Valeriana phu 'Aurea,' up to 3 ft (90 cm) high and 2 ft (60 cm) wide, has deeply cut, bright yellow leaves, turning greener as they age. It bears dense, 6 in (15 cm) long sprays of white tubular flowers in late summer.

Cultivation

Plant in midfall or early spring in ordinary garden soil in full sun or partial shade. Stake the taller species in early spring, especially

Valeriana officinalis

on exposed sites and in moist soil. Remove the faded flower stems in midfall.

Propagation Divide and replant the roots in midfall or in early spring.

V. officinalis is easily raised from seed, though the named cultivars will not reproduce true to type. Sow the seeds outside in midspring. When the seedlings are large enough to handle, prick out into a nursery bed. Set the young plants out in midfall in the permanent site.

Pests/diseases Generally trouble free.

Veratrum

false hellebore, helleborine

Veratrum album

❏ Height 3-7 ft (90-210 cm)
❏ Planting distance 1½-2½ ft (45-75 cm)
❏ Flowers mid- to late summer
❏ Moist, light soil
❏ Sun or partial shade
❏ Herbaceous
❏ Zones 3-9

False hellebore has stiff, narrow spikes or sprays of dense, minute flowers and large, fanlike pleated leaves. The roots of all species are poisonous.

Popular species

Veratrum album, up to 4 ft (120 cm) high and 1½ ft (45 cm) wide, has light green leaves and green-white flowers.

Veratrum nigrum, an American native that reaches up to 5 ft (150 cm) high, has mid- to dark green leaves. Dense maroon-black flower spikes grow up to 3 ft (90 cm) long in late summer; attractive seed heads follow.

Veratrum viride reaches 7 ft (210 cm) in height, with mid-green leaves and sprays of yellow-green flowers in midsummer.

Cultivation

Plant in midfall or early spring in moist, light soil in sun or partial shade.

Propagation Divide and replant in midfall or early spring to midspring.

Sow seeds when mature or in midfall in a cold frame. When seedlings are large enough to handle, prick out and grow on in a nursery bed. The plants reach flowering size in 3-4 years .

Pests/diseases Trouble free.

Verbascum

mullein

Verbascum 'Cotswold Queen'

Verbascum longifolia

Verbascum 'Pink Domino'

- ❏ Height 2-5 ft (60-150 cm)
- ❏ Planting distance 1-2 ft (30-60 cm)
- ❏ Flowers early summer to late fall
- ❏ Any well-drained ordinary garden soil
- ❏ Sunny or lightly shaded site
- ❏ Herbaceous
- ❏ Zones 5-10

Mullein, with its strong, branching flower spikes, is a majestic feature for beds and for semiwild settings. The plant, which has several bushy dwarf forms, bears saucer-shaped flowers in shades of yellow, pink, purple, or white. The leaves are lance-shaped or oblong and mid- to dark green or gray-green. Both the leaves and the stems may be matted with white or yellow hairs.

Popular species/hybrids
Verbascum chaixii, up to 3 ft (90 cm) high, has tongue-shaped, gray-green woolly leaves and yellow flowers with purple stamens, borne in branched spikes in mid- to late summer. 'Album' has white flowers.
Verbascum densiflorum (syn. *V. thapsiforme)* is up to 5 ft (150 cm) high and 2 ft (60 cm) wide. It is rosette forming, with crinkly, midgreen oblong leaves densely covered with yellow hairs. Tapering spikes of yellow flowers appear throughout summer.
Verbascum × hybridum is a group of summer-flowering hybrids with 3-4 ft (90-120 cm) flower spikes. Some cultivars include 'Cotswold Gem' (terra-cotta and yellow), 'Cotswold Queen' (amber with buff center), 'Gainsborough' (primrose-yellow with gray leaves), 'Letitia' (bright yellow with velvety blue leaves), and 'Pink Domino' (deep rose with dark leaves).
Verbascum longifolia is up to 4 ft (120 cm) high and 2 ft (60 cm) wide. It has hairy, lance-shaped basal leaves, up to 2 ft (60 cm) long, and bears golden yellow flowers in dense spikes throughout summer.
Verbascum olympicum is an imposing plant, 5 ft (150 cm) or more tall. Long-lived and suitable for wild gardens, the tall stems rise from rosettes of hairy, lance-shaped gray leaves and carry bright golden yellow flowers in widely branched spikes from early summer into fall.

Cultivation
Plant in early fall or in early spring to midspring in any well-drained soil in full sun or light shade. Stake tall varieties in exposed sites. Remove the flower spikes as they fade to encourage later blooms and to prevent self-seeding.
Propagation Increase the true species, which often seed themselves, from seed sown in midspring in a cold frame or other protected spot. When they are large enough to handle, prick the seedlings out into a nursery bed and grow on until early fall, then move them to their flowering sites.

Increase cultivars, which do not come true from seed, with 3 in (7.5 cm) long root cuttings taken in late winter or early spring. Root in a cold frame or protected shaded bed, then transfer them to a sunny nursery bed. Grow on until early fall, when they can be moved to permanent sites.
Pests/diseases Trouble free.

Verbena

verbena

Verbena × *hybrida* 'Sissinghurst'

Verbena × *hybrida*

❏ Height ½-6 ft (15-180 cm)
❏ Planting distance 1-3 ft (30-90 cm)
❏ Flowers early summer to midfall
❏ Any well-drained fertile soil
❏ Sun
❏ Hardiness variable; herbaceous
❏ Zones 3-10

Originally from South America, verbenas vary in their tolerance for cold. The popular garden hybrids are winter hardy only in truly frost-free areas (zone 10), but some of the species overwinter successfully in zone 3. Even the least hardy kinds, however, can be carried over from year to year by cuttings brought indoors in fall.

The mid- to dark green leaves are generally ovate and prominently toothed. The fragrant flowers resemble primroses but are borne in showy clusters.

Popular species/hybrids

Verbena bonariensis is 4-6 ft (120-180 cm) tall and hardy to zone 7. Its strong, hairy branching stems are set with rough-textured dark green leaves and topped with purple-lilac flower clusters from early summer onward.
Verbena canadensis (rose verbena) is a sprawling plant, reaching a height of 1½ ft (45 cm) and spreading to 2-3 ft (60-90 cm), rooting as it goes. It is valuable for edging and ground cover. The flowers are in shades of rose-pink and lilac, sometimes white. The plant is hardy to zone 5.

Verbena hastata (blue vervain), up to 4-5 ft (120-150 cm), produces a clump of bicolored pink-and-purple flowers from late summer into early fall. It is hardy to zone 3.
Verbena × *hybrida* is a large group of colorful verbenas, popular for summer bedding. These bushy plants, 6-18 in (15-45 cm) tall, have dark green toothed and often finely divided leaves. They are ideal for planting in large groups in borders and beds, with tight flower clusters that begin to open in early summer and continue until the first frost. Color selections include 'Sissinghurst' (to 1 ft/30 cm; rose-pink) and 'Sparkle Hybrids' (6 in/15 cm; scarlet, pink, and purple with white centers).
Verbena rigida (syn. *V. venosa*) is hardy from zones 8-10, having escaped from gardens to go native from North Carolina to Florida. It grows up to 2 ft (60 cm) tall from tuberous roots and bears erect stems with dark green, narrowly ovate, stiff and finely toothed leaves. The compact claret-purple flower clusters are about 2 in (5 cm) wide. 'Flame,' a dwarf 6 in (15 cm) in height, bears masses of scarlet flowers.

Cultivation

Plant verbenas in late spring, in any good, humus-rich, well-drained soil in full sun. Because they are fast growing, floriferous,

and resistant to drought, these plants are very valuable to water-conserving gardeners. Most verbenas will not tolerate continually wet soils. Pinch out the growing points to induce side-branching and deadhead regularly to prolong the flowering season.

Propagation Take stem cuttings that are 2-3 in (5-7.5 cm) long in midspring with hardy types. To overwinter tender verbenas, take cuttings in early fall. Root them, preferably in a propagator, at a temperature of 50-55°F (10-13°C). Pot the rooted cuttings singly and plant out when the danger of frost is past.

Plants of *V. bonariensis* and *V. rigida* can be increased by division of the roots when new growth is evident.

All verbenas can be raised from seed sown indoors from midwinter to early spring at a temperature of 64-70°F (18-21°C). Germination is erratic and may take several weeks. Prick out the seedlings into flats and harden them off before planting out in late spring or early summer.

Pests/diseases Aphids may infest young plants and check growth.

Veronica

speedwell

Veronica gentianoides

- ❏ Height ⅔-7 ft (20-210 cm)
- ❏ Planting distance 9-24 in (23-60 cm)
- ❏ Flowers late spring to early fall
- ❏ Well-drained, humus-rich, moisture-retentive garden soil
- ❏ Sun or partial shade
- ❏ Herbaceous
- ❏ Zones 3-10

Grown for its profusion of long-blooming spikes or sprays of flowers in a range of outstanding blues, speedwell is a beautiful soft-textured plant. It is an ideal plant for borders and for edging.

The following species are of upright habit and bear oval to lance-shaped leaves that are generally mid- to dark green, and sometimes silvery or gray-green. The long-lasting saucer-shaped flowers are each composed of a short tube opening out into four irregularly shaped petals. Borne on terminal spikes, they come in shades of purple and pink as well as white.

Popular species

Veronica gentianoides, up to 2 ft (60 cm) high and 1½ ft (45 cm) wide, forms a mat of glossy dark green leaves and bears loose, very pale blue flower spikes in early summer. It is suitable for edging. The cultivar 'Variegata' has leaves marbled with cream-white. *Veronica incana* (woolly speedwell) is sometimes sold as *V. candida*. Growing up to 2 ft (60 cm) high and 1½ ft (45 cm) wide, it has toothed, lance-shaped silvery leaves and loose spikes of midblue flowers, which are 6 in (15 cm) long and produced in succession throughout the summer. Some cultivars include 'Rosea' (flowers flushed pink), 'Sarabande' (up to 1½ ft/45 cm; violet-blue), and

Veronica longifolia 'Icicle'

Veronica spicata 'Pavanne'

Veronica incana

Veronica teucrium 'Shirley Blue'

'Wendy' (up to 2 ft/60 cm; pale blue).

Veronica latifolia (syn. *V. teucrium*) is up to 1½ ft (45 cm) high and 1 ft (30 cm) wide, with short sprays of blue to reddish flowers. Some cultivars include 'Crater Lake Blue' (to 15 in/38 cm; ultramarine blue), 'Shirley Blue' (deep blue), and 'Trehane' (up to 8 in/20 cm; golden green leaves and deep blue flowers).

Veronica longifolia, up to 4 ft (120 cm) high and 1½ ft (45 cm) wide, has toothed, oblong to lance-shaped mid- or dark green leaves and spikes of deep purple-blue flowers that are 6 in (15 cm) long from early to late summer. Cultivars and hybrids include 'Foerster's Blue' (to 2½ ft/75 cm; deep blue), 'Icicle' (to 2 ft/60 cm; white), 'Sunny Border Blue' (long blooming; dark violet), and *V. subsessilis* (syn. *V. longifolia subsessilis* or *V. hendersonii*; to 3 ft/90 cm; branched spikes; royal blue flowers).

Veronica spicata is up to 1½ ft (45 cm) high and 1 ft (30 cm) wide. It forms a neat clump of toothed midgreen leaves and bears dense spikes up to 6 in (15 cm) long of blue flowers from early to late summer. Cultivars include 'Alba' (white), 'Barcarolle' (rose-pink), 'Blue Fox' (bright lavender-blue), 'Pavanne' (tall grayish foliage with pink flowers), and 'Red Fox' (reddish pink).

Veronica virginica (syn. *Veronicastrum virginicum*), up to 7 ft (210 cm) high and 2 ft (60 cm) wide, has whorls of pointed midgreen leaves and branched sprays up to 10 in (25 cm) long of pale blue flowers from midsummer to early fall. Cultivars include 'Album' (white) and 'Roseum' (pink).

Cultivation

Plant speedwell in midfall or midspring in well-drained garden soil, enriched with compost. The soil should be moisture-retentive and the site in full sun or partial shade. Stake or support with twiggy sticks in exposed positions and cut all stems down to just above ground level after flowering or in late fall.

Propagation Lift and divide perennial species every 3 years in early spring to midspring.

Pests/diseases Powdery mildew may turn the foliage gray-white and disfigure it.

Viola

viola, violet, violetta

Viola hybrid

❏ Height 2-12 in (5-30 cm)
❏ Planting distance 4-15 in (10-38 cm)
❏ Flowers late winter to midsummer
   and fall
❏ Any moist, well-drained fertile soil
❏ Sun or partial shade
❏ Hardiness varies with species;
   herbaceous or evergreen
❏ Zones 3-10

Violas, violettas, and violets are delightful perennial plants for edging, ground cover under trees, raised beds, and rock gardens.

Their profuse five-petaled flowers, which appear from late winter to midsummer and sometimes again in fall, are renowned for their intense violets and deep blues, but also come in shades of mauve, paler blue, yellow, pink, and white. They are close relations of the annual summer- and winter-flowering pansies. Violas and violettas have flat flowers with overlapping petals, but violettas are smaller than violas. Violets have narrower petals with spurs at the back.

The leaves, which range from pale to dark green, may be oval or heart-shaped and are often lobed. The species described are herbaceous unless otherwise stated.

Viola odorata

Viola tricolor

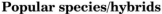

Viola cornuta 'Lilacina' and 'Alba'

Popular species/hybrids

Viola blanda (sweet white violet), a diminutive species up to 2 in (5 cm) tall, bears perfumed, purple-veined white flowers. Its spreading habit makes it useful and attractive ground cover for moist, shaded sites.

Viola canadensis (Canada violet) forms a neat tuft up to 1 ft (30 cm) tall and wide. From spring into early summer, it bears short-spurred flowers that shade from purplish brown on the edges, through white, to a yellow eye at the center. It is the hardiest viola, overwintering reliably in zone 3.

Viola cornuta (horned violet), 4-12 in (10-30 cm) high and up to 15 in (38 cm) wide, has midgreen leaves with rounded teeth, and in early summer and midsummer bears deep lavender, 1 in (2.5 cm) wide narrow-petaled flowers with slender spurs. Cultivars include 'Alba' (white), 'Arkwright Ruby' (bright maroon with yellow eyes), 'Blue Perfection' (pale blue), 'Chantreyland' (large apricot flowers), 'Lilacina' (soft lilac),

and 'Scottish Yellow' (lemon-yellow shading to orange at center).

Viola cucullata, syn. *V. obliqua* (marsh violet), forms a mat 3-6 in (7.5-15 cm) high and 1 ft (30 cm) wide. It has pale green heart-shaped leaves and fragrant violet-like flowers up to 1 in (2.5 cm) wide, ranging from white to violet with darker veining on the lower

petals. It blooms in late spring and early summer. The cultivar 'Freckles' has large pale blue flowers flecked with purple.

Viola hederacea, up to 3 in (7.5 cm) high and 10 in (25 cm) wide, is only moderately hardy. It has white-edged, violet-blue, almost spurless violet-shaped flowers that appear from late spring into early fall.

Viola labradorica 'Purpurea' is an evergreen species, 4-5 in (10-13 cm) high and 1 ft (30 cm) wide, with purplish-green leaves and purple flowers in late spring.

Viola lutea (mountain pansy), up to 8 in (20 cm) high and 15 in (38 cm) wide, has evergreen foliage and yellow flowers with brown or purple veins in late spring and early summer.

Viola odorata (sweet violet), 4-8 in (10-20 cm) high and 1 ft

Viola labradorica 'Purpurea'

Woodsia

woodsia

Viola 'Molly Sanderson'

Viola cucullata

Woodsia obtusa

(30 cm) or more wide, spreads by runners. It forms evergreen mats of heart-shaped mid- to dark green leaves and, from late winter to midspring, produces violet-shaped flowers in shades of purple to white, and sometimes pink. Single-flowered hybrids include 'Alba' (white), 'Czar' (fragrant, violet-purple), 'Rosea' (soft pink), 'Rosina' (bright, deep pink), and 'White Czar' (fragrant, white feathered with violet and yellow). Double-flowered hybrids (Parma violets) include 'Duchess de Parme' (very fragrant, mauve) and 'Marie Louise' (very fragrant, violet and white).

Viola tricolor is commonly grown as an annual but it will perennialize in favorable locations, bearing tricolor flowers that combine white, purple, and yellow.

Viola hybrids are usually up to 6 in (15 cm) high and 15 in (38 cm) wide with fragrant flowers up to 2 in (5 cm) wide in late spring and early summer. They include 'Blue Elf' (deep violet and light blue with golden eyes), 'Jersey Gem' (purple-blue), and 'Molly Sanderson' (near-black).

Violetta hybrids grow up to 6 in (15 cm) high and 1 ft (30 cm) wide. Fragrant flowers that are 1 in (2.5 cm) wide appear in late spring. A hybrid is 'Rebecca' (cream flecked with violet).

Cultivation

Plant violas in early fall to midfall

or early spring to midspring in a sunny or partially shaded site. They thrive in any moist but well-drained fertile soil.

Propagation In early spring or midsummer, sow seeds outdoors in a damp, shaded site. Transplant the seedlings to a nursery bed and grow on until early to midfall. Or germinate seeds in a cold frame. Prick out into pots, and plant out as before.

Named cultivars are best propagated from basal shoots that are 1-2 in (2.5-5 cm) long in midsummer and rooted in a cold frame or cool, shaded bed. Pot and plant out from early fall to early spring.

Pests/diseases Slugs and caterpillars may devour the plants. Red spider mites may weaken and disfigure them. Anthracnose fungus may cause browning or blotching of the leaves, sometimes killing the plant. Downy mildew may cover the undersides of the leaves with a gray feltlike growth, especially in wet conditions; subsequently, the leaves rot and the whole plant wilts.

VIRGINIA COWSLIP — see *Mertensia*
WELSH POPPY — see *Meconopsis*
WILD GINGER — see *Asarum*
WILD MARJORAM — see *Origanum*
WOOD POPPY — see *Stylophorum*

❏ Height 4-16 in (10-40 cm)
❏ Planting distance 8-16 in (20-40 cm)
❏ Foliage plant
❏ Gritty, moist soil
❏ Partial shade
❏ Herbaceous
❏ Zones 4-9

Woodsia, a small fern with a tuft of dull green or grayish-green fronds, is a good ground cover.

Popular species

Woodsia ilvensis has dull green lacy fronds on reddish stalks. It is hardy to zone 4.

Woodsia obtusa, up to 16 in (40 cm) high and wide, has grayish-green fronds covered with hairs. As hardy as *W. ilvensis*, but more heat tolerant, it grows in southern states into zone 9.

Cultivation

Plant in midspring in partial shade, in gritty, moist soil or in wall crevices. *W. obtusa* thrives in limestone soils.

Propagation Lift and divide in spring. Alternatively, sow the dustlike spores in early spring or mid- to late summer.

Pests/diseases Trouble free.

WORMWOOD — see *Artemisia*
YARROW — see *Achillea*
YELLOW ARCHANGEL — see *Lamium*
YELLOW ASPHODEL — see *Asphodeline*

ACKNOWLEDGMENTS

Photographer's credits
Gillian Beckett 49(tl), 69(tr), 92(tr), 123(tl), 132(tr), 133(tr), 138(tr). Biofotos/Heather Angel 29(tr), 34(tr), 92(tl), 125(tl), 142, 143(tl), 152(tr), 164(tr). Boys Syndication (Jacqui Hurst) 144(tr). Bruce Coleman (Hans Reinhard) 161(tr). Eric Crichton 9(t), 12(b), 20(tl), 21(b), 22(tl), 23(tl,b), 24(tr), 25(tr), 26(tl), 27(tr), 30, 31(tr), 32(t,c), 33, 34(tl,b), 35(c), 36(tl,tr), 37(tl), 38, 39(tc,c), 40(b), 41(tc,tr), 42(tl,tr,b), 43(tl,tr), 44(t,bl), 45(tr), 46(tl), 48(tl), 52(tr), 56(tl), 59(tl), 60(tl), 61(tl,c),62, 66(tr), 67(tr), 68, 71(tl,tr,b), 73(tl,tc), 74(tr), 75(tr), 76(b), 78(t,c), 79(c), 80(tr), 81, 85(tr), 86(tl), 87(tl), 88(b), 89(tl,tr), 90(tl,b), 92(tc), 93(tl,tr), 94(tr,b), 95(tl,b), 96(tl,tr), 97(c), 98(tr), 100(c), 101(tr), 102(tr), 103(tr), 104(tl), 105(tl,tr), 106(tl), 107(tl,tc), 108(tl), 109(l), 110, 111(tl), 112(tl,tc), 113(tl,c), 115(tr), 116(tl), 117(tl,tc,tr), 118(tr,c), 120(c), 122(tl), 126(tr), 127(tc), 128(tl,tr), 131(tl,tr), 133(tl), 135(tl,tr), 136(tr), 137(tr), 138(tl), 138(b), 139(tl,c), 140(l,r), 141(tr,c), 143(c), 144(tl), 145(b), 149(tl,tc), 150(tl), 153(tr), 154(tr), 156(b), 160(t), 161(b), 167(l,r), 170(tr), 171(t,b), 172(tr). Derek Fell 26(br), 35(tr), 53(tr), 54(tl,tr), 55, 58(tl), 61(tr), 74(tl), 77(bl), 97(br), 104(tr), 113(tr), 119(b) 120(tr), 122(tr), 123(tr), 124(t), 126(tl), 129(tl), 141(tl), 143(tr), 174(tr), 175(tc). Philippe Ferret 82(t), 84(tl,b). Garden Picture Library (Brian Carter) 36(c), 39(tr), 48(tr), 59(tr), 60(tr), 87(tc), 111(tr), 127(tl), 148(tl), 168(tr), (John Glover) 1, 157(t), (Carole Hellman) 151(tl), (Michelle LaMontagne) 121, (Clay Perry) 2-3, (David Russell) 19(tl), 36(tc), 50(tl), (Ron Sutherland)10(b), 11(t), 75(tc), 156(t), (Brigitte Thomas) 14,

(Didier Willeby) 27(tl). John Glover front cover(bc,br), 40(tr), 46(b), 115(tl), 153(tl). Derek Gould 69(tl), 82(b), 89(b), 124(b). Derek & Lyn Gould 131(tl), 169(tr). Insight Picture Library 130(b). Michelle LaMontagne 22(tr), 100(tr), 101(tl), 106(tc). Andrew Lawson 125(tr), 166(tr). Donald Lowndes 135 (br). S & O Mathews front cover(tc), 25(l), 37(tr), 63(tl), 67(tl), 70(tl), 72(t), 76(t), 85(tl), 106(tr), 119(tr,cr), 158, 175(tl), back cover. Tania Midgley 24(b), 39(tl,b), 41(tl), 65(tr), 77(br), 86(tr), 94(tl), 95(tr), 100(tl), 102(tl), 108(tr,c), 116(tr), 118(b), 119(tl), 120(tl,tc), 122(c), 148(tr), 165(l). Natural Image (Bob Gibbons) 161(tc), 162(tr), 168(c), (Liz Gibbons) 161(tl), 173(t). Philippe Perdereau 66(tl). Photo Nats (Liz Ball) 31(tl). (Robert Lyons) 56(tr), 87(tr), 98(tl), 141(tc), (Ann Reilly) 57(tl), 98(bl), 126(tc). Photos Horticultural 175(tr). Photos Horticultural/Michael Warren front cover (tl,tr,cl,cc,cr,bl), 4-5, 16(l,r), 17(tl,tr,b), 18(tl,b), 19(tr,b), 20(tr), 24(tl), 28(tl), 35(tl), 44(br), 47(tl,tr), 50(tr), 52(tl), 53(tl), 57(tr), 58(tr), 61(tr), 63(tr), 64(c), 65(tl,c), 69(c), 70(tr), 72(b), 73(tr), 74(tc), 77(t), 79(t), 80(tl), 83(t), 86(b), 88(t), 90(tr), 91, 97(tl,tr), 98(b), 99(tr), 101(b), 107(b), 112(tr), 114(tl,tr), 118(tl), 127(tr), 129(b), 130(tl,tr), 132(tc), 133(b), 134(tr), 136(tl,b), 137(tl,c), 144(bl,br), 145(tl,tr), 146(tl,tr), 150(tr,b), 151(tc,tr), 152(tl), 155, 157(b), 159(tl,tr), 160(b), 161(tr), 162(tl,tc), 163(tl,tc), 164(tl,b), 165(r), 166(tl), 168(tl), 170(tl), 172(c), (Andrew Lawson) 163(tr), 174(tl,b). Positive Images (Karen Bussolini) 173 (b), (Jerry Howard) 23(tr). (Lee Campbell) 67(b). Harry Smith Collection 16(c), 25(cr), 26(tr), 28(tr), 29(tl), 31(b), 37(tc), 40(tl), 45(tl), 49(tr), 51(tl), 58(b), 64(t), 75(tl), 99(tl,tc), 103(tl), 105(b), 107(tr), 109(r), 129(tr), 134(tl,c), 139(tr), 147,149(tr), 154(tl), 166(c), 169(tl), 170(c), 172(tl). Harry Smith Collection/Polunin Collection 18(tr). David Squire 21(t). Brigitte Thomas 12(t). EWA 9(b), (Clare College) 8, (Jerry Harpur) 10(t), 12-13(t), 13(b). EWA/Jenkyn Place (Jerry Harpur) 6-7.

Illustrators
Reader's Digest 11(b), (Shirley Felts) 83(b). Anne Winterbotham 84(tr).